Urban Mobility Systems in the World

SCIENCES

Geography and Demography, Field Director – Denise Pumain

Infrastructure and Mobility Networks Geography,
Subject Heads – Hadrien Commenges and Florent Le Néchet

Urban Mobility Systems in the World

Coordinated by
Gaële Lesteven

WILEY

First published 2023 in Great Britain and the United States by ISTE Ltd and John Wiley & Sons, Inc.

Apart from any fair dealing for the purposes of research or private study, or criticism or review, as permitted under the Copyright, Designs and Patents Act 1988, this publication may only be reproduced, stored or transmitted, in any form or by any means, with the prior permission in writing of the publishers, or in the case of reprographic reproduction in accordance with the terms and licenses issued by the CLA. Enquiries concerning reproduction outside these terms should be sent to the publishers at the undermentioned address:

ISTE Ltd
27-37 St George's Road
London SW19 4EU
UK

www.iste.co.uk

John Wiley & Sons, Inc.
111 River Street
Hoboken, NJ 07030
USA

www.wiley.com

© ISTE Ltd 2023

The rights of Gaële Lesteven to be identified as the author of this work have been asserted by her in accordance with the Copyright, Designs and Patents Act 1988.

Any opinions, findings, and conclusions or recommendations expressed in this material are those of the author(s), contributor(s) or editor(s) and do not necessarily reflect the views of ISTE Group.

Library of Congress Control Number: 2023938913

British Library Cataloguing-in-Publication Data
A CIP record for this book is available from the British Library
ISBN 978-1-78945-154-2

ERC code:
SH2 Institutions, Values, Environment and Space
    SH2_8 Energy, transportation and mobility
    SH2_9 Urban, regional and rural studies

Contents

Introduction: Diversity and Evolution of Urban Mobility Systems........ xiii
Gaële LESTEVEN

Part 1. Urban Mobility and Socio-Economic Characteristics..... 1

Chapter 1. Getting Around the City: Overview of Urban Mobility Around the World........ 3
Gaële LESTEVEN

    1.1. Describing urban mobility systems........ 3
        1.1.1. Definitions........ 3
        1.1.2. Population growth and urban transition........ 5
        1.1.3. Mobility and urban forms........ 6
        1.1.4. Social trends........ 8
    1.2. Observing urban mobility........ 9
        1.2.1. Household equipment and personal mobility........ 9
        1.2.2. A diversity of modal share........ 10
    1.3. Modes of transport: areas of relevance, urban planning and local policies........ 13
        1.3.1. The predominance of private cars........ 13
        1.3.2. High urban density and public transport........ 15
        1.3.3. Active transport in the heart of the city........ 17
    1.4. Conclusion........ 18
    1.5. References........ 19

Chapter 2. Unevenly Distributed Mobility, Spotlight on Brazil 23
Benjamin MOTTE-BAUMVOL

2.1. Introduction. 23
2.2. Income and access to the automobile, main determinants
of low mobility 24
   2.2.1. Decreasing inequalities of motorization. 24
   2.2.2. Decoupling of motorization and automotive mobility 25
   2.2.3. Automobile dependency as a source of inequalities. 26
2.3. Low mobility as a source of exclusion 27
2.4. The effects of accessibility and low densities. 28
2.5. Room for maneuver with respect to *transport poverty* 29
2.6. In Brazil, increased inequality and *transport poverty*? 32
   2.6.1. Low mobility, a question of measurement?. 32
   2.6.2. With motorization, inequalities in mobility increase 33
   2.6.3. Slow public transport. 34
   2.6.4. Geographical confinement. 35
   2.6.5. Highly mobile poor neighborhoods 36
2.7. Conclusion 37
2.8. References 37

Chapter 3. Going Out Without Getting By? Mobility and
Poverty in Dakar 45
Lourdes DIAZ OLVERA, Didier PLAT and Pascal POCHET

3.1. Field and tools 46
3.2. Who are the poor? 48
3.3. A specific mobility in situations of poverty 50
   3.3.1. Essential mobility 50
   3.3.2. Costly mobility 51
   3.3.3. Local mobility 53
3.4. Going to study: degraded conditions of access to institutions 55
3.5. Shopping for food: a little further, a little less easy 57
3.6. Living in the outskirts, working in the neighborhood instead of
downtown Dakar 59
3.7. Restricted access to the city 62
3.8. Conclusion 63
3.9. References 64

Chapter 4. Children's Mobility: Comparative Perspectives Between France and Quebec ... 67
Sylvanie GODILLON

- 4.1. Introduction. ... 67
- 4.2. Children as mainly passengers in individual motorized modes ... 68
  - 4.2.1. School as structuring family organization. ... 68
  - 4.2.2. The predominance of motorized modes for getting to school ... 69
  - 4.2.3. Walking and cycling, modes used less and less ... 71
- 4.3. Important health, safety and environmental issues. ... 71
  - 4.3.1. Physical inactivity impacts children's health. ... 71
  - 4.3.2. Parental fears of accidents and assaults ... 72
  - 4.3.3. A difficult but necessary change faced with climate issues. ... 74
- 4.4. Actions to encourage modal change for daily mobility ... 74
  - 4.4.1. Organizing accompaniment of children on foot ... 75
  - 4.4.2. Pedestrianizing the streets around schools ... 76
  - 4.4.3. Developing children's cycling skills. ... 77
- 4.5. Conclusion ... 78
- 4.6. References ... 78

Part 2. Urban Public Transport ... 83

Chapter 5. Mobility, Public Transportation and Super-Aging in Japan ... 85
Sophie BUHNIK

- 5.1. Introduction: Japan or the efficiency of urban transport faced with super-aging ... 85
- 5.2. Geographies of super-aging in Japan and their influence on public transport networks and daily mobilities. ... 88
  - 5.2.1. The deepening depopulation of Japan's peripheries. ... 88
  - 5.2.2. An aging of suburban fringes reinforced by changes in residential preferences ... 90
- 5.3. The influence of passengers' sociodemographic characteristics and location on transportation reconfigurations ... 93
  - 5.3.1. Changes in rail traffic: key figures and explanations ... 93
  - 5.3.2. Unpacking the factors behind the rise in motorization rates in aging and shrinking Japan. ... 96

5.4. Seniors' exposure to urban decline and the changing role
of station neighborhoods in aging agglomerations 97
    5.4.1. Attachment to station neighborhoods tested by the decline
    in rail traffic and commercial devitalization 97
    5.4.2. Between automobile dependence and new places of
    sociability for senior suburban households 99
    5.4.3. Questioning the present and future strategies of railway
    companies 101
5.5. Maintaining accessibility in aging cities and regions: transport
policies at the crossroads of care and local autonomy 103
    5.5.1. Integration of public and private actors in compact city
    policies 104
    5.5.2. Institutionalization of volunteering to curb the shrinkage
    of transport. 107
5.6. Conclusion 108
5.7. References 109

Chapter 6. From Calcutta to Delhi and Hyderabad: Genealogy of Indian Metros 113
Bérénice BON

6.1. Introduction. 113
6.2. The first metro in Calcutta: jewel for rail engineers, burden
for urban policies 114
    6.2.1. The birth of the Calcutta metro: emerging urban transport
    policies across India 115
    6.2.2. The Calcutta metro, jewel of railway engineers 118
6.3. Construction of a political and technical model around the
Delhi metro 119
    6.3.1. Delhi, capital of India and center of experimentation
    for major urban projects 120
    6.3.2. National sectoral reforms, a favorable context for metros
    at local level 122
    6.3.3. Building a metro but also a political and technical model 123
6.4. Private firms and regional states: counterweights to the Delhi
metro model 126
    6.4.1. The controversial arrangements of the Hyderabad metro. 127
    6.4.2. Mumbai's hybrid model 129
6.5. Conclusion 131
6.6. References 132

Chapter 7. Non-Centralized Urban Transport: An Illustration Based on the Case of Jakarta... 135
Rémi DESMOULIÈRE

7.1. Introduction... 135
7.2. Words and things: terminological issues... 137
    7.2.1. Paratransit, a functional approach... 137
    7.2.2. Informal transport and artisanal transport: from the socioeconomic to the political... 140
    7.2.3. Centralization, decentralization and non-centralization... 142
7.3. Operating and controlling non-centralized transport... 143
    7.3.1. Fragmented structures of operation... 143
    7.3.2. The ambivalent role of public authorities... 145
    7.3.3. Intermediary organizations: popular companies or cartels?... 147
7.4. What place for non-centralized transport in contemporary metropolises?... 149
    7.4.1. "Gearboxes for metropolization?" Questions of flexibility and adaptability... 149
    7.4.2. Integration of non-centralized transport: experiences and sticking points... 152
7.5. Conclusion... 153
7.6. References... 154

Part 3. Active Modes of Transport and Infrastructure Policies... 157

Chapter 8. The Infrastructure of Walking: The Case of Mexico City Sidewalks... 159
Ruth PÉREZ LÓPEZ, Jérôme MONNET and Guénola CAPRON

8.1. Introduction: sidewalks, a special element of urban pedestrian infrastructure... 159
8.2. In Mexico City, the place of walking in the mobility system reflects social inequalities... 161
8.3. The social and material production of sidewalks: methodology... 165
8.4. The diversity of sidewalk functions... 166
8.5. Competition and conflict between sidewalk uses... 169
8.6. From uses to actors' games: the production of a negotiated order... 172

8.7. Conclusion: Towards inclusive and adaptive sidewalk layouts?. 176
8.8. References 177

Chapter 9. Cycling Policies in Europe: The Case of Greater Lyon and Hamburg 181
Manon ESKENAZI

9.1. Introduction. 181
9.2. Cycling infrastructure at the heart of cycling policies 183
9.3. Hamburg: cycling planning to support the development
of practices. 184
    9.3.1. Integrating cycling into the urban strategy of the
    sustainable city: the carrot-without-the-stick approach. 185
    9.3.2. Cycling infrastructure at the heart of cycling strategy 187
    9.3.3. Cycling services to build intermodality 189
9.4. Greater Lyon: relaunching practice through policies,
a missed bet?. 191
    9.4.1. A cycling policy of plans 191
    9.4.2. Infrastructure and services as the pillars of public
    cycling action 194
9.5. Conclusion 197
9.6. References 199

Part 4. Circulation of Urban Mobility Analysis Tools and Public Policy Models. 203

Chapter 10. Categorical Pitfalls for Analyzing Urban Mobility 205
Hadrien COMMENGES and Florent LE NÉCHET

10.1. Introduction. 205
10.2. Which type of data for analyzing urban mobility? 207
    10.2.1. Typology of mobility data 207
    10.2.2. From local surveys to attempts at international
    harmonization. 211
10.3. Which objects describe mobility?. 213
    10.3.1. The trip 213
    10.3.2. The mode of transport 215
    10.3.3. The city 218

10.4. Categorical pitfalls: balancing diversity and comparability 223
    10.4.1. The category of transport: modes and purposes for travel 224
    10.4.2. Temporal categories: the typical working day 227
    10.4.3. The spatial category: local urban systems 228
    10.4.4. Categories reconstructed for harmonization: ad hoc
    mechanisms 231
10.5. Discussion 233
10.6. References 234

Chapter 11. Geographical Inequalities in the Analysis of Urban Mobility 243
Florent LE NÉCHET

11.1. Introduction 243
11.2. Analysis of the implementation of CEREMA-type surveys
in France 245
11.3. Size effects and context effects explaining why an HTS
is carried out 248
11.4. Bibliometric analysis of research on urban mobility 251
11.5. Global heterogeneity of urban mobility analysis 253
11.6. Thematic specializations revealing issues for local action
on mobility 257
11.7. Discussion 259
11.8. References 260

Chapter 12. Circulation of Models in Africa: The Example of Bus Rapid Transit in Cape Town 265
Solène BAFFI

12.1. Introduction 265
12.2. The diffusion of BRT in Africa 266
    12.2.1. Diffusion of an efficient transport model as a planning
    and urban planning tool 266
    12.2.2. Stakeholders supporting this model 268
    12.2.3. Limits of the circulation of the model in Africa 270
12.3. South Africa, laboratory for urban mobility projects 272
    12.3.1. A long-awaited reform 272
    12.3.2. BRT: symbol of post-apartheid South Africa 275
    12.3.3. The Capetonian version of the BRT project: MyCiti 276

12.4. Between strong appropriation and poor adaptation, MyCiti's mixed record 279
    12.4.1. An international model reappropriated to assert local power 279
    12.4.2. A project ill-suited to South African specificities 280
    12.4.3. Feedback effects at different levels 282
12.5. Conclusion 284
12.6. References 285

List of Authors 291

Index 293

Introduction

Diversity and Evolution of Urban Mobility Systems

Gaële LESTEVEN
*Laboratoire Aménagement Économie, Transports (LAET),
Université de Lyon, ENTPE, France*

This volume of the *Infrastructure and Mobility Networks Geography* set offers insight into the geographical organization of urban mobility systems around the world. Infrastructure networks, transport services and the travel practices of populations constitute the mobility system. Contributions to this book are varied. Some are based on one case study in particular, while others put several urban contexts into perspective, analyze travel practices or study mobility policies and services. All of them focus on better understanding the different aspects of mobility systems.

This book is multidisciplinary. It comprises 12 chapters, organized into four parts and written by 16 researchers from the fields of geography, sociology, urban planning, socioeconomics and political science. The book aims to highlight the geographical diversity of mobility systems, based on case studies in Africa, North and South America, Asia and Europe.

Urban mobility systems are evolving. For more than a century, the demand for mobility has risen. This is due to population growth at a global level, an increase in living standards and better transport efficiency, thanks to technological progress – primarily the motorization of vehicles and the transformation of industry and society. The shift from transport to mobility, from a world of cities and countryside to a predominantly urban world, is leading to paradigm shifts that have impacted

Urban Mobility Systems in the World,
coordinated by Gaële LESTEVEN. © ISTE Ltd 2023.

mobility systems. These changes are both a reflection of structural transformations and the source of new questions.

I.1. From transport to mobility

For several years now, the term "mobility" has been gradually replacing the term "transport". Transport referred to the world of engineers, road planning and construction, vehicle design and traffic flow prediction. The user was considered to be outside the system. This technical-economic approach held sway during the 20th century. It was characterized by the use of cost–benefit analysis and the implementation of a science of traffic (Gallez and Kaufmann 2009). The oil crises of the 1970s and the economic slowdown that followed, along with the beginnings of environmental awareness, called into question this supply-oriented approach to transport. A new field of analysis then emerged: the socioeconomics of transport (Commenges 2013). This subject borrows methods and concepts from economics, sociology and geography. It seeks to better know and understand individual travel practices. The notion of travel replaces that of flow. A segmented approach in terms of transport networks gives way to the disaggregated study of individual travel behaviors and to systemic analysis that studies spatial interactions between travel demand and transport supply (Gallez and Kaufmann 2009). It is in this context that the term "mobility" tends to impose itself (Commenges 2013). The mobility approach puts the user at the heart of the analysis. It focuses on individual lifestyles and the travel practices that they induce. In France, the adoption of the Mobilities Orientation Law (*Loi d'Orientation des Mobilités* – LOM) in 2019, replacing the Inland Transport Orientation Law (*Loi d'Orientation des Transports Intérieurs* – LOTI) of 1982, has endorsed this paradigm shift.

Defining the term "mobility" is not easy. Mobility has become a portmanteau word in everyday language. Its definition varies according to the discipline in which it is discussed. In general, it refers to a process of change that characterizes the behavior of individuals or groups of individuals (Meissonnier et al. 2020). The geographical approach to mobility distinguishes between different fields of study based on the spatial scales mobilized (local, national, international) and the temporalities to which it relates (Drevon and Kaufmann 2022). Reversible mobilities (Kaufmann 2005) are organized around an anchor point; the home. They are opposed to non-reversible mobilities, which require a change of residence (migration, residential mobility). Among the reversible mobilities, some involve long-distance movements, over several days or weeks (travel, multi-residence). Most of them take place during the day, in the context of the everyday life of the individuals studied (Orfeuil 2002). These daily mobilities are the subject of this book.

Mobility refers to the possibility and fact of a person moving in space between an origin and a destination; over time and at a certain speed; with a given reason for travel (work, shopping, leisure, etc.); with one or more modes of transport and on networks adapted to these modes; depending on the resources and skills available to the person. Knowledge tools such as household travel surveys collect information about weekday trips, and the demographic and socioeconomic characteristics of the households and individuals who make them. Individual mobility can be understood along five axes (Massot and Orfeuil 2005). A first axis involves social interaction. It is measured in terms of the number of trips made per day per inhabitant, depending on the type of activities carried out. A second axis refers to spatial interaction, according to the size of the space frequented. This is estimated by the total distance traveled per day by each inhabitant. The third axis involves the costs of individual mobility through studying the budget of time and money devoted to transport. Then comes the intensity of use of the different transport modes by individuals. The last axis refers to the ability of individuals to organize their own mobility, conditioned in particular by their level of income and their place of residence (motorization, access to public transport services, etc.).

I.2. From city to urban space

The second semantic change concerns the transition from "city" to "urban space". If urban space has today become generalized (Brenner 2014), it is however not homogeneous, in what it comprises nor in its contours.

The city is the place of an organized power, whether central or local. It is delimited by its administrative boundaries. During the 20th century, as populations grew and the built-up fabric expanded, demographic and morphological criteria progressively replaced administrative criteria (Guérois and Paulus 2002). Urban space is defined based on a threshold of inhabitants and continuity of the built-up area. In contrast to rural areas, it is characterized by an intensity of land occupation. Housing units are close together; constructions are multi-storey; ground and underground use is intense. The resulting population densities may be high, even very high, such as in the centers of major Asian cities. The democratization of the automobile and suburban housing that took place during the 1960s in industrialised countries generated a phenomenon of suburbanization, blurring the boundaries between town and country. Demographic and morphological criteria have proved insufficient to characterize the urban space expanded by everyday use of the automobile. A functional criterion based on the home-to-work commute complements the demographic and morphological criteria. Thus, as urban expansion has progressed, the criteria that characterize the city have gradually been redefined (Guérois and Paulus 2002).

Urban density and functional mix influence the organization of daily trips and the distances traveled. The concentration of employment most often translates into a concentration of wealth, infrastructure and equipment, as opposed to less well-equipped rural and suburban areas. "The city starts where the beer is cold", they say in West Africa, where there is electricity to power the fridges (Choplin 2020, p. 23). Both the concentration of population and activities and urban sprawl are consequences of urban growth. Densities thus tend to decrease with distance from the center of the city.

Urban expansion transforms cities, and cities are indeed evolving (Pumain 1997). The increase in the speed of travel expands the size of people's daily environment. The increasing size of cities makes their organization more complex. It reinforces inequalities within and between them. It confronts them with issues of social, economic and environmental sustainability in the organization of their mobility systems.

These criteria of density and urban concentration, which are conventionally adopted by urban research, are increasingly giving way to the concepts of accessibility, attractiveness and diversity. They confirm the fact that urban sprawl is concomitant with the extension of networks (Brès and Devisme 2020) and a strengthening of the urban hierarchy with the domination of global cities (Sassen 1991). Other forms are emerging, such as in West Africa, where an "urbanization without a city, without services, urbanity or centrality" is spreading (Choplin 2020, p. 136).

I.3. From monograph to comparison

The study of urban mobility may be carried out through monographs or from a comparative perspective, mobilizing specific approaches.

Applied at an international scale, comparison makes it possible to understand the diffusion of urban models and to distinguish the different scales involved in contemporary urban dynamics. It provides a more general point of view, through the search for regularities or divergences between case studies, and it constitutes support for conceptualization (Vigour 2005). International comparison encourages a change of perspective, while promoting the appropriation of new tools and concepts (Authier et al. 2019). It is not exempt from risks, such as the difficulty of adopting a general position given the uniqueness of each case, concentration of research on the most globalized cities, a tendency to standardize certain ways of thinking and survey methods (Authier et al. 2019) or a better knowledge of one of the fields of study among those selected for comparison.

The urban scale offers fertile ground for understanding territorial and organizational changes in the supply of mobility. The mobility systems of Western metropolises (Europe, North America) have been the subject of more study, since more data are available, and the academic potential is greater. However, J. Robinson calls for a broader comparative gesture. The challenge is to become aware of the diversity of situations (Robinson 2011), including metropolises in the Global South (Asia, Africa, Latin America). The colonial legacy and the economic and social changes experienced by most of these countries have perpetuated large inequalities in income, life expectancy and access to resources (Dados and Connell 2012) that condition daily mobility practices.

I.4. Organization of the book: between a systemic approach and modal diversity

Following this introduction, this book is organized into four parts and 12 chapters.

Part 1 focuses on urban mobility in general and then considers the role played by the socioeconomic and demographic determinants of individuals in their mobility practices.

After defining urban mobility systems and their characteristics, Chapter 1 presents an overview of the daily mobility of urban populations at a global scale. Gaële Lesteven reviews the use of the main modes of transport and their links with urban development and policies implemented in different geographical contexts. Then, using American and European case studies, Benjamin Motte-Baumvol shows in Chapter 2 how social inequalities affect the dynamics of household car ownership and their mobility practices in Brazil. Mobility is unequally distributed between individuals. Low mobility limits access to many urban resources, particularly jobs. This reflection is in line with work on the relationship between poverty and daily travel. In Chapter 3, Lourdes Diaz Olvera, Didier Plat and Pascal Pochet study the mobility of the urban poor and characteristics based on the case of Dakar in Senegal. When daily travel is difficult, it hampers efforts to emerge from poverty. It is by improving walking conditions and access to public transport that transport policies can improve the travel of the urban poor. Not only do socioeconomic determinants play a role in travel practices – demographic determinants do too. In Chapter 4,

Sylvanie Godillon focuses on the mobility of children based on a cross-analysis between France and Quebec. Since the 1980s, children have walked less in both France and Quebec. The motorization of travel weakens children's ability to develop urban and social experience. Reduced pedestrian mobility has health consequences (sedentary lifestyle), cognitive consequences (less autonomy) and environmental consequences (more kilometers traveled). Faced with this observation, actions have been put in place to encourage walking and cycling.

Part 2 focuses on the role of public transport in urban mobility systems.

In Chapter 5, Sophie Buhnik examines how Japanese cities have developed around railway infrastructure. Depopulation and the aging of the population are having an impact on their structure. The number of loss-making railway lines is increasing in the suburbs where population renewal has ceased, while public policies encourage the rehousing of the elderly in central station districts. It shows the limits of the scenario of urban compactness, which benefits the most dynamic cities, without solving the causes of loneliness in elderly residents. Unlike Japan, India is characterized by a young population, growing cities and public transport networks that are under construction. In Chapter 6, Bérénice Bon looks at the construction of metros in Indian cities. She addresses the institutional, technical and human components of these major infrastructures. She highlights the difficult adjustment of competences between India's central government, supported by international donors and local urban authorities. In many major cities, particularly in developing countries, rail and metro networks are either non-existent or unable to meet the growing demand for mobility. Minibuses, shared taxis and motorcycle taxi services develop to meet this demand on a day-to-day basis. Then, based on the case study of Jakarta in Indonesia, Rémi Desmoulière shows in Chapter 7 that these "non-centralized" networks pre-exist centralized public transport networks, and are indicative of a different regime of production and the government of urban spaces. Faced with the absence or failure of public authorities, these modes can be seen as forms of innovation that help reduce urban divides.

Complementing the section on collective modes, Part 3 looks at policies dedicated to walking and cycling infrastructures.

In Chapter 8, Ruth Pérez López, Jérôme Monnet and Guénola Capron focus on sidewalks based on the case study of Mexico City. They show that sidewalks have a diversity of functions and spatial configurations, while public authorities usually consider sidewalks only as support for pedestrian traffic. Allowing a variety of uses on sidewalks means making room for a diversity of users, especially the most vulnerable: children, the elderly or those whose survival depends on street resources.

Adding to the discussion in Chapter 3 on the links between poverty and daily mobility based on the case of Dakar, they recall the role of walking and the importance of taking it into account in public policies. Chapter 9 is devoted to cycling policies in Europe based on the cases of Lyon in France and Hamburg in Germany. Manon Eskenazi reports on the growing importance of cycling facilities and cycling measures in the mobility policies of many European cities. The comparison of Hamburg and Lyon highlights the paradox that, even if the objective of building cycling infrastructure seem to have been achieved, the use of bicycles is increasing but only weakly. The technical approach to cycling policies struggles to grasp the complexity of bicycle use and its social context.

Part 4, the final part of the book, discusses how tools for analysing urban mobility and public policy models circulate.

In Chapter 10, Hadrien Commenges and Florent Le Néchet discuss the tools used and the type of data collected to describe and compare urban mobility systems. They highlight categorical pitfalls, such as the delimitation of the area of study, in understanding urban issues. They illustrate their point by citing the case of the Randstad, between Amsterdam and Rotterdam, in the Netherlands. Each of these cities, taken on separately, is a virtuous example of urban planning that promotes sustainable mobility. However, travel between these cities is mainly done by car and contributes to significant traffic congestion at a regional level. In Chapter 11, Florent Le Néchet continues the discussion by looking at geographical inequalities in the analysis of urban mobility. He shows that a fragmentation of urban mobility knowledge tools leads to a fragmentation of knowledge about mobility. On the one hand, he observes that the importance given to the analysis of mobility is very uneven from one city to another and does not depend solely on city size. On the other hand, he notes that the study of daily mobility reveals a diversity of public policy models. In Chapter 12, Solène Baffi looks back on a public policy model that has become iconic in recent years: Bus Rapid Transit (BRT). Invented in Latin America, the BRT was established in Cape Town, South Africa, in the 2000s. Promoted by international donors and quickly appropriated by the public authorities, it is ill-suited to the local context, whether in terms of the difficulty of integrating pre-existing transport modes or of targeting the urban poor. However, the introduction of BRT marks a key stage in the post-apartheid reform of transport. It has made South African cities laboratories for urban transformation across the African continent, contributing to the spread of BRT to other cities on the continent.

Presenting one or more local situations, these chapters highlight the diversity of daily mobility on an urban scale, the challenges encountered and the solutions offered. A better knowledge of urban mobility systems and their specificities may reveal paths of innovation for policy makers and city dwellers. It will hopefully contribute to the implementation and promotion of inclusive and sustainable mobility.

I.5. References

Authier, J.-Y., Baggioni, V., Cousin, B., Fijalkow, Y., Launay, L. (eds) (2019). *D'une ville à l'autre. La comparaison internationale en sociologie urbaine*. La Découverte, Paris.

Brenner, N. (2014). Introduction: Urban theory without an outside. In *Implosions/Explosions. Towards a Study of Planetary Urbanization*, Brenner, N. (ed.). Jovis, Berlin.

Brès, A. and Devisme, L. (2020). L'urbain, à ses limites. In *Pour la recherche urbaine*, Adisson, F., Barles, S., Blanc, N., Coutard, O., Frouillou, L., Rassat, F. (eds). CNRS Éditions, Paris.

Choplin, A. (2020). *Matière grise de l'Urbain : la vie du ciment en Afrique*. MétisPresses, Geneva.

Commenges, H. (2013). L'invention de la mobilité quotidienne. Aspects performatifs des instruments de la socio-économie des transports. PhD Thesis, Université Paris-Diderot-Paris VII.

Dados, N. and Connell, R. (2012). The Global South. *Contexts*, 11, 12–13.

Drevon, G. and Kaufmann, V. (2023). *Mobility and Geographical Scales*. ISTE Ltd, London, and John Wiley & Sons, New York.

Gallez, C. and Kaufmann, V. (2009). Aux racines de la mobilité en sciences sociales : contribution au cadre d'analyse socio-historique de la mobilité urbaine. In *De l'histoire des transports à l'histoire de la mobilité ?*, Flonneau, M. and Guigueno, V. (eds). Presses Universitaires de Rennes.

Guérois, M. and Paulus, F. (2002). Commune centre, agglomération, aire urbaine : quelle pertinence pour l'étude des villes. *Cybergeo*, 212, 15.

Kaufmann, V. (2005). Mobilités et réversibilités : vers des sociétés plus fluides ? *Cahiers internationaux de sociologie*, 118, 119–135.

Massot, M.-H. and Orfeuil J.-P (2005). La mobilité au quotidien, entre choix individuel et production sociale. *Cahiers internationaux de sociologie*, CXVIII, 81–100.

Meissonnier, J., Vincent, S., Rabaud, M., Kaufmann, V. (2020). *Connaissance des mobilités : hybridation des méthodes, diversification des sources*. Cerema, Bron.

Orfeuil, J.-P. (2002). Les sens de la mobilité. In *Dictionnaire de l'habitat et du logement*, Segaud, M., Brun, J., Driant J.-C. (eds). Armand Colin, Paris.

Pumain, D. (1997). Pour une théorie évolutive des villes. *Espace Géographique*, 26(2), 119–134.

Sassen, S. (1991). *The Global City: New York, London, Tokyo*. Princeton University Press, NJ.

Robinson, J. (2011). Cities in a world of cities: The comparative gesture. *International Journal of Urban and Regional Research*, 35(1), 1–23.

Vigour, C. (2005). *La comparaison dans les sciences sociales. Pratiques et méthodes*. La Découverte, Paris.

PART 1

Urban Mobility and Socio-Economic Characteristics

1
Getting Around the City: Overview of Urban Mobility Around the World

Gaële LESTEVEN
*Laboratoire Aménagement Économie, Transports (LAET),
Université de Lyon, ENTPE, France*

This chapter provides an overview of urban mobility around the world. It reviews the main trends related to the use of different modes of transport in the city. Without claiming to be exhaustive, it aims to adopt a broad perspective, revealing similarities but also contrasts and specificities according to the geographical context.

The first part of the chapter presents urban mobility systems and their characteristics. The second part provides an overview of daily mobility and the use of modes of transport at an international scale. The third part reviews modes of transport and their links with urban development and the policies implemented.

1.1. Describing urban mobility systems

1.1.1. Definitions

Based on the study of technical networks, Dupuy (2008) defines a "network" as a collection of lines and nodes serving a given geographical unit. Technical networks (roads, power lines, sewers, etc.) form territorial systems (mobility systems, electricity distribution systems, sanitation systems, etc.). It is networks – and no longer zoning – that define a territory. The organization into these networks, established at the beginning of the 19th century, gradually prevailed over the traditional organization into zones. Gabriel Dupuy defines three levels of networks and operators, which interact with each other to organize the system. The first-level operator is in charge of the infrastructure network. The second-level operator manages the production and consumption networks, which are based on the infrastructures. Finally, households constitute the third-level operators (Dupuy 2008).

We shall apply this organization, in three levels of networks, to the urban mobility system.

At the first level, the public authorities mobilize technical and financial resources to develop and maintain a network of transport infrastructures: road networks, railways, waterways, cycle paths, footpaths, etc. Transport infrastructures have a local spatial influence: they connect different points of the territory but also create barrier effects. In many agglomerations, a local authority is in charge of developing and organizing transport policy. The local transport authority "determines the role assigned to the various modes of transport, the major investments to be made, their financing and that of their operation, the pricing and the means of encouraging users towards the objectives that have been set" (Merlin and Choay 2010). The boundaries of the authority's jurisdiction may vary from city to city, as may the infrastructure and modes of transport which it regulates and supervises.

At the second level, public or private operators provide transport services based on the existing infrastructure. The use of infrastructure by different modes of transport produces effects at global level, such as the emission of greenhouse gases. It also produces local effects in terms of accessibility, but also noise, air pollution and accidents. Indicators of the quality of transport provision vary according to the services offered. For example, public transport indicators are based on the spatial service of the mode, the temporal frequency of the services offered and their patronage. An improvement in provision leads to better travel conditions.

At the third level, households act as operators. They travel to different points of the territory for social and economic activities: work, visiting friends or family, shopping, etc. The demand for travel refers to the set of travel practices of a population in a given urban territory. It is possible to characterize the situation of mobility based on the data concerning the spatial organization of the territory, its demographic and economic dynamics, the distribution of places of employment and residence and daily trips. This characterization may apply to the whole population, considering the spatiotemporal distribution of trips and their share among the modes of transport used or "modal share". It can also be performed at the level of an individual or a group of individuals for a social category or a particular area within the scope of study. A mobility rate is calculated as the number of trips per day per person. A travel time budget is determined based on the time spent each day by each individual traveling, including the share of income spent each month on travel.

The intersection between travel demand and transport supply determines usage, but also traffic conditions and the quality of service. The system functions through interactions between the elements comprising it. Any change in conditions of mobility, resulting from new regulations or the introduction of new transport services, leads to systemic reactions: modal shift, induced or reduced mobility, changes in itineraries, longer term strategies for the relocation of households and businesses, etc.

While the organization of the urban mobility system is the same everywhere, the interactions between infrastructure networks, transport supply and demand for travel vary from city to city. These variations are a function of internal elements of the system, but also of external factors of a demographic, spatial, economic, social or political nature, as described below.

1.1.2. *Population growth and urban transition*

After growing very slowly for millennia, the world's population began to increase rapidly two centuries ago. It increased from nearly a billion human beings in 1800 to 7.7 billion in 2019. According to United Nations projections, it should continue to grow and reach 10.9 billion inhabitants in 2100 (UN 2019). Most of this future growth will take place in the countries of the Global South, especially in Africa, where it is expected to double by 2050. The continent would then exceed 2 billion inhabitants. With 1.6 billion inhabitants, India would be the most populous country in the world at that time, followed by China with 1.4 billion inhabitants (UN 2019).

The phenomenon of demographic transition explains this rapid population growth over a short period of time. A new equilibrium where low fertility is associated with low mortality is gradually replacing the old equilibrium of high fertility and high mortality. The demographic transition is much faster in Africa, Asia and Latin America than it has been in Western countries and explains their growing demographic weight. In many industrialized countries, low net immigration and longer life expectancy, combined with a fertility rate lower than population renewal, have led to an ageing population, and in some cases to demographic decline. For example, more than a quarter of the Japanese population is 65 years of age or older, while in Sub-Saharan Africa, 40% of the population is under 15 years of age (UN 2019). This change in the age curve determines the current and future demand for travel and the use of transport networks.

Population growth translates into urban growth. Today, 55% of the world's population live in cities. According to the United Nations, the urban population will constitute 68% of the global population by 2050 (UN 2018). The strongest level of urban growth is expected in Asia, especially in India and China, as well as in Africa, especially in Nigeria (UN 2018). Echoing the notion of demographic transition, urban transition refers to a phenomenon of rapid urbanization. In the first phase, the growth of cities is due to rural exodus. In the second, the number of births in cities becomes more significant than the number of immigrants from rural areas. Faced with this rapid population growth, cities change scale and become difficult to manage, plan and regulate (Steck 2006).

At the local level, urban spaces sprawl out towards the peripheries and/or densify in the center. The city centers of Cairo in Egypt, Mumbai in India or Dhaka in Bangladesh contain more than 50,000 inhabitants per square kilometer, double the densities of central Paris, France. Conversely, urban decline is also a real phenomenon (Fol and Cunningham-Sabot 2010). It may be linked to an aging population, as in Japan, or to a recomposition of economic activity at national level, as in the United States.

Finally, while the largest population growth occurs in cities of a few million, cities of multi-millions also continue to grow. Today, one in eight urban dwellers live in one of the 33 cities of more than 10 million inhabitants that exist on earth. There were only 10 in 1990, and they are expected to increase to 43 by 2030, most of them in the Global South (UN 2018). These human concentrations call into question the ability of road and public transport networks to satisfy an ever-increasing demand for mobility.

1.1.3. *Mobility and urban forms*

The distribution of populations and activities in urban space conditions travel, just as the development of infrastructure, transport services and travel flows influence urban forms.

The development of the railway in the 19th century challenged the historic city surrounded by its fortifications. Urbanization extended along the new railway lines. In the city center, electric trams and, in larger cities, metro systems gradually replaced horse-drawn public transport. This sociotechnological heritage partly explains the modal split in many cities in industrialized countries, but also the developing world. In Mumbai, India, railway lines built in the 19th century to transport cotton were transformed a century later into suburban train lines for commuting.

The development of the automobile system during the 20th century transformed the city into "automotive territories" (Dupuy 1995). Cars have allowed, people to travel faster, and therefore further. Time savings are converted into space savings for households who leave the city centers. Wiel (1999) subtitled his work on urban transition "the transition from the pedestrian city to the motorized city". Residential areas and shopping centers are built on the outskirts and are served by motorway networks. Theorized by *The Athens Charter* (Le Corbusier 1973), functional town planning promotes the separation of flows, through the zoning of activities and the hierarchy of urban roads. Car mobility becomes a territorial issue. The growth of car traffic leads to improvements in road infrastructure, which promote the spreading out of the built-up area. This leads to an increase in distances and growing use of the car and therefore, once again, an increase in car traffic (Wiel 1999).

After studying more than 30 cities around the world at the end of the 1980s, Peter Newman and Jeffrey Kenworthy published a famous curve, linking urban density to distances traveled through the volume of fuel used in daily travel (Newman and Kenworthy 1989). The curve highlights the automobile cities. Located in North America and Australia, they are characterized by low densities and long distances traveled. They contrast with densely populated Asian cities, and to a lesser extent European cities, in which fuel consumption is lower due to prevalence of walking and the use of public transport. It should be noted that African and South American cities were absent from this analysis, which limits its scope.

The first criticisms of "all-car policy" emerged in the 1960s. These noted that urban space is first and foremost a place of living before being a space of circulation (Buchanan 1963); the street can accommodate a multitude of uses that have been gradually erased by automobile traffic (Jacobs 1961). The oil shocks of 1970 and the ensuing slowdown in the global economy reinforced this questioning of the car-based city in favor of a revival of public transport, while environmental issues begin to gain importance. In the proliferating theories of the sustainable city, daily mobility has a central role. These theories argue for the compact city (Beaucire 2005) or the "appropriate speed of travel" city (Wiel 2005) instead of the low-density city, which encourages long distance journeys by car and therefore greenhouse gas emissions. Some theories, such as New Urbanism, advocate a return to urban density where the travel share of the private car would be reduced in favor of public transport, walking and cycling (Henderson 2012). Other theories go further. Combining urban density and mixed functions, they advocate a return to proximity in the "quarter-hour city", where all services would be accessible in less than 15 min (Moreno and Garnier 2020). At the metropolitan level, they promote urban and transport planning coordination through transit-oriented development (TOD). TOD refers to a concept that encourages urban development close to public transport networks in order to reduce car use (Gallez et al. 2015). While some researchers see in these urban models the possibility of a "post-automobile" future (Dennis and Urry 2012), others point to contradictory policies (Reigner et al. 2009) in which the calming of urban centers, particularly in European cities, is coupled with improvements in road infrastructure on the periphery.

1.1.4. Social trends

In addition to demographic dynamics and urban forms, other factors contribute to the evolution of urban mobility systems on a global scale, such as the digital revolution, consideration of climate change and increasing inequalities.

The development of mobile Internet and real-time geolocation during the 2000s made information the keystone of the mobility system. With a smartphone, the user has access to a growing number of varied and individualized services which deliver geolocated and real-time information on timetables, routes, modes of transport and opportunities available in the territory. The consequences are manifold. Users become actors in their own mobility, both consumers and producers of data (Lesteven 2018). The spread of digital technology also changes the supply of transport. It promotes the emergence of new actors in the transport sector, often virtual, such as digital platforms. It allows existing operators to improve their productivity and efficiency by optimizing operation and maintenance. It opens up opportunities in terms of coordinated pricing and multimodal integration. Thanks to these functions, coupled with complete passenger information, it becomes possible for public or private operators to offer a range of networked mobility services, in the form of Mobility-as-a-Service (MaaS). The use of digital technology in urban areas is found on all continents. Its dissemination fuels the debate on the sustainable city, with the concept of the smart city presented as one of the possible models.

Climate change is relevant to long-distance mobility, which contributes significantly to greenhouse gas emissions, but also everyday mobility. Events related to global warming impact the proper functioning of transport systems. Increasingly frequent severe climatic episodes, such as floods or heat waves, make roads impassable and damage railway lines. In the long term, rising sea levels and rising temperatures bring into question the sustainability of certain areas of settlement. At the local level, other transport externalities must also be considered: air pollution, whose effects are harmful to health, noise pollution, congestion, community severance and lack of road safety.

Finally, income gaps between households are indicative of differentiated access for urban residents to individual and public transport. Many poor households live on the outskirts of large cities, particularly in the countries of the Global South, in neighborhoods with little or no public transport access, while jobs are still located in central areas. At the global level, despite an overall improvement in living standards, 10% of the world's population still lived below the poverty line in 2015, on less than $1.90 per person per day, the majority of whom were in Sub-Saharan Africa (WB 2018). The Covid-19 pandemic has been harsh for the urban poor, leading to increases in inequality (Narayan et al. 2022). This state of affairs highlights the concept of social exclusion related to transport, especially in developing cities where the majority of the population faces financial and travel difficulties (Lucas 2011).

1.2. Observing urban mobility

The second part of the chapter offers an overview of urban mobility at a global level. The data used comes from the meta-observatory of mobilities[1]. It presents existing information and does not claim to be exhaustive. It shows various figures, in particular equipment rates and modal shares, for a sample of major cities around the world. My colleagues and I examined about 100 urban agglomerations, their transport infrastructure, public transport services, vehicle fleet, travel demand, regulation and air quality. For each agglomeration, we collected information on an incremental and regular basis, drawing on locally available sources (Eskenazi et al. 2017). The use of secondary sources raises methodological issues such as the low availability of certain data, their poor quality or even inappropriate scales (see Chapter 10) that limit an exhaustive collection.

1.2.1. *Household equipment and personal mobility*

Globally, the motorization rate is 182 cars per 1,000 inhabitants (OICA 2015). But it varies greatly from one continent to another, and from one country to another. In the United States, the motorization rate exceeded 800 cars per 1,000 inhabitants in 2015, while it was below 600 in Europe and below 50 in Africa (OICA 2015). Locally, variations are even greater. In Europe, large conurbations are often less motorized than secondary towns, and their historic centers are even less so. This is

---

[1] The meta-observatory of mobility was developed at LVMT/ENPC as part of research funded by IMD Renault-ParisTech (2016–2020) that I coordinated.

particularly marked in the Paris region, France, especially the city of Paris where the motorization rate is below the world average. Conversely, some large cities in emerging countries are home to most of the country's car fleet, reflecting the urban concentration of wealth. For example, in Senegal, the passenger car fleet is concentrated in the capital region of Dakar (ANSD 2018). Even within urban areas, car ownership is not homogeneously distributed and reflects the sociospatial distribution of wealth. Traffic jams are concentrated in the affluent parts of city centers, while many households cannot afford a second-hand car. In places where public transport has a low service quality, as in Africa, some urban dwellers turn to motorbikes. Less costly than a car to buy and to maintain, motorized two-wheelers are well adapted to the local context, which is often characterized by poor road conditions in peripheral areas and significant car congestion in accessing the city center (Pochet et al. 2017).

The comparison of motorization rates and urban density makes several city profiles stand out. It is based on a panel of 52 agglomerations from the meta-observatory, dispersed over all the continents and presenting contrasting levels of economic development (Trouvé et al. 2020). Cities in North America and Australia are the most motorized and also the least dense. Conversely, large cities in Africa or South Asia have high levels of density and low rates of motorization, even if these cities contain most of their country's automobile fleet. On the other hand, these cities often have high motorcycle motorization rates, particularly in Asia and some African countries. These rates may exceed 600 motorcycles per 1,000 inhabitants. Traditionally considered as a stage in the motorization of households (Gwilliam 2002), the motorized two-wheeler has the advantages of the automobile at a lower cost, while being well adapted to rapid extensions of the urban fabric and to congested and lower quality roads. Unlike car ownership, urban form is not the explanation for differences in motorcycle ownership from a statistical point of view (Trouvé et al. 2021).

1.2.2. *A diversity of modal share*

City dwellers use different modes of transport to travel from one point to another. Household travel surveys collect information on all trips made the day before the survey. Trip aggregation makes it possible to estimate the use of different modes of transport on a particular day of the week. Modal share is calculated in terms of the number of trips and in terms of the distances traveled.

The modes of transport used differ from one agglomeration to another. The basic forms (walking, cycling, private car, bus, individual taxis, etc.) are present in most urban areas. Other forms are specific to certain contexts (car sharing, minibuses, shared taxis, tricycles with or without engines, motorcycle taxis).

Figure 1.1 compares the modal distributions of daily travel in 25 major cities around the world. The data is drawn from the latest household travel survey available for each city. Cities are identified by colour according to their geographical affiliation. African cities are in orange, Asian cities in green, European and Near Eastern cities in pink, North American cities in dark blue and South American cities in light blue.

Modes of transport are classified into three categories on the graph.

The first category, entitled "active transport", refers to walking, comprising the bulk of this category, to which cycling is added. In many surveys, short walking trips are not counted, which tends to underestimate the real share of walking in daily travel. Similarly, in the case of intermodal trips – those involving two or more transport modes during the same trip – it is often the motorized mode that prevails to the detriment of walking which again is not counted.

Motorized modes fall into two categories. The second category called "public transport" includes all motorized transport for commercial use, from mass transit (metro, commuter train, bus rapid transit (BRT)) to paratransit (taxis, motorcycle taxis, etc.). For some modes, such as carpooling when presented as a separate modality in surveys, the distinction between collective mode and personal mode is not obvious. The preference here is to integrate it into the category of public transport.

The third category includes motorized individual modes for personal use, mainly the private car, as both driver and passenger, and motorized two-wheelers. The latter is recorded as a personal mode, but may also be used as a motorcycle taxi. Here again, the categorization is not obvious; the way the mode is used is rarely specified in the surveys (Pochet and Lesteven 2023). The modal shares obtained for each of the three categories are distributed on each of the three axes of the graph. The value on each axis is obtained by projection, parallel to the previous axis.

Reading this graph makes it possible to distinguish groups of cities. Active transport, especially walking, dominates in African cities (in orange), while the use of personal motorized modes is still low, below 20%. Motorized public transport represents 20–40% modal share. Walking remains the main mode of transport in these cities, especially for the urban poor. Most of the population of the global poor is concentrated on the African continent. For Nairobi in Kenya or Cape Town in South Africa, it is possible that the share of walking is underestimated in the surveys. One hypothesis would be that some of the walking in the large slum of Kibera in Nairobi and the townships of Cape Town is not counted.

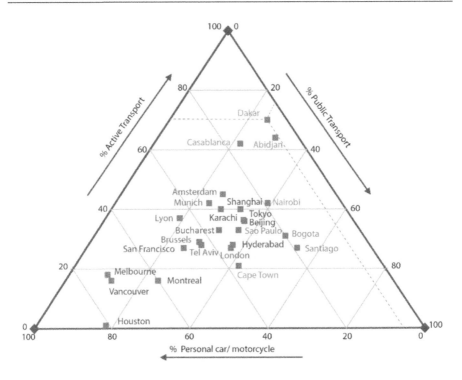

Figure 1.1. *Ternary graph of modal share of daily trips (a reading: the value on each axis is obtained by projection parallel to the previous axis. For example, in Dakar, Senegal, active transport represents 70.5% of trips, public transport 24% and personal motorized modes 5.5% – data from the 2015 EMTASUD survey). For a color version of this figure, see www.iste.co.uk/lesteven/urban.zip*

South American cities (in light blue) come next. The public transport share is high. It accounts for half or more of daily trips, as in Bogotá in Colombia or Santiago in Chile.

At the opposite end of the graph are the North American and Australian cities with a very high share of travel by private car. In Houston, United States, walking is almost nonexistent and most public transport trips involve carpooling. San Francisco, also in the United States, has a slightly different profile and is closer to European cities.

European cities with Asian cities form the middle group, with an active transport share around 30–40%. In European cities, the share of the private car is still significant, ranging between 30% and 50% of trips. The gap is widening for the cities of Northern Europe where, alongside walking, cycling has a modal share of 15–20%. In Asian cities, often more densely populated, the share of public transport dominates. They are often very large cities, with multi-million populations, most of them equipped with high-capacity public transport networks. São Paulo, Brazil, is, in this sense, close to Asian cities.

Public transport represents the majority of motorized trips in Africa, Latin America and Asia. By allowing high occupancy rates, it emits less greenhouse gases than personal transport modes. It contributes to more sustainable mobility, even if its cost limits access to part of the urban population in the Global South.

1.3. Modes of transport: areas of relevance, urban planning and local policies

The last part of the chapter looks at the areas of relevance of transport modes, the urban development they require and their regulation. This first section focuses on personal motorized modes, private cars and motorcycles, which are distributed very unevenly on a global scale, and which generate social differentiation and inequalities in mobility.

1.3.1. *The predominance of private cars*

Following the invention of the combustion engine at the end of the 19th century, it took almost a century for the automotive system to become established in the more industrialized countries. The automotive system refers to a set of elements – infrastructure, vehicle fleet, etc. – which contribute to ensuring motorized travel, to which is added a set of rules that organize its operation (Dupuy 1995). In the countries of the Global South, the stock of vehicles continues to grow, while it stagnates in the industrialized countries. For many Western urban dwellers, owning a car is no longer a sign of progress compared to the previous generation (Massot and Orfeuil 2005). The dynamics of motorization result in renewal of the fleet (Kuhnimhof et al. 2014), or even, in some cases, by de-motorization when life trajectories induce a decrease in regular use (Cacciari and Belton-Chevallier 2020). Conversely, the countries of the Global South, particularly in Asia, are experiencing an explosion in demand for cars. This strong growth of the fleet is explained by wealthier households, urban sprawl and cheaper cars. Perceived as an external sign of wealth, the car is one of the attributes of the middle classes of large cities, allowing them to settle on the periphery while accessing more distant jobs. This growth in the fleet also applies to motorized two-wheelers. Like the automobile, but without the same prestige, the motorcycle also represents a marker of social status.

As a step or outcome in the process of motorization of households, it is also becoming an alternative to the private car, while commercial motorcycle taxi services are developing massively. Despite its high human cost, mobility in motorized two-wheelers often lacks consideration by public authorities in emerging countries, such as Brazil (Vasconcellos 2018).

The corollary of this growth in individual motorization is the reinforcement of negative externalities. Urban sprawl reinforces automobile dependency. In France, with the exception of the urban area of Paris, more than 60% of metropolitan trips are made by car, which represents 80% of the kilometers traveled (SDES 2022) and the same proportion of greenhouse gas emissions. The average vehicle occupancy rate remains below two occupants per vehicle and decreases during rush hour. The massive use of automobiles leads to situations of congestion. Suburban lifestyles bring the possibility of sustainable mobility into question. Their inhabitants use cars to access services and amenities. The dominance of cars in mobility systems reinforces sociospatial inequalities, between the households and territories that can liberate themselves from the automobile, and those which remain dependent on it. In emerging countries, the growth of personal motorization does not necessarily lead to an increase in use, particularly among low-income households, as has been observed in Brazil (Motte et al. 2016). On the contrary, car ownership tends to be concentrated among the richest households, as is the case in Dakar, Senegal (Diaz Olvera et al. 2020a). The role of the automobile in African metropolises is more significant than its relative rarity suggests in practice. Additionally, various forms of sharing, even limited sharing, bring certain parts of the population closer to car access.

Faced with socially and spatially differentiated uses, only ambitious public action can allow for the reconsideration of the role of the automobile (Godillon and Lesteven 2020). However, many policies do not rethink its place in public space or in use. They are limited to sectoral guidelines, supporting a car industry that provides technical and technological innovations, or to local projects to improve the road network, by building new sections or dealing with traffic black spots. In addition to a high cost in investment and operation, the creation of new road infrastructures or their optimized management creates induced demand, while reinforcing the negative externalities of the automobile.

It is by acting upon the infrastructure that public authorities can change the role of the car in the city. This includes the creation of carpooling lanes, reserved for vehicles carrying at least two people, as in the United States since the 1980s. Public authorities may also constrain automobile use by reconfiguring existing roads to reduce speeds and limit barrier effects: transformation of tunnels into urban boulevards, suppression of overpasses, reduction of the number of lanes, etc. These practices of reconfiguration of living spaces are found in the centers of many cities from the United States to Asia. An iconic example is the demolition of the Cheonggyecheon motorway viaduct in the heart of Seoul, South Korea. The covered river has been restored and the place has become a major recreational area for the agglomeration, while land values have soared and car traffic has evaporated (Lecroart 2013). This reconfiguration of the road system may go hand in hand with a desynchronization or even removal of traffic lights and lower speed limits. In Paris, traffic speeds have been limited to 30 km/h since 2021. Complementary to a road reconfiguration policy, the parking policy is an effective lever to constrain automobile use and encourage modal shift. Designed in line with the supply of parking in private places (car parks, company parking, etc.) and at the metropolitan level, it frees up public space for other uses: pedestrian mobility and cycle paths. Parking pricing also frees up resources for the community, as does road pricing. As a measure often discussed in the media, road pricing makes the motorist pay for access to the area or its traffic. It may take the form of a congestion charge, as in London or Singapore, or an environmental charge, as in Italy. Enacted in the 1980s to preserve the historic centers of Italian cities damaged by pollution, low-emission zones are now multiplying in many European cities.

These policies are not exhaustive and mainly involve Western cities. Many cities in the Global South are today characterized by intense congestion in their central spaces, which are poorly adapted to cars. As the fleet of vehicles grows and the roading network becomes more extensive, congestion and pollution spread out to the peripheries (Lesteven 2012). Faced with this automotive transition and in a context of demographic pressure, public authorities have a major role to play in the development of public transport and the rehabilitation of active transport. They have at their disposal a repertoire of policies to implement while taking the local context into account; if not, there is a risk of discrepancies between the policies desired on paper and those deployed on the ground (Olivier de Sardan 2021).

1.3.2. *High urban density and public transport*

Mass transit refers to modes that move a significant number of passengers in the same vehicle at the same time, most often on dedicated infrastructures. Suitable for high demand, they perform well on radial and internal links for the city center, where the highest population densities are found. Their capacity is all the more justified by their operation in networks with feeder lines involving buses, minibuses or collective taxis, which carry many passengers.

Several types of mass transit exist and are distinguished by their type of infrastructure, rolling stock and operating conditions. Running on their own dedicated route, underground or elevated, permanently guided, metro systems allow high traffic flows and speeds. It has grown continuously since the end of the 19th century and is present today in 182 cities around the world and is planned for more than 30. The 2010s saw the commissioning of 45 new metro networks, including 33 in Asia (UITP 2018). In contrast to the metro, though also permanently guided, a tramway runs on its own partially dedicated route. With less capacity than the metro, it also has a lower operating speed, due to intersections. Developed during the 19th century, trams were first pulled by horses and were then electrified. It reached a peak in the 1920s with more than 3,000 networks worldwide. Many of them were dismantled during the 20th century, competing with the automobile. Today, tram networks exist in 389 cities around the world, more than half of which are in Europe (UITP 2019). This renewed interest in the tram is partly explained by a coupling with urban planning policies. Reclaiming the streets, the tramway reduces the role of the automobile in the city while encouraging a reconfiguration of public space. Finally, BRT travels on reserved lanes and stops at pre-established stops. Invented in Brazil in the 1980s, BRT is cheaper than rail, while achieving high levels of capacity. It retains the flexibility of the bus, with relatively short commissioning times. Note that 181 cities around the world have a BRT network, one-third of which are in Latin America[2]. International donors, led by the World Bank, encourage the deployment of BRT lines in many cities, with the prerequisite of setting up a transport authority at metropolitan level (Cirolia et al. 2020).

In addition to public transport operating on its own route, public and private bus companies and commercial services using individual motorized modes provide public transport of a lesser capacity. Their operating speeds may be limited by car traffic and their quality of service may be lower. Shared taxis, motorcycle taxis, motor tricycles, and minibuses are the only means of collective transport in many Southern metropolises. As intermediate modes between private cars and mass transit, they satisfy a growing demand in neighborhoods which are less dense or not as well served by public transport, while being more flexible than high-capacity modes. In Latin America, Africa and Asia, they have developed massively since the 1980s, following neoliberal reforms that led to the withdrawal of the state and the bankruptcy of public bus companies. Motorcycle taxis are now present in more than half of the cities on the African continent (Diaz Olvera et al. 2020b). Intermediate modes are also experiencing a revival in cities of the North, under the influence of environmental injunctions, budgetary constraints and the diffusion of digital technologies and the platform economy. Car-sharing and ride-sharing services are developing alongside e-hailing platforms, which, like Uber, connect drivers and passengers in real time. Most commonly based on private initiative, these services

---

2 Available at: https://brtdata.org/ [Accessed 3 March 2022].

raise the question of how to regulate them, which is illustrated in the choice of terms used to designate them. Besides the term "paratransit" (Behrens et al. 2016), the term "informal transport" is used in contrast to institutional public transport. In India, household travel surveys list them under the label of intermediate public transport (Kunhikrishnan and Srinivasan 2018).

These modes have a spatial footprint, embodied in particular by pick-up locations, formalized or not. In the outskirts of Dakar, shared taxis, locally called clandestine taxis or clandos, circulate between the different pick-up locations, on routes that are generally fixed and well known to users. They also involve a social aspect, allowing the greatest possible number to access motorized mobility, even on a casual basis. Inhabitants of the outskirts of Dakar, especially women, use the clando in their neighborhoods to access health services, visit relatives, go to the market, etc. Workers, on the other hand, most often use clandos as a means of transferring to other public transport to get to work (Lesteven et al. 2022).

1.3.3. *Active transport in the heart of the city*

Non-motorized modes are still rarely considered as modes of transport in their own right by public authorities. They are rarely the subject of dedicated mobility policies. Yet walking is the most commonly used mode of transport on a daily basis in many cities around the world (see section 1.2). As a mode used by poor populations in cities of the Global South, it has experienced a revival in many European cities over the past 20 years (Lavadinho 2011). This revival is accompanied by urban planning operations at different scales in order to make urban residents aware that it is sometimes just as fast but more pleasant to walk than to take public transport for a few stops. Urban density, which was criticized for limiting the fluidity of car traffic, becomes favorable to the practice of walking, especially when barrier effects are eliminated, obstacles are removed and elevators, ramps or spaces for sitting are installed. These facilities enable access to walking for elderly people or people with disabilities. But in many cities, walking remains uncomfortable and dangerous. Dedicated facilities such as footpaths, pedestrian crossings or footbridges across roadways, stairs, etc., are often missing or poorly maintained. Their markings are unsuitable or the lighting is absent. This state of infrastructure makes access to public transport and the city more difficult and makes pedestrians particularly vulnerable to motorized traffic.

Besides walking, cycling is also experiencing a revival at the global level, even if its modal share remains much lower. Its low-cost equipment makes it the preferred mechanized mode for low-income populations, especially rural populations in poor countries. In Western cities, cycling is promoted as a utilitarian mode and not just a leisure mode. Many cities offer bike sharing services while dedicated infrastructure is built: bike paths, secure crossings, bike parking, etc. Multimodal policies integrate cycling into possible combinations, notably with trains. The development of electric bikes reinforces this trend, as do scooters and other personal mobility devices (Segways, self-balancing unicycles, skateboards, etc.) which increase the speed of pedestrian traffic (Monnet 2019). These infrastructure policies are more effective when linked to proximity-related policies, for example, by maintaining local shops and services and by allowing urban residents, young or old, to access them on foot or by bicycle.

1.4. Conclusion

This overview of urban mobility systems around the world allows us to approach the diversity of systems. Demographic and urban transitions amplify differences between systems, while globalization erases others.

Mobility policies influence urban forms, just as urban forms influence mobility policies. Depending on the modes favored by mobility policies, the populations involved are not the same. The development of road infrastructure favors motorized travel, which often concerns middle-class and affluent households. In the cities of the Global South, the development of mass transit raises the question of service to outlying districts and the ability of users to pay. Active transport is too often neglected, although walking remains the main mode of daily travel. In some areas, walking and cycling may offer interesting prospects for modal shift if accompanied by developments in public space suitable for their uses. Multimodal policies promote mobility practices in which city dwellers can switch from one mode to another depending on their reasons for travel or their destination. The construction of dedicated infrastructures such as multimodal hubs and the implementation of integrated ticketing encourage these multimodal practices.

But the reality remains that many urban dwellers do not have access to quality daily mobility. For many of them, getting around the city has a high monetary and time cost. The issue of spatial equity complements the issue of social equity. Daily travel is not the same for urban residents of peripheries not served by public transport as for those living in urban centers, close to amenities. Despite policies limiting car access in the city and encouraging a shift to collective and active modes, the private car remains the main means of travel for many city dwellers in Western cities. Promoting sustainable mobility that emits less greenhouse gases requires policies that promote local travel by foot or bicycle, encourage car sharing and the use of intermediate public transport modes, or even promote a decrease in certain trips. Not all cities are in the same stage of their demographic, urban and automotive transitions, and there are still many challenges in moving toward more sustainable urban mobility systems.

1.5. References

ANSD (2018). Situation économique et sociale du Sénégal en 2015. Report, Agence Nationale de Statistique et de la Démographie, Dakar.

Beaucire, F. (2005). La ville compacte est-elle importable en France ? In *Les sens du mouvement. Modernité et mobilité dans les sociétés contemporaines*, Allemand, S., Allemand, A.F., Levy, J. (eds). Belin, Paris.

Behrens, R., McCormick, D., Mfinanga, D. (2016). *Paratransit in African Cities Operations, Regulation and Reform*. Routledge, New York.

Buchanan, C. (1963). *Traffic in Towns*. Penguin Books, Harmondsworth.

Cacciari, J. and Belton Chevallier, L. (2020). Beyond the mobility biographies, the social production of travel choices: Socialization, space and social relations. *Flux*, 119–120(1–2), 59–72.

Cirolia, L.R., Harber, J., Croese, S. (2020). Position paper: The state of knowledge and research. Governing mobility in Sub-Saharan African cities. Paper, Volvo Research and Educational Foundations, Gothenburg.

Dennis, K. and Urry, J. (2012). Post-car mobilities. In *Car Troubles: Critical Studies of Automobility and Auto-mobility*, Conley, J. and Mclaren, A.T. (eds). Ashgate Publishing, Farnham.

Diaz Olvera, L., Plat, D., Pochet, P. (2020a). Access to the car in the cities of Sub-Saharan Africa: Practices and users in Dakar. *Flux*, 119–120, 73–89.

Diaz Olvera, L., Plat, D., Pochet, P. (2020b). Looking for the obvious: Motorcycle taxi services in Sub-Saharan African cities. *Journal of Transport Geography*, 88, 102476.

Dupuy, G. (1995). *Les territoires de l'automobile*. Anthropos-Economica, Paris.

Dupuy, G. (2008). *Urban Networks: Network Urbanism*. Techne Press, Amsterdam.

Eskenazi, M., Lesteven, G., Leurent, F. (2017). Meta-observatory of mobility at country and city scale. In *Transportation Research Board (TRB) 96th Annual Meeting*, 8–12 January, Washington, DC.

Fol, S. and Cunningham-Sabot, E. (2010). "Déclin urbain" et Shrinking Cities : une évaluation critique des approches de la décroissance urbaine. *Annales de géographie*, 674(4), 359–383.

Gallez, C., Maulat, J., Roy-Baillargeon, O., Thébert, M. (2015). Le rôle des outils de coordination urbanisme – Transports collectifs dans la fabrique politique urbaine. *Flux*, 101–102, 5–15.

Godillon, S. and Lesteven, G. (2020). The death and life of automobile mobility? Between resistance and change. *Flux*, 119–120(1–2), 1–4.

Gwilliam, K. (2002). Cities on the move. A World Bank urban transport strategy review. Report, World Bank, Washington, DC.

Henderson, J. (2012). The politics of mobility: De-essentializing automobility and contesting urban space. In *Car Troubles: Critical Studies of Automobility and Auto-mobility*, Conley J. and Mclaren A.T. (eds). Ashgate Publishing, Farnham.

Jacobs, J. (1961). *The Death and Life of Great American Cities*. Vintage, New York.

Kuhnimhof, T., Rohr, C., Ecola, L., Zmud, J. (2014). Automobility in Brazil, Russia, India, and China quo vadis? *Transportation Research Record: Journal of the Transportation Research Board*, 2451, 10–19.

Kunhikrishnan, P. and Srinivasan, K. (2018). Investigating behavioral differences in the choice of distinct Intermediate Public Transport (IPT) modes for work trips in Chennai city. *Transport Policy*, 61, 111–122.

Lavadinho, S. (2011). Le renouveau de la marche urbaine : terrains, acteurs et politiques. Thesis, École normale supérieure de Lyon – ENS Lyon.

Le Corbusier (1973). *The Athens Charter*. HarperCollins, New York.

Lecroart, P. (2013). *Séoul : Cheonggyecheon Expressway – La ville après l'autoroute : études de cas*. IAU, Ile-de-France.

Lesteven, G. (2012). Les stratégies d'adaptation à la congestion automobile dans les grandes métropoles : analyse à partir des cas de Paris, São Paulo et Mumbai. Thesis, Université Paris 1 Panthéon-Sorbonne.

Lesteven, G. (2018). La transformation numérique des mobilités. In *Le nouveau monde de la mobilité*, Landau, B. and Diab, Y. (eds). Presses des Ponts, Paris.

Lesteven, G., Cissokho, D., Pochet, P., Diongue, M., Sakho, P. (2022). Daily mobility in urban peripheries: The role of clandestine taxis in Dakar, Senegal. *Sustainability*, 14, 6769.

Lucas, K. (2011). Making the connections between transport disadvantage and the social exclusion of low-income populations in the Tshwane region of South Africa. *Journal of Transport Geography*, 19, 1320–1334.

Merlin, P. and Choay, F. (eds) (2010). *Dictionnaire de l'urbanisme et de l'aménagement*. PUF, Paris.

Massot, M.-H. and Orfeuil, J.-P. (2005). La mobilité au quotidien, entre choix individuel et production sociale. *Cahiers internationaux de sociologie*, CXVIII, 81–100.

Monnet, J. (2019). #12 / Marcher en ville : technique, technologie et infrastructure (s)lowtech ? *Urbanités* [Online]. Available at: https://www.revue-urbanites.fr/12-monnet/ [Accessed 21 March 2022].

Moreno, C. and Garnier, M. (2020). Livre blanc n°2. La ville du 1/4 d'heure. Du concept à la mise en œuvre. White paper, Chaire ETI – IAE Paris, Université Paris 1 Panthéon Sorbonne.

Motte, B., Aguilera, A., Bonin, O., Nassi, C. (2016). Commuting patterns in the metropolitan region of Rio de Janeiro. What differences between formal and informal jobs? *Journal of Transport Geography*, 51, 59–69.

Narayan, A., Cojocaru, A., Agrawal, S., Bundervoet, T., Davalos, M.E., Garcia, N., Lakner, C., Mahler, D.G., Montalva Talledo, V.S., Ten, A., Yonzan, N. (2022). COVID-19 and economic inequality: Short-term impacts with long-term consequences. Policy research working paper, World Bank Group, Washington, DC [Online]. Available at: http://documents.worldbank.org/curated/en/219141642091810115/COVID-19-and-Economic-Inequality-Short-Term-Impacts-with-Long-Term-Consequences [Accessed 21 February 2022].

Newman, P. and Kenworthy, J. (1989). *Cities and Automobile Dependence: A Sourcebook*. Gower Technical, Brookfield.

OICA (2015). World vehicles in use by country and type 2005–2015 [Online]. Available at: http://www.oica.net/category/vehicles-in-use [Accessed 21 February 2022].

Olivier de Sardan, J.-P. (2021). *La revanche des contextes*. Karthala, Paris.

Pochet, P. and Lesteven, G. (2023 (in press)). La moto personnelle dans les villes d'Afrique subsaharienne : diffusion, usages et utilisateurs. *Géotransports*.

Pochet, P., Diaz Olvera, L., Plat, D., Adoléhoume, A. (2017). Private and public use of motorcycles in Sub-Saharan African cities. In *Public Transport Trends 2017*, UITP (ed.). UITP, Brussels.

Reigner, H., Hernandez, F., Brenac, T. (2009). Circuler dans la ville sûre et durable : des politiques publiques contemporaines ambiguës, consensuelles et insoutenables. *Métropoles*, 5 [Online]. Available at: http://journals.openedition.org.inshs.bib.cnrs.fr/metropoles/3808 [Accessed 21 March 2022].

SDES (2022). Résultats détaillés de l'enquête mobilité des personnes de 2019. Study, Données et Études Statistiques, Ministère de la Transition Écologique [Online]. Available at: https://www.statistiques.developpement-durable.gouv.fr/resultats-detailles-de-lenquete-mobilite-des-personnes-de-2019?rubrique=60&dossier=1345 [Accessed 21 February 2022].

Steck, J.-F. (2006). Qu'est-ce que la transition urbaine ? Croissance urbaine, croissance des villes, croissance des besoins à travers l'exemple africain. *Revue d'économie financière*, 86, 267–283.

Trouvé, M., Lesteven, G., Leurent, F. (2020). Worldwide investigation of private motorization dynamics at the metropolitan scale. *Transportation Research Procedia*, 48, 3413–3430.

Trouvé, M., Nemett, L., Lesteven, G. (2021). Motorisation motocycliste dans le monde : dynamiques métropolitaines et caractérisation socio-économique. In *Connaissances scientifiques pour les motocycles*, Subirats, P., Ragot-Court, I., Serre, T., Lanfranchi, M. (eds). L'Harmattan, Paris.

UITP (2018). World Metro Figures 2018. Statistics report, International Association of Public Transport, Brussels.

UITP (2019). Light rail and tram: The European outlook. Statistics report, International Association of Public Transport, Brussels.

UN (2018). World urbanization prospects. The 2018 revision, highlights. Report, United Nations Department of Economic and Social Affairs [Online]. Available at: https://population.un.org/wup/Publications/Files/WUP2018-Report.pdf [Accessed 21 February 2022].

UN (2019). World population prospects 2019, highlights. Report, United Nations Department of Economic and Social Affairs [Online]. Available at: https://population.un.org/wpp/Publications/Files/WPP2019_Highlights.pdf [Accessed 21 February 2022].

Vasconcellos, E. (2008). Urban transport policies in Brazil: The creation of a discriminatory mobility system. *Journal of Transport Geography,* 67, 85–91.

WB (2018). Poverty and shared prosperity 2018: Piecing together the poverty puzzle. Summary report, World Bank, Washington, DC [Online]. Available at: https://pubdocs.worldbank.org/en/911401537279777945/PSPR2018-Ch1-Summary-EN.pdf [Accessed 21 March 2020].

Wiel, M. (1999). *La transition urbaine ou le passage de la ville pédestre à la ville motorisée.* Mardaga, Sprimont.

Wiel, M. (2005). *Ville et mobilité : un couple infernal ?* Éditions de l'Aube, La Tour d'Aigues.

2

Unevenly Distributed Mobility, Spotlight on Brazil

Benjamin MOTTE-BAUMVOL
ThéMA, CNRS, Université de Bourgogne, Dijon, France

2.1. Introduction

We are not all equal when it comes to everyday mobility. Disparities may be explained by multiple factors, such as age, gender, income, household composition, or areas of residence and travel. But not all of these disparities reflect the same social issues. In terms of inequalities, low mobility, which particularly concerns poor individuals, has been the subject of much research as it is likely to threaten access to many important resources for individuals, and is therefore a factor of exclusion. Lucas (2012, 2019) uses the term *transport poverty* to refer to low mobility and its social challenges related to the restriction of individuals' access to goods and services, and indeed to other social resources such as social networks and therefore social capital. Accordingly, *transport poverty* does not pertain to the absolute value of indicators of daily travel, but rather to the relationship between lower mobility, in terms of numbers of trips or distances traveled, and degraded access for individuals to important social resources. Kenyon et al. (2002, p. 210) define this link as "the process by which people are prevented from participating in the economic, political and social life of the community due to reduced accessibility of opportunities, services and social networks, due wholly or partly to insufficient mobility in a society and environment built around an assumption of high mobility".

In this context, drawing in particular on existing works to which the present author has contributed, the objective of this chapter is to show that low mobility

Urban Mobility Systems in the World,
coordinated by Gaële LESTEVEN. © ISTE Ltd 2023.

takes on different forms depending on the social and spatial context, and that it results in different forms of exclusion for the individuals experiencing it. In order to document these contextual effects, we make use of an overview of different European countries, North America, Australia and more specifically, Brazil. Brazil is characterized by a much lower level of per capita income and very marked sociospatial inequalities compared to the other countries studied in this chapter. Analysis of mobility in Brazil thus offers a very stark contrast and makes a more detailed study of certain forms of endemic inequalities in the countries of the north possible, without losing sight of the specificities of these observations in relation to the local context.

2.2. Income and access to the automobile, main determinants of low mobility

While income is reportedly the main determinant of low mobility, it is not tackled head on in the literature. Instead, it is addressed by way of its association with access to automobiles. Indeed, income limits access to the automobile in terms of use but primarily in terms of ownership (Giuliano and Dargay 2006). This approach is particularly well developed in British, American and Australian studies. The point is proven in two stages: first by highlighting the correlation between household income and car ownership, and second by highlighting the link between non-ownership of a vehicle and low mobility, as characterized by short distances of travel and a low number of trips (Pucher and Renne 2005; Wixey et al. 2005; Delbosc and Currie 2012).

2.2.1. Decreasing inequalities of motorization

In France, the growth of automobile ownership by households has slowed over recent decades (Grimal et al. 2013). Since all sections of the population are increasingly motorized, room for further expansion is now limited. The young adult generations in France and elsewhere are attracting the attention of many researchers because they seem to make different choices in terms of transport compared to previous generations. In many developed countries, people born in the year 2000 take longer to obtain a driver's license, own fewer cars and drive less than their elders (Kuhnimhof et al. 2012). However, more recent results reveal a diversity of situations depending on the country and/or city, with no clear overall trend emerging in the end as to a possible decline in sustainable car ownership for young adults (Delbosc and Ralph 2017; Delbosc et al. 2019).

As a result, inequality in car ownership according to income, which was very high in the 1970s, is far lower today. Low-income households are still characterized by lower average ownership per adult (Collet et al. 2013), but the gap in relation to the richest has narrowed considerably. In France, the household motorization gap between the first income quartile (those with the lowest incomes) and the other three quartiles is 10 points (75% vs. 85%) (Collet et al. 2013). Collet et al. (2013) believe that this gap will narrow further, as their forecast models estimate that the level of motorization of the poorest should grow faster than that of the richest, which has almost reached its limit.

In addition to the extent of motorization, inequalities in ownership according to income also concern the type and age of cars (Bhat et al. 2009; Coulangeon and Petev 2012), the type of insurance (Taylor et al. 2008) and maintenance and repairs (Hivert 2001). These inequalities weigh particularly on the poorest and on immigrants in the United States (Priya and Uteng 2009). Finally, low-income motorized households are distinctive in their automotive mobility in that they avoid parking charges and road tolls (Taylor et al. 2008), sometimes forcing them to make longer and more tiring trips.

2.2.2. Decoupling of motorization and automotive mobility

While consideration of motorization provides an initial approach to mobility inequalities, it only serves as an approximation. Indeed, the link between motorization and automotive mobility is not straightforward, since it is not absolutely necessary to own a car to enjoy access to automotive mobility. Households or individuals who do not own a car can get a lift with friends and family or from car-pooling services, and they may borrow or rent a vehicle through car-sharing services. In the United States, individuals living in a household without a car nevertheless make about one-third of their trips by car (Lovejoy and Handy 2011). In France, one-third of non-motorized adults travel by car on weekdays, as a passenger and/or driver (Motte-Baumvol et al. 2010). Furthermore, households are not necessarily permanently non-motorized. Klein and Smart (2017) show that poor households in the United States frequently alternate between motorization and non-motorization. Car ownership in poor households is therefore not always permanent.

In addition, motorization does not always make it possible to take full advantage of automotive mobility. Thus, even when motorized, poor households make extremely moderate use of the automobile (Orfeuil 2004). In France, adults in the lowest income quartile travel an average of 6,500 km per year by car, compared with more than 8,000 km for adults in the second quartile and more than 10,000 km for adults in the highest quartile (Grimal et al. 2013). In Britain, motorized households in the highest quintile annually travel distances three times greater than those in the lowest quintile (Wixey et al. 2005). In other countries, differences in automotive mobility according to income are also observed and are often more pronounced, as in the United States (Renne and Bennett 2014) or in Australia (Delbosc and Currie 2012).

2.2.3. *Automobile dependency as a source of inequalities*

While inequalities in motorization are lessening in some respects, the automobile remains a lasting source of inequalities in that a situation of dependence has become established (Goodwin 1997; Dupuy 1999). Now, this dependence tends to place people who do not travel by car, who are in principle ever fewer in number, in an increasingly acute position of exclusion.

For Dupuy, the basis of automobile dependence is the existence of a sufficiently developed automotive system (Hall 1988), that is, a whole array of mass-produced devices, and of services, infrastructures, rules and regulations essential to automobile travel as we know it today. Without this environment, the automobile could not be a rapid and accessible mode of transport for the greatest number of people. The system thus functions like a club that produces greater effects the more members it has. Dupuy (1999) estimates that for the population as a whole, a "1% increase in motorization provides, all other things being equal, a gain in accessibility on the order of 2%". The strong development of the automotive system and the club effects that it fosters generate a form of *radical monopoly* as formulated by Illich (1974). In other words, the development of automotive mobility comes at the expense of other modes of transport. The expansion of the automotive system and the accessibility gains offered by automotive mobility downgrade the accessibility and availability of other modes of transportation. This downgrading may be relative in some cases, that is, the levels of accessibility and supply of other alternative modes do not decrease, but these levels continue to soar for the automobile. The gaps between modes widen to the advantage of the automobile. For example, during the final two decades of the 20th century, the availability and accessibility of public transport increased throughout France's major urban areas. However, that increase was slower than for the automobile, resulting in the strengthening of the *radical monopoly* and automobile dependency.

Ultimately automotive dependence is an eminently global process affecting society and territories as a whole. Automotive mobility imposes a norm in travel practices and has become the condition for "normal" inclusion in social life, particularly in areas of lower population density (Cervero 2002). For Dupuy, non-motorized households are the major losers in car dependency, precisely because they are not members of the club. Indeed, society is dependent on the automobile, and those who cannot use one suffer from a form of exclusion. The same applies to motorized households that limit their mobility or their car ownership for reasons of cost (Grimal et al. 2013). The *radical monopoly* imposed by the automobile is manifested by the exclusion of an entire fringe of the population, in particular the poorest and the oldest (Dupuy 1999). These populations would no longer be able to carry out their activities (work, shopping, family visits, etc.), nor satisfy their aspirations, if they did not have a private car, or more broadly, if they could not use one when needed.

While automobile dependence is global, for some authors (Goodwin 1995; Stradling et al. 2000; Motte-Baumvol 2007) it is also subject to spatial and individual contexts. Local and individual contexts modulate automobile dependence depending in particular on the availability of alternative modes and local resources, the program or places of individual activity. Car dependence thus affects territories and individuals differently. Its challenges must therefore be assessed in both these dimensions. The challenges of automobile dependence are reflected by the capacity of households to cope with constraints on access to the resources they need depending on the territory. Motte-Baumvol (2006, p. 43) thus proposes a change in the definition of automobile dependence: "A process in which the superior performance of the private car compared to other modes tends to give it a growing and hegemonic place. This process, which varies in intensity over time and depending on the territory, leads to a form of exclusion for households who are unable to motorize or who struggle to take full advantage of the possibilities offered by the private car".

2.3. Low mobility as a source of exclusion

Beyond the determinants of inequalities, and in particular the role of the automobile, many studies focus on the observation of these inequalities and the processes of social marginalization to which these inequalities may lead for the poorest individuals. Thus, for poor households as a whole, whether motorized or not, the distances traveled annually are lower than for households on higher incomes. On a daily basis, poor households limit the range of their travel by favoring closer destinations for daily activities other than work (Gray et al. 2001; Diaz Olvera et al. 2004). In the United States, the ratio between the daily distances traveled by rich households (more than $100,000 per year) and poor households (less than $20,000 per year) exceeds 1.7, with 18 miles and 32 miles, respectively, per day (Pucher and Renne 2003). In Great Britain, the ratio between the distances traveled by the highest and lowest income quintiles is greater than 2: poor households tend to limit their trips, including for employment, and generally live closer to their place of work

(Wixey et al. 2005). This is also the case in France, where the working poor work more often in their municipality of residence and make trips over shorter distances (Orfeuil 2004).

In addition to constraining travel distances, the mobility difficulties of the poorest also limit the number of trips they make. In France, rich households make only 10% more trips than poor households (Diaz Olvera et al. 2004). But the gap reaches 35% in Great Britain (Wixey et al. 2005) and almost 50% in the United States, with 4.8 daily trips for rich households compared to 3.3 for poor households (Pucher and Renne 2003).

In addition, households with limited incomes have less varied reasons for travel. This is especially the case for French peri-urban areas, where travel for shopping and leisure is particularly rare when income is limited (Motte-Baumvol et al. 2010). Since they make fewer trips, individuals on low incomes tend to limit their travel to the strict minimum and focus on access to employment, education and whatever is necessary to support the family. They thus have fewer opportunities to enjoy the other resources offered by the city, which, while not essential, are nonetheless useful for social integration (Ureta 2008). In Île-de-France, travel for leisure by non-motorized and low-income individuals is rarer, being partially offset by more visits to family or friends (Motte-Baumvol et al. 2010). Diaz-Olvera et al. (2004) find the same trends in Lyon. Blumenberg and Agrawal (2014) show that poor households tend to minimize the number of trips they make by reorganizing their activities to combine their trips and group their destinations.

2.4. The effects of accessibility and low densities

While low mobility tends to limit the activities of individuals, this tendency is accentuated in certain areas (Motte-Baumvol et al. 2010; Jouffe et al. 2015), mainly due to the diminished geographical accessibility of resources for low-income households.

Constraints and limitations on the mobility of low-income households are particularly marked in peripheral areas where automobile dependency is more pronounced, as shown by Morency et al. (2011) in the case of Canada or Mattioli et al. (2019) for England. Indeed, the disparities in access between central areas and urban peripheries are very significant and tend to increase, as also shown by studies of French urban areas (Caubel 2006; Motte-Baumvol 2008). In Canada, the peripheral location of a portion of social housing is the main explanation for very limited levels of access to services and facilities for half of social housing residents (Apparicio and Seguin 2006). Even for motorized households, the gains in accessibility related to owning a car are lower in peripheral areas (Paez et al. 2010). In the Australian context, Currie and Delbosc (2010) show that transport and accessibility issues are more likely to be a source of ill-being and social exclusion in rural and peri-urban areas than in central areas. Indeed, less-motorized households living in peripheral areas poorly served by public transport are forced to reduce their daily mobility, which reduces their participation in many activities and their opportunities for social integration (Delbosc and Currie 2012).

In the greater Barcelona area, Cebollada (2009) highlights the importance of territorial differences in terms of mobility and access to employment. He shows that if non-motorized households have access to a more limited labor market and employment opportunities, and are less likely to find and keep a job, these inequalities may be partly offset, in the dense area of the agglomeration, by the proximity of jobs and the use of public transport. On the other hand, in the periphery, households without cars are forced to resort to precarious, unsustainable or even dangerous arrangements to get to work, like those individuals who cross a freeway on foot every day. In peri-urban areas, women, who are more often without a car at their disposal, are forced to give up working or confine themselves to local, under-qualified and poorly paid jobs (Camarero and Oliva 2008; Ortar 2008).

Social and territorial conditions therefore combine to constrain daily mobility and limit the accessibility of poor households, particularly in peri-urban areas. This context raises even more questions in that a proportion of low-income households have a strong propensity to settle in peri-urban areas. Kneebone and Garr (2010) show that in most large North American cities, the poor population is growing faster in the peri-urban areas than in the suburbs. In France (Cavailhès and Selod 2003) and Australia (Currie 2010), there is also a rapid growth of low-income households in peri-urban areas, attracted by lower land and housing costs. Residing in the outskirts, however, results in increased pressure on the budget of low-income households, due in particular to the costs of automotive mobility (Polacchini and Orfeuil 1999; Berri 2007; Dodson and Sipe 2007; Coulombel and Leurent 2013).

2.5. Room for maneuver with respect to *transport poverty*

Individuals with low mobility, whatever its characteristics, short distances traveled and/or few trips, seem irremediably trapped in this situation, mainly by the costs associated with the automobile and by the locations in which they live. However, there is room for maneuver for these households to escape *transport poverty* and "participate in the economic, political and social life of the community" (Kenyon et al. 2002, p. 210), despite their lower accessibility and mobility.

These margins of maneuver consist, on the one hand, of traveling at a lower cost in order to gain the means to travel as much as is affordable for them. On the other hand, this room for maneuver is based on mobilization of social networks to avoid travel, for example, by exchanging services for shopping or childcare. Despite limited access to many resources, low-income individuals deploy multiple forms of organization allowing them to reduce their high mobility costs, notably by restricting their travel (Blumenberg and Agrawal 2014; Ortar 2018).

In order to minimize travel costs, journeys are limited in number and distance according to a criterion of strict necessity, and the least expensive modes of transport are preferred. In addition, automotive mobility is reduced in favor of walking, public transport, car sharing (Blumenberg and Agrawal 2014; Molin et al. 2016) and cycling (Martens 2013). Other arrangements are implemented by individuals of modest means, particularly the use of social networks, which are widely mobilized to enable many trips to be made (Hine and Grieco 2003). This results in intensive practices of carpooling or borrowing cars (Charles and Kline 2006; Blumenberg and Smart 2010; Lovejoy and Handy 2011; Ortar 2018). Thus, even for non-motorized people, the automobile has a central place in mobility (Rogalsky 2010). Spatial proximity to social networks is one of the conditions for this solution, which is sometimes accompanied by monetary compensation or exchanges of services (Lovejoy and Handy 2011), and which needs to be carefully arranged and planned (Clifton 2004).

Social networks are mobilized to avoid travel without giving up access to certain activities, while ensuring the well-being of low-income households (Delbosc and Currie 2011). Child minders are thus widely sought after within the family circle, which is a major provider of services and mutual aid, in particular childcare and accommodation (Barnes 2003). In general, poor households live close to their families (Bonvalet et al. 1999) and devote a large part of their free time to them, in particular with regard to the services they provide to each other. However, maintaining the social network generates its own mobility requirements. Orfeuil and Soleyret (2002) show that weekend visits to family and friends account for a clearly larger share of travel for poor households than for wealthy households.

Beyond social networks, the mobility of poor individuals relies on intensive practices of local space. Proximity lies at the heart of their mobility and accessibility strategies, but also at the heart of their residential and working lives. Indeed, poor households have relational networks that are mainly based on proximity, which fosters much stronger local anchoring than for most other social categories (Fol 2009). These forms of social capital that can be mobilized locally have the effect of reducing the residential mobility of poor households. For example, blue-collar workers are less likely to move when they estimate their chances of becoming integrated elsewhere to be low (Retière 1994). While professionals assert their social identity by moving away from their families, blue-collar workers demonstrate their social belonging by staying close to the family nucleus. The residential choices of poor households are also linked to the need to maximize accessibility to shops, amenities and services. Non-motorized individuals live closer to shops than those who are motorized (Clifton 2004). Poor households thus make residential choices that allow them to balance their mobility and accessibility, given a limited budget (Currie et al. 2010).

Proximity to employment is also sought after by poor households. Immergluck (1998) shows that the availability of jobs nearby has a decisive impact on the process of leaving unemployment for poor households. The work of both Kawabata and Shen (2007) for the United States and Korsu and Wenglenski (2010) for France indicates that the least qualified individuals tend to work in a much more local job market. Indeed, this local area is largely favored in the search for employment, because of the (low) gains and (high) costs that poor households can expect from geographical mobility, given their qualification profile, in the United States (Chapple 2001) as in France (Vignal 2005; Sigaud 2015). These adjustments are thus characterized by voluntary limitation of both the scope of the job search and of the distance at which jobs are likely to be accepted (Chapple 2001; Vignal 2005; Fol 2009).

Many studies emphasize that poor households value anchoring, although it is linked to an adjustment of subjective expectations to objectively unequal opportunities (Passeron and Bourdieu 1968). Effects on social mobility may be negative depending on individuals' social networks (Pinkster 2007) and nearby resources (Curley 2010). It is also the effectiveness of anchoring as compensation for difficulties of access that encourages its valorization. Particularly in sparsely populated areas, urban mobility appears disconnected from well-being, which arises more from strong ties forged in proximity (Delbosc and Currie 2011). Many studies (Gieryn 2000; Morel-Brochet and Motte-Baumvol 2010) highlight the subjective attachment of inhabitants to their place of residence. The valorization of local anchoring finally appears as another form of adjustment to inequalities in mobility, insofar as it frees inhabitants from the need for mobility (Coutard et al. 2002; Bacqué and Fol 2007).

A system of constraints weighs on the movements of certain individuals, in particular the poorest, in connection with lower car ownership and their residential location in sparsely populated peripheral areas. But, as we have just seen, these individuals have room for maneuver that allows them to moderate the effects of mobility inequalities. Our work (Belton-Chevallier et al. 2018) characterizes these margins of maneuver as expedients and groups them into three types: limitation of movements and their concentration in local space; the intensive use of social networks; residential relocation. It has been shown, on the one hand, that these arrangements are articulated to form a system of practices creating an alternative to excessively expensive automotive mobility, and, on the other hand, that they are constructed collectively and at different scales: the couple, household and social network. The collective nature of the arrangements implemented by households makes this alternative system more efficient because it allows them to withstand the particularly strong constraints of an environment dominated by automotive mobility by giving them sufficient access to urban resources. But at the same time, it weakens this alternative insofar as raising a challenge to only one of the components of the system is likely to destroy the complex equilibrium of the interactions upon which it is based (Cacciari and Belton-Chevallier 2020).

2.6. In Brazil, increased inequality and *transport poverty*?

In large Brazilian cities, daily mobility is lower than in large North American or European cities. The number of daily trips observed in Rio de Janeiro or Sao Paulo is around two compared to nearly four in cities in the United States or Île-de-France. Poverty is advanced as an explanation for these very low levels of mobility in Brazilian cities (Vasconcellos 2005). In the context of highly segregated Brazilian cities, this leads to neighborhoods, even entire areas of cities, characterized by low mobility and with difficulties in accessing employment and other urban resources. In Brazil, the term fragmentation is used to describe this situation (Santos 1990). Fragmentation goes beyond the spatial separation of social groups since it expresses a more rigid separation along geographical boundaries that may be impossible to erase (Chétry 2013). Santos (1990) highlights the isolation created by fragmentation – particularly for certain poor neighborhoods wedged between rich neighborhoods – infrastructure and the physical environment. The author sees the relative immobility of a large part of the population in these neighborhoods as relating not only to poverty and low wages, but also to the conditions of the area. He concludes that the low mobility of such a large number of people transforms the city into a muddle of ghettos and what was fragmentation becomes disintegration. We are faced here with extreme forms of *transport poverty* that our work largely relativizes.

2.6.1. *Low mobility, a question of measurement?*

But this very marked difference in the measurement of travel can be explained by several factors linked to the methods of observing mobility, as opposed to being the outcome of inequalities. First, there is the question of how Brazilian travel surveys measure mobility. Indeed, the surveys do not count non-motorized journeys of less than 300 m in their observations, meaning that the number of journeys made is largely underestimated, in particular in very densely populated and poor neighborhoods such as favelas, where many trips are made on foot within a short radius. Second, the lower number of trips observed may be understood in relation to the lower income levels in Brazil. Thus, in the Metropolitan Region of Sao Paulo, individuals with income levels above the median have levels of travel somewhat closer to those observed in Île-de-France (2.8 versus 3.8 trips), in particular when it comes to the number of journeys by individual motorized modes (1.5 in both cases), which are counted in the same way in both surveys. On the other hand, for the poorest, the number of trips is much lower, with only 1.5 trips per day and in particular, less than 0.5 trips by individual motorized modes. In French cities, the number of trips is comparable between poor and rich households, with the exception of travel related to work. In large Brazilian cities such as Sao Paulo and Rio de Janeiro, the number of trips made by the poorest populations is nearly half that of the richest (Vasconcellos 2005; CENTRAL 2014). Inequalities in mobility related to income are therefore much greater there.

2.6.2. *With motorization, inequalities in mobility increase*

Between 2001 and 2015, Brazil experienced a period of strong economic growth. This growth led to a general improvement in the standard of living of the population, as noted by Neri (2008) in the middle of the period. This resulted in a process of social mobility that allowed the transition of a large part of the population from the lower class (low income) to the middle class (middle income) (Anderson 2011) and had a significant impact on daily mobility, especially with regard to access to motorization (Rodrigues 2013). Indeed, the Brazilian government encouraged the growing motorization of households in order to develop an automotive industry that has been important to the country's economy since the 1950s (Lopes 2005). For example, the government temporarily reduced taxes on popular new cars, combined with credit and financing facilities (Wilbert et al. 2014). These measures encouraged many households to use motor vehicles for the first time (Neri 2008; Pereira and Schwanen 2013). However, motorization remains much lower than in European or North American cities. In Sao Paulo in 2017, only 52.9% of households were motorized, compared to 49.5% in 2007 (SETM 2019). To households owning a car, we must add the estimated 8% of households owning motorized two-wheelers. Taking into account both cars and motorcycles, the household motorization rate reaches 60% in Sao Paulo, with very high inequalities. For the richest 15% of households, motorization reaches 93% compared to only 27% for the poorest quarter of households. In Rio de Janeiro, our work also shows marked inequalities for working people, with only 27% of poor working people being motorized compared to 78% for the richest (Motte-Baumvol et al. 2017).

2.6.3. Slow public transport

Even when motorized, poor Brazilian households cannot take full advantage of automotive mobility as it remains too expensive. Thus, travel by the poor is characterized by fewer and shorter trips. Our work on commuting in Rio de Janeiro shows that only 9% of poor working people drive to their workplace, or barely one-third of the motorized poor (Motte-Baumvol et al. 2017). Automotive mobility remains too expensive on a daily basis for the vast majority of motorized households. Apart from the costs of maintenance and fuel, parking is limited and very expensive in the central neighborhoods of Rio de Janeiro (Torres 2013) and parking on public roads is rarely possible for reasons of security and theft (Musumeci and Conceiçao 2007). The alternative to the car is public transport in particular, but this poses several problems. There are serious difficulties with unreliable services and overloaded vehicles, especially at peak times in outlying metropolitan areas. In addition, poor neighborhoods are often poorly served by public transport, while a large part of the population still cannot afford to travel by bus. In 2014, a typical monthly bus ticket cost about 17% of the national minimum wage (Vasconcellos 2018).

Beyond that, public transport is particularly slow in many Brazilian cities as it is based mainly on a vast network of bus lines, only rarely benefiting from portions of dedicated lanes or having right-of-way at intersections, and it is therefore affected by the high and growing congestion that marks the main arterial routes. Buses contribute to this increasing congestion, in that their traffic has increased sharply with demand. In fact, higher capacity and faster modes of transport, such as trains and metros, still account for only 10% of daily public transport journeys in major Brazilian cities. The recent move toward high-level service buses (BHLS) is developing strongly and improving both the availability and speed of public transport. But its development is still limited and there is (as is already the case for the metro) a risk of "elitism", with high-quality BHLS in city centers and a substandard bus system in outlying areas – where, in addition, road infrastructure is generally more degraded and/or unpaved.

Thus, workers who travel to work by public transport have longer travel times than those observed by car. The differences here are not insignificant; commutes of more than an hour represent 41% of journeys by public transport compared to 22% of journeys by car or motorbike in Rio de Janeiro. In fact, the working poor have travel speeds 20% lower than the richest. In some poor neighborhoods of Rio de Janeiro, these durations have increased further as bus travel speeds have deteriorated due to increasing congestion.

2.6.4. Geographical confinement

Beyond the difficulties encountered in public transport, the poor, who to a large extent use non-motorized modes, are very severely hampered in their mobility. Indeed, non-motorized transport has always been neglected by the public authorities (Vasconcellos 2018). There are no clear policies for sidewalk construction and maintenance. In all cities, landowners are responsible for the sidewalks in front of their properties. As regulations are not strict and enforcement is weak, sidewalks are in a poor state-of-repair and in some peripheral areas they are simply non-existent. Finally, cycling is very dangerous because cyclists have to share unsuitable roads with motorized vehicles and only rarely have dedicated cycle lanes.

Other obstacles are placed in the way of non-motorized modes. These are the effects of severance due to physical barriers. There are several kinds of severance effects. The first, which are well documented, are high-traffic streets. These particularly affect the practices of residents who are separated from each other by infrastructure and have fewer neighborly relations, use public space around their homes less and whose lives are more confined to their homes (Appleyard et al. 1981). These severance effects vary in intensity with the type of barriers and the difficulties of crossing them, among which are very busy streets, freeways or railways. James et al. (2005) emphasize that these physical barriers also have a psychological dimension, as they produce an atmosphere (unpleasant, insecure, etc.) and nuisances (noise, smell, traffic, etc.), which form obstacles to local travel. Moreover, severance effects are not unique to transport infrastructures, but apply to all major single-use rights-of-way (Jacobs 1961), such as industrial areas, airports, stadiums or port areas. The natural environment can also form physical barriers. In Rio de Janeiro, such barriers include steep hillsides, the coastline, the islands, the bay and the protected forest, the latter two being located in the heart of the metropolitan space.

The existence of a barrier is not necessarily detrimental to travel beyond the immediate vicinity of the right-of-way, if each of the areas separated from the others by the boundary is large enough to be adequately multifunctional (Héran 2009). But when the neighborhoods are too small or fragmented and/or the barrier is very difficult to cross, the whole area is then subject to a severance effect and sees the degree of mobility of the residents decline. For Heran (2011), the indirect effects of severance are a loss of interest in walking and cycling, a decline in neighborly relations, and a deterioration in health and in the living environment. Thus, for this author, the populations most vulnerable to severance are children, people with reduced mobility, pedestrians and cyclists. Indeed, severance subjects them, among other things, to detours, changes in elevation, additional energy expenditure and/or dangerous passages with which these populations and users of these modes of transport find it more difficult to cope.

Based on a statistical analysis of data from the Rio de Janeiro Travel Survey of 2003, using a geographically weighted regression model, we were able to highlight the effects of these severances on individual movements (Motte-Baumvol et al. 2016). Thus, in several districts of the city, marked by physical barriers (transport infrastructure, single-use rights-of-way, walls, rugged terrain), the model revealed a lower probability of travel. Also, the model points to the poorest populations in these neighborhoods as being most impacted by these severance effects. Indeed, poor residents in these neighborhoods travel almost exclusively on foot. Severance imposes detours and additional efforts which limit their travel, especially since public transport is less accessible due to its cost (Gomide 2003). For the better-off workers who travel by public transport or car, the effects of physical barriers are much more limited or even non-existent. Thus, in a middle-class neighborhood (Ilha do Governador), although located on an island to which access is restricted in particular by the presence of the international airport, the movement of working people does not seem to be hampered by the double effect of severance due to access to motorized mobility (cars, motorcycles and public transport).

2.6.5. *Highly mobile poor neighborhoods*

We must be careful, however, not to overgeneralize and conclude that these results show a lower probability of moving around in poor neighborhoods. Undoubtedly, these effects only concern certain poor neighborhoods that are particularly marked by physical barriers, and do not provide material for the literature on possible neighborhood effects, especially since this study focused on the case of *favelas* located on hillsides above rich neighborhoods, that is, a small part of the poor neighborhoods of Rio de Janeiro. For these neighborhoods, we postulated severance effects due to perceived and symbolic barriers (Capron 2002) corresponding to the very strong sociospatial segregation of Rio de Janeiro. Santos (2009) highlights the isolation created by fragmentation, especially for some poor neighborhoods wedged between wealthy neighborhoods, infrastructure and physical barriers. In these neighborhoods, the relative immobility of a large part of the population is, for the author, due to poverty, low wages and local conditions. But our work (Motte-Baumvol et al. 2016) highlights that in the case of favelas located in the heart of rich neighborhoods, fragmentation leads to increased mobility. These neighborhoods are those where the probability of being immobile is the lowest, in particular for working people. Indeed, the wealthy neighborhoods nearby offer many job opportunities for low-skilled and poor workers, particularly in commerce or home services. Conversely, the inhabitants of the city's richest district (Leblon) are marked by greater immobility. We hypothesize that these individuals, surrounded by poorer people, remain in their own neighborhood, where the shops, services and jobs intended for them are located.

2.7. Conclusion

The study of inequalities in mobility has been the subject of substantial research, some of which focuses on individuals with low mobility and provides a better understanding of the issues in terms of social insecurity for the individuals concerned. Thus, low mobility has characteristics and an intensity in terms of travel that vary with the individual, in particular with their level of income, their access to a car or their residential location. Low mobility is generally characterized by a restricted range of travel, as well as fewer trips and less varied travel patterns. This results in serious limitations in access to many resources, including work, preventing some people from sustainably keeping, changing or finding employment because of difficulties in traveling regularly and in suitable conditions to certain locations. However, there is room for maneuver to at least partially overcome *transport poverty*, in particular by seeking more favorable residential locations and the use of solidarity networks that are often offered by relatives and families. But these margins of maneuver do not allow us to completely overcome the social issues of *transport poverty*, especially in a country like Brazil, where very strong sociospatial segregation requires poor populations to be able to move at the risk of a sociospatial fragmentation of society, as suggested by Santos (2009).

2.8. References

Anderson, P. (2011). O Brasil de Lula. *Novos Estudos-CEBRAP*, 91, 23–52.

Apparicio, P. and Seguin, A.-M. (2006). Measuring the accessibility of services and facilities for residents of public housing in Montreal. *Urban Studies*, 43(1), 187–211.

Appleyard, D., Gerson, M.S., Lintell, M. (1981). *Livable Streets, Protected Neighborhoods*. University of California Press, Berkeley.

Bacqué, M. and Fol, S. (2007). L'inégalité face à la mobilité : du constat à l'injonction. *Revue suisse de sociologie*, 33(1), 89–104.

Barnes, S. (2003). Determinants of individual neighborhood ties and social resources in poor urban neighborhoods. *Sociological Spectrum*, 23(4), 463–497.

Belton-Chevallier, L., Motte-Baumvol, B., Fol, S., Jouffe, Y. (2018). Coping with car dependency: A system of expedients used by low-income households on the outskirts of Dijon and Paris. *Transport Policy*, 65, 79–88.

Berri, A. (2007). Residential location and household expenditures on transport and housing: The example of the Greater Paris Region. *World Conference on Transportation Research*. WCTR, Berkeley.

Bhat, C.R., Sen, S., Eluru, N. (2009). The impact of demographics, built environment attributes, vehicle characteristics, and gasoline prices on household vehicle holdings and use. *Transportation Research Part B: Methodological*, 43(1), 1–18.

Blumenberg, E. and Agrawal, A.W. (2014). Getting around when you're just getting by: Transportation survival strategies of the poor. *Journal of Poverty*, 18(4), 355–378.

Blumenberg, E. and Smart, M. (2010). Getting by with a little help from my friends and family: Immigrants and carpooling. *Transportation*, 37(3), 429–446.

Bonvalet, C., Gotman, A., Grafmeyer, Y. (1999). *La famille et ses proches : l'aménagement des territoires*. INED/PUF, Paris.

Cacciari, J. and Belton-Chevallier, L. (2020). La démotorisation des ménages comme analyseur de la diversité des expériences de socialisation à la "norme automobile". *Flux*, 119120(1), 59–72.

Camarero, L.A. and Oliva, J. (2008). Exploring the social face of urban mobility: Daily mobility as part of the social structure in Spain. *International Journal of Urban and Regional Research*, 32(2), 344–362.

Capron, G. (2002). Accessibility to modern public spaces in Latin-American cities: A multi-dimensional idea. *GeoJournal*, 58(2–3), 217–223.

Caubel, D. (2006). Politique de transports et accès à la ville pour tous ? Une méthode d'évaluation appliquée à l'agglomération lyonnaise. PhD thesis, Université Lumière Lyon 2.

Cavailhès, J. and Selod, H. (2003). Ségrégation sociale et périurbanisation. *INRA Sciences Sociales*, 1–2(3), 1–4.

Cebollada, À. (2009). Mobility and labour market exclusion in the Barcelona Metropolitan Region. *Journal of Transport Geography*, 17(3), 226–233.

CENTRAL (2014). Plano diretor de transporte urbano 2011 da região metropolitana do Rio de Janeiro: Resultados da pesquisa origem e destino. Report, Governo do Estado do Rio de Janeiro, Rio de Janeiro.

Cervero, R. (2002). Built environments and mode choice: Toward a normative framework. *Transportation Research Part D: Transport and Environment*, 7(4), 265–284.

Chapple, K. (2001). Time to work: Job search strategies and commute time for women on welfare in San Francisco. *Journal of Urban Affairs*, 23(2), 155–173.

Charles, K.K. and Kline, P. (2006). Relational costs and the production of social capital: Evidence from carpooling. *The Economic Journal*, 116(511), 581–604.

Clifton, K.J. (2004). Mobility strategies and food shopping for low-income families. *Journal of Planning Education and Research*, 23(4), 402–413.

Collet, R., Madre, J.L., Hivert, L. (2013). Diffusion de l'automobile en France : vers quels plafonds pour la motorisation et l'usage ? *Economie et statistiques*, 457-458, 1–17.

Coulangeon, P. and Petev, I.D. (2012). L'équipement automobile, entre contrainte et distinction sociale. *Economie et statistique*, 457(1), 97–121.

Coulombel, N. and Leurent, F. (2013). Les ménages arbitrent-ils entre coût du logement et coût du transport : une réponse dans le cas francilien. *Economie et statistique*, 457, 57–72.

Coutard, O., Dupuy, G., Fol, S. (2002). La pauvreté périurbaine : dépendance locale ou dépendance automobile ? *Espaces et sociétés*, 108–109, 155–172.

Curley, A.M. (2010). Relocating the poor: Social capital and neighborhood resources. *Journal of Urban Affairs*, 32(1), 79–103.

Currie, G. (2010). Quantifying spatial gaps in public transport supply based on social needs. *Journal of Transport Geography*, 18(1), 31–41.

Currie, G. and Delbosc, A. (2010). Modelling the social and psychological impacts of transport disadvantage. *Transportation*, 37(6), 953–966.

Currie, G., Richardson, T., Smyth, P., Vella-Brodrick, D., Hine, J., Lucas, K., Stanley, J., Morris, J., Kinnear, R., Stanley, J. (2010). Investigating links between transport disadvantage, social exclusion and well-being in Melbourne – Updated results. *Research in Transportation Economics*, 29(1), 287–292.

Delbosc, A. and Currie, G. (2011). The spatial context of transport disadvantage, social exclusion and well-being. *Journal of Transport Geography*, 19(6), 1130–1137.

Delbosc, A. and Currie, G. (2012). Choice and disadvantage in low-car ownership households. *Transport Policy*, 23, 8–14.

Delbosc, A. and Ralph, K. (2017). A tale of two millennials. *Journal of Transport and Land Use*, 10(1), 903–910.

Delbosc, A., McDonald, N., Stokes, G., Lucas, K., Circella, G., Lee, Y. (2019). Millennials in cities: Comparing travel behaviour trends across six case study regions. *Cities*, 90, 1–14.

Diaz Olvera, L., Mignot, D., Paulo, C. (2004). Daily mobility and inequality: The situation of the poor. *Built Environment*, 30(2), 153–160.

Dodson, J. and Sipe, N. (2007). Oil vulnerability in the Australian city: Assessing socioeconomic risks from higher urban fuel prices. *Urban Studies*, 44(1), 37–62.

Dupuy, G. (1999). *La dépendance automobile : symptomes, analyses, diagnostic, traitements.* Anthropos, Paris.

Fol, S. (2009). *La mobilité des pauvres.* Belin, Paris.

Gieryn, T.F. (2000). A space for place in sociology. *Annual Review of Sociology*, 26, 463–496.

Giuliano, G. and Dargay, J. (2006). Car ownership, travel and land use: A comparison of the US and Great Britain. *Transportation Research Part A: Policy and Practice*, 40(2), 106–124.

Gomide, A. (2003). *Transporte urbano e inclusão social: elementos para políticas públicas.* IPEA, Brasília.

Goodwin, P. (1992). *Car Dependence.* RAC Foundation for Motoring and the Environment, Feltham.

Goodwin, P. (1997). Mobility and car dependence. In *Traffic and Transport Psychology*, Rothengatter, J.A. and Carbonell Vaya, E. (eds). Pergamon Press, Oxford.

Gray, D., Farrington, J., Shaw, J., Martin, S., Roberts, D. (2001). Car dependence in rural Scotland: Transport policy, devolution and the impact of the fuel duty escalator. *Journal of Rural Studies*, 17(1), 113–122.

Grimal, R., Collet, R., Madre, J.-L. (2013). Is the stagnation of individual car travel a general phenomenon in France? A time-series analysis by zone of residence and standard of living. *Transport Reviews*, 33(3), 291–309.

Hall, P. (1988). Impact of new technologies and socio-economics trends on urban forms and functioning. Report, OECD, Paris.

Héran, F. (2009). Des distances à vol d'oiseau aux distances réelles ou de l'origine des détours. *Flux*, 76–77(2), 110–121.

Héran, F. (2011). *La ville morcelée : effets de coupure en milieu urbain.* Economica, Paris.

Hine, J. and Grieco, M. (2003). Scatters and clusters in time and space: Implications for delivering integrated and inclusive transport. *Transport Policy*, 10(4), 299–306.

Hivert, L. (2001). Le parc automobile des ménages, étude en fin d'année 1999 à partir de la source "Parc Auto" SOFRES. Report, INRETS, Arcueil.

Illich, I. (1974). *Energy and Equity.* Marion Boyars Publishers Ltd., London.

Immergluck, D. (1998). Neighborhood economic development and local working: The effect of nearby jobs on where residents work. *Economic Geography*, 74(2), 170–187.

Jacobs, J. (1961). *The Death and Life of Great American Cities.* Random House, New York.

James, E., Millington, A., Tomlinson, P. (2002). Understanding community severance I: Views of practitioners and communities. Report, Department for Transport, London.

Jouffe, Y., Caubel, D., Fol, S., Motte-Baumvol, B. (2012). Faire face aux inégalités de mobilité. Tactiques, stratégies et projets des ménages pauvres en périphérie parisienne. *Cybergeo: European Journal of Geography*. doi: 10.4000/cybergeo.26697.

Kawabata, M. and Shen, Q. (2007). Commuting inequality between cars and public transit: The case of the San Francisco Bay Area, 1990–2000. *Urban Studies*, 44(9), 1759–1780.

Kenyon, S., Lyons, G., Rafferty, J. (2002). Transport and social exclusion: Investigating the possibility of promoting inclusion through virtual mobility. *Journal of Transport Geography*, 10(3), 207–219.

Klein, N.J. and Smart, M.J. (2017). Car today, gone tomorrow: The ephemeral car in low-income, immigrant and minority families. *Transportation*, 44(3), 495–510.

Kneebone, E. and Garr, E. (2010). The suburbanization of poverty: Trends in metropolitan America, 2000 to 2008. Metropolitan policy program, Brookings, Washington, DC.

Korsu, E. and Wenglenski, S. (2010). Job accessibility, residential segregation, and risk of long-term unemployment in the Paris region. *Urban Studies*, 47(11), 2279–2324.

Kuhnimhof, T., Armoogum, J., Buehler, R., Dargay, J., Denstadli, J.M., Yamamoto, T. (2012). Men shape a downward trend in car use among young adults – Evidence from six industrialized countries. *Transport Reviews*, 32(6), 761–779.

Lopes, S.P. (2002). Development of mathematics models for analysis, evaluation and forecast of the motorisation behavior in Brazil. PhD thesis, Federal University of Rio de Janeiro.

Lovejoy, K. and Handy, S. (2011). Social networks as a source of private-vehicle transportation: The practice of getting rides and borrowing vehicles among Mexican immigrants in California. *Transportation Research Part A: Policy and Practice*, 45(4), 248–257.

Lucas, K. (2012). Transport and social exclusion: Where are we now? *Transport Policy*, 20, 105–113.

Martens, K. (2013). Role of the bicycle in the limitation of transport poverty in the Netherlands. *Transportation Research Record: Journal of the Transportation Research Board*, 2387, 20–22.

Mattioli, G., Philips, I., Anable, J., Chatterton, T. (2019). Vulnerability to motor fuel price increases: Socio-spatial patterns in England. *Journal of Transport Geography*, 78, 98–114.

Molin, E., Mokhtarian, P., Kroesen, M. (2016). Multimodal travel groups and attitudes: A latent class cluster analysis of Dutch travelers. *Transportation Research Part A: Policy and Practice*, 83, 14–29.

Morel-Brochet, A. and Motte-Baumvol, B. (2010). Les périurbains franciliens : stratégies résidentielles, tactiques du quotidien et résistance des modes d'habiter. In *Mobilités et modes de vie métropolitains, les intelligences du quotidien*, Massot, M.H. (ed.). L'oeil d'or, Paris.

Morency, C., Paez, A., Roorda, M.J., Mercado, R., Farber, S. (2011). Distance traveled in three Canadian cities: Spatial analysis from the perspective of vulnerable population segments. *Journal of Transport Geography*, 19(1), 39–50.

Motte-Baumvol, B. (2006). La dépendance automobile pour l'accès aux services aux ménages en grande couronne francilienne. PhD thesis, Université Paris I Panthéon Sorbonne.

Motte-Baumvol, B. (2007). La dépendance automobile pour l'accès des ménages aux services : le cas de la grande couronne francilienne. *Revue d'économie régionale et urbaine*, 5, 897–919.

Motte-Baumvol, B. (2008). L'accès des ménages aux services dans l'espace périurbain francilien. *Strates*, 14, 149–164.

Motte-Baumvol, B., Massot, M.-H., Byrd, A.M. (2010). Escaping car dependence in the outer suburbs of Paris. *Urban Studies*, 47(3), 604–619.

Motte-Baumvol, B., Bonin, O., David Nassi, C., Belton-Chevallier, L. (2016). Barriers and (im)mobility in Rio de Janeiro. *Urban Studies*, 53(14), 2956–2972.

Motte-Baumvol, B., Nassi, C.D., Coelho de Morais Neto, G., Lopes, L., de Aquino Lannes Brites, P. (2017). Motorisation croissante et évolution des déplacements domicile-travail à Rio de Janeiro entre 2002 et 2012. *Cybergeo : European Journal of Geography*. doi: 10.4000/cybergeo.27916.

Musumeci, L. and Conceiçao, G. (2007). Geografia dos roubos de veículos na cidade do Rio de Janeiro: análise das ocorrências registradas pela Polícia Civil e das denúncias feitas ao Disque-Denúncia no período 2002-2002. Report, UFRJ, Rio de Janeiro.

Neri, M.C. (2008). *A nova classe média*. FGV/IBRE, Rio de Janeiro.

Orfeuil, J.-P. (2004). Accessibilité, mobilité, inégalités : regards sur la question en France aujourd'hui. In *Transports, pauvretés, exclusions : pouvoir bouger pour s'en sortir*, Orfeuil, J.-P. (ed.). Editions de l'Aube, La Tour d'Aigues.

Orfeuil, J.-P. and Soleyret, D. (2002). Quelles interactions entre les marchés de la mobilité à courte et à longue distance ? *Recherche – Transports – Sécurité*, 76, 208–221.

Ortar, N. (2008). Entre ville et campagne, le difficile équilibre des périurbaines lointaines. *Métropoles*, 3. doi: 10.4000/metropoles.1642.

Ortar, N. (2018). Dealing with energy crises: Working and living arrangements in peri-urban France. *Transport Policy*, 65, 72–78.

Paez, A., Gertes Mercado, R., Farber, S., Morency, C., Roorda, M. (2010). Relative accessibility deprivation indicators for urban settings: Definitions and application to food deserts in Montreal. *Urban Studies*, 47(7), 1415–1438.

Passeron, J.-C. and Bourdieu, P. (1968). L'examen d'une illusion. *Revue française de sociologie*, 9(1), 227–253.

Pereira, R.H.M. and Schwanen, T. (2013). *Tempo de deslocamento casa-trabalho no Brasil (1992-2009): Diferenças entre regiões metropolitanas, níveis de renda e sexo*. Instituto de Pesquisa Econômica Aplicada (IPEA), Brasília.

Pinkster, F.M. (2007). Localised social networks, socialisation and social mobility in a low-income neighbourhood in the Netherlands. *Urban Studies*, 44(13), 2587–2603.

Polacchini, A. and Orfeuil, J.-P. (1999). Les dépenses des ménages franciliens pour le logement et les transports. *Recherche Transports Sécurité*, 63, 31–46.

Priya, T. and Uteng, A. (2009). Dynamics of transport and social exclusion: Effects of expensive driver's license. *Transport Policy*, 16(3), 130–139.

Pucher, J. and Renne, J.L. (2002). Rural mobility and mode choice: Evidence from the 2001 National Household Travel Survey. *Transportation*, 32(2), 165–186.

Pucher, J. and Renne, J.L. (2003). Socioeconomics of urban travel: Evidence from the 2001 NHTS. *Transportation Quarterly*, 57(3), 49–77.

Renne, J.L. and Bennett, P. (2014). Socioeconomics of urban travel: Evidence from the 2009 National Household Travel Survey with implications for sustainability. *World Transport Policy & Practice*, 20(4), 7–27.

Retière, J. (1994). *Identités ouvrières*. L'Harmattan, Paris.

Rodrigues, J.M. (2013). Evolução da frota de automóveis e motos no Brasil 2001-2012. Report, INCT Observatório das Metrópoles, Rio de Janeiro.

Rogalsky, J. (2010). Bartering for basics: Using ethnography and travel diaries to understand transportation constraints and social networks among working-poor women. *Urban Geography*, 31(8), 1018–1038.

Santos, M. (2009). *Metropole corporativa fragmentada: o caso de São Paulo*. Editora Edusp, São Paulo.

SETM, S. (2019). A mobilidade urbana da região metropolitana de São Paulo em detalhes. Report, Governo de São Paulo, São Paulo.

Sigaud, T. (2012). Accompagner les mobilités résidentielles des salariés : l'épreuve de l'"entrée en territoire". *Espaces et sociétés*, 162(3), 129–142.

Stradling, S., Meadows, M., Beatty, S. (2000). Helping drivers out of their cars. Integrating transport policy and social psychology for sustainable change. *Transport Policy*, 7(3), 207–212.

Taylor, J., Barnard, M., Neil, H., Creegan, C. (2008). The travel choices and needs of low income households: The role of the car. Report, Department for Transport, London.

Torres, H.M. (2013). Uma nova política de estacionamento para o Rio de Janeiro. *19º Congresso Brasileiro de Transporte e Trânsito*, ANTP, Brasília.

Ureta, S. (2008). To move or not to move? Social exclusion, accessibility and daily mobility among the low-income population in Santiago, Chile. *Mobilities*, 3(2), 269–289.

Vasconcellos, E.A. (2002). Transport metabolism, social diversity and equity: The case of São Paulo, Brazil. *Journal of Transport Geography*, 13(4), 329–339.

Vasconcellos, E.A. (2018). Urban transport policies in Brazil: The creation of a discriminatory mobility system. *Journal of Transport Geography*, 67, 85–91.

Vignal, C. (2002). Logiques professionnelles et logiques familiales : une articulation contrainte par la délocalisation de l'emploi. *Sociologie du travail*, 47(2), 153–169.

Wilbert, M.D., Serrano, A.L.M., de Souza Gonçalves, R., Alves, L.S. (2014). Redução do imposto sobre produtos industrializados e seu efeito sobre a venda de automóveis no Brasil: uma análise do período de 2006 a 2013. *Revista Contemporânea de Contabilidade*, 11(24), 107–124.

Wixey, S., Jones, P., Lucas, K., Aldridge, M. (2002). Measuring accessibility as experienced by different socially disadvantaged groups. Working paper, Transport Studies Group, University of Westminster, London.

3

Going Out Without Getting By? Mobility and Poverty in Dakar

Lourdes DIAZ OLVERA, Didier PLAT and Pascal POCHET
*Laboratoire Aménagement Économie, Transports (LAET),
Université de Lyon, ENTPE, France*

There are many ways to study poverty, but due to its multidimensional nature, none of them allow us to grasp the totality of its manifestations and implications (Deaton 1997; Herpin and Verger 1997; Paugam 2005; Razafindrakoto and Roubaud 2005; Damon 2014; Alkire et al. 2015). Three main theoretical currents can be identified. The monetary approach examines the level and variability of economic resources within the population and sets a threshold below which households (or individuals) are considered poor. In order to make relevant comparisons between households, income or expenditure should be related to household needs, which vary according to size and composition. An approach based on the living conditions or essential needs of households considers that the ability to acquire various goods from one's income, even in societies where access to goods and services is essentially based on monetary transactions, gives only a truncated view of situations of poverty. These in fact arise from a combination of handicaps that degrade living conditions, including both material aspects (food, housing, etc.) and social aspects (access to education, employment, health, etc.). The subjective approach to poverty contrasts with these first two approaches, which adopt an external, "objectified" point of view toward households and individuals in order to qualify their situations. According to this line of thought, it is the opinion of the persons being interviewed that matters – their own appreciation of their situation and well-being. Each of these

Urban Mobility Systems in the World,
coordinated by Gaële LESTEVEN. © ISTE Ltd 2023.

approaches presents its own methodological difficulties, whether it involves precisely identifying available resources, or distinguishing between preferences or aspirations, on the one hand, and needs or necessities, on the other hand.

Studies on Sub-Saharan African cities that concern the links between poverty and daily mobility do not generally feature in the theoretical debate that we have just mentioned. They adopt an objective definition of poverty, either in terms of a monetary threshold or in terms of living conditions (Bryceson et al. 2003; Salon and Gulyani 2010; Salon and Aligula 2012; Sietchiping et al. 2012; Diaz Olvera et al. 2013; Boyer and Delaunay 2017). Empirical observations show that, for poor populations, often located in poorly served areas, being able to travel to places that offer jobs and urban amenities is essential. In rapidly expanding cities, access to motorized transport, individual or collective, appears increasingly necessary to reach destinations that are increasingly beyond walking distance. However, few households possess cars and motorized two-wheelers, public transport is often insufficient, and regular use of private or public motorized transport costs dearly compared to the incomes of poor households. A spatial poverty trap is thus liable to close upon poor populations, contributing to the reproduction of urban poverty. Leaving home in search of everyday resources does not seem to systematically enable one to leave situations of poverty.

Our objective here is to extend this research through the study of the mobility of poor populations in the metropolis of Dakar. Two questions underlie our approach. Does being poor influence the travel practices of urban dwellers and if so, what are the distinctive features of the mobility of the poor? Are the mobility practices of the poor likely to lift them out of poverty, or to lock them in? We first present the study area and the empirical data used, then the definition of situations of poverty. We then examine the mobility of poor populations, before analyzing access to three essential activities: school, shopping and work.

3.1. Field and tools

The metropolis of Dakar, due to its spatial development and the geographical characteristics of its location, shows a strong separation between places of activity and residential locations (Sakho 2002; Lombard et al. 2006). In 2015, the Dakar Region, its administrative name, comprised four departments: Dakar, Guédiawaye, Pikine and Rufisque (Figure 3.1). At the 2013 census, it had more than 3 million inhabitants, with the departments of Dakar and Pikine together accounting for nearly three quarters of the population. Rufisque accounted for 16% and Guédiawaye 10% (Agence Nationale de la Statistique et de la Démographie 2014). Urbanization has spread unidirectionally from the department of Dakar, first to Pikine, then to

Guédiawaye, then Rufisque (Sakho 2002, 2014) and has often developed in unplanned areas. Even today, in the southern tip of the department of Dakar, the Plateau, there is a concentration of a number of administrative, economic and service activities, which generates an imbalance between residence and employment and significant travel flows.

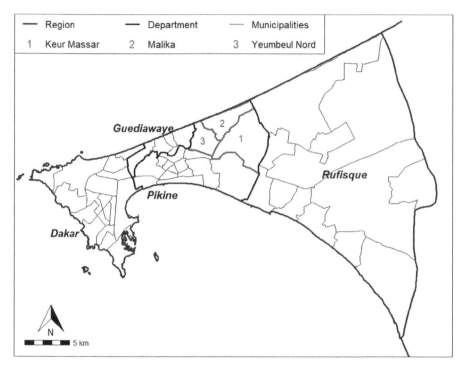

Figure 3.1. *The Dakar Region. For a color version of this map, see www.iste.co.uk/lesteven/urban.zip*

In 2015, possession of personal vehicles remained uncommon, as in other African capitals. Only one in seven households owned at least one car, and bicycles and motorbikes are even rarer. The availability of public transport is extremely varied, from personal cars operated as shared taxis to articulated buses, from individual artisanal activity to large companies dominated by public capital (Lombard 2015). However, it is the informal supply of public transport that predominates, despite the efforts to restructure the sector undertaken by the public authorities since the late 1990s. These efforts have been partially successful as the buses that they have promoted, colloquially known as Tatas (named after the Indian bus manufacturer), now receive half of the demand for public transport. But, victims of their own success, these buses are usually crowded and their customers are dissatisfied (Sitrass-Curem 2016).

The analyses presented here are based on data from the EMTASUD 2015[1], a household mobility survey conducted in May–June 2015 on behalf of CETUD (Sitrass-Curem 2016). The survey sample, representative of the population after statistical weighting, is based on a division of the Dakar Region into 41 zones, a random selection of 419 census districts within these zones and finally, a random selection of households to be surveyed within each selected census district. A total of 3,176 households and 13,415 individuals aged 11 and over from those households were interviewed. The information collected therefore makes it possible to identify the mobility of Dakar residents and to relate it to situations of poverty[2].

3.2. Who are the poor?

As the household survey was not designed to specifically study poor populations, it is necessary a posteriori to establish operational criteria to define these populations based on the available data. Although there is relative agreement today in seeing poverty as a multidimensional phenomenon and the monetary dimension remains very significant, the scientific literature does not propose a consensual definition of poverty. In this chapter, we choose to define situations of poverty according to the economic resources of households, and where necessary, we identify, among the poor, the "deprived" populations based on additional data about their living conditions.

The monetary approach we have adopted, which is standard (Deaton 1997), is based on a classification of households according to per capita income (the sum of

---

1 EMTASUD is the Dakar Survey on Mobility, Transport and Access to Urban Services.
2 The information collected concerns the household as a whole, on the one hand, and its members aged 11 and over, on the other. At the household level, the main themes relate to its composition, housing characteristics, goods owned (including vehicles), neighborhood environment, conditions of access to essential resources and services (water, electricity, education, health, markets, etc.). At the individual level, the information concerns socio-demographic characteristics, education, activity status, characteristics of employment (occupation, function, sector), income (which was collected in detail in a dedicated section (Diaz Olvera et al. 2015) and opinions on the public transport modes they use. An exhaustive description of every trip undertaken the previous day was collected (origin and destination, purpose, places and times of departure and arrival, modes of transport, amount paid for public transport). This type of survey is also used in other geographical contexts and has been adapted specifically to Sub-Saharan cities (for a perspective on household mobility surveys and initial transpositions in African contexts, see Godard et al. 2001).

the incomes of all members of the household divided by the total number of people in the household). Poor households are therefore those at the bottom of the income scale, in the first two quintiles, that is, the 40% of households with the lowest per capita incomes. By extension, poor individuals are the members of these households. Non-poor households, and correspondingly non-poor individuals, are those classified in the following three quintiles, that is, the 60% of households with the highest per capita incomes.

To identify, among poor households, those with significantly worse living conditions and increased vulnerability, we focus only on households in the first quintile, and take into account unmet food and health needs over the past year, based on two relevant survey questions ("In the last 12 months, has your household skipped a meal due to lack of resources?" and "In the last 12 months, has anyone in your household been unable to receive health care due to lack of resources?"). Among poor households, those in the first quintile who answered "Yes" to at least one of the two questions, and by extension the individuals belonging to them, will be referred to as "deprived". They represent 9% of all households in the region.

These three groups differ from each other primarily, of course, because of their monetary resources. On average, the incomes of poor households represent 62% of those of non-poor households, while those of deprived households represent only 20%. Higher housing costs in the Dakar department, and to a lesser extent in Guédiawaye, explain why poor households are proportionally much more concentrated in Pikine and Rufisque (Table 3.1). Regardless of the department, they live more often in flood-prone and less secure areas, to which access is difficult (+12 points for the poor, +19 points for the deprived). Dwellings, built with lower quality materials, are less often connected to running water and electricity networks.

	Non-poor	Poor	*of which* Deprived
Dakar	55	30	24
Guédiawaye	9	10	8
Pikine	26	43	53
Rufisque	10	17	15

Table 3.1. *Households' department of residence according to poverty (%)*

Poor households own fewer durable goods. This is particularly the case for transport vehicles (Table 3.2). Possession of bicycles and motorcycles is very limited, but this is also the case for non-poor households. The gap is much larger when it comes to cars – they are available for one in four households among the non-poor, but only one in 18 among the poor, and zero among the deprived.

	Non-poor	Poor	*of which* Deprived
Bikes (Nb)	0.03	0.03	0.01
Motorcycles (Nb)	0.08	0.04	0.00
Cars (Nb)	0.25	0.06	0.00
Households with car (%)	16.5	4.5	0.0

Table 3.2. *Number of vehicles per household and car ownership rate, according to household poverty*

The population of poor households is more female and younger, with these traits even more pronounced for deprived households. Among adults, illiteracy and low levels of education (dropping out of primary school) are more common. Still compared to the non-poor, the share of the active population is lower among the poor (-10 points). They are also more dependent on the informal economy: fewer salaried and permanent jobs, more self-employed, itinerant or home-based workers. How do these distinct population profiles translate into mobility behavior?

3.3. A specific mobility in situations of poverty

Given the great contrasts in housing conditions and strong inequalities regarding access to modes of transport according to household income, can poverty be associated with mobility difficulties, reduced mobility, or even immobility? Conversely, can greater and more diverse mobility be linked to less difficult living conditions? Based on data collected in the EMTASUD, levels of mobility by mode and by purpose make it possible to question, clarify and provide nuance for these relationships.

3.3.1. *Essential mobility*

In terms of the total number of trips and the time spent traveling during the day, the average levels of mobility for poor and non-poor individuals are very close. Poor individuals make a daily average of 3.3 trips for a total of 60 min, compared to 3.4 trips for a total of 64 min for the non-poor, due to a slightly higher proportion of poor people who did not travel (17% versus 14%, respectively). For women and men, the time spent traveling is the same at a given level of household poverty. However, deprived men and women are affected differently (Figure 3.2). The mobility of deprived men is somewhat more restricted than that of the other two groups, due to less travel for work corresponding to lower activity rates in this group. On the other hand, deprived women move around a little more than other women, because their trips for daily chores (food purchases, formalities and services) and sociability more than compensate for low mobility in connection with work. Among the deprived, the similar levels of mobility between men and women are therefore not accompanied by a convergence in their out-of-home activities. As has been shown in other African cities, strong economic constraints are a powerful "generator of mobility", as they lead individuals to multiply trips related to the management of daily life, a sphere of activity that most often falls to women. This includes smaller and more frequent purchases due to a lack of resources, visits to seek help or to try to solve a problem, or care for children in parallel with a small business activity (Grieco et al. 1996; Mandel 2004; Diaz Olvera et al. 2013).

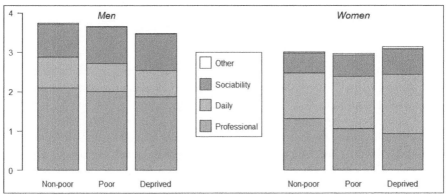

Professional: work or study. Daily: purchases, formalities and services, health, support. Sociability: visits, leisure, associations. Other: other purposes.

Figure 3.2. *Average number of trips per day, by major sphere of activity according to household poverty. For a color version of this figure, see www.iste.co.uk/lesteven/urban.zip*

3.3.2. Costly mobility

While overall levels of mobility are similar between poor and non-poor individuals, the means used to achieve this mobility differ quite a lot (Table 3.3). Walking is the most frequently used mode, most often for short distance trips[3] (590 m on average for the non-poor, 650 m for the poor, 680 m for the deprived). Its share is greater among the poor, for both men (three out of four trips) and women

---

3 All distances are "as the crow flies" distances between neighborhood centroids.

(four out of five). Poor people are not able to compensate for their low vehicle ownership rate by using public transport more frequently. All these traits are reinforced for deprived men and women.

	Non-poor	Poor	*of which* Deprived
Walking	64.7	77.7	81.5
PT 1 leg	25.1	18.1	14.7
Intermodal	2.7	2.7	3.3
Personal modes	7.5	1.6	0.6

Walking: trip made entirely on foot
PT 1 leg: trip made using a single public transport (PT) mode
Intermodal: several PT legs or, very rarely, one leg by PT and one by a personal mode
Personal modes: car (mainly), motorized two-wheelers, bicycle

Table 3.3. *Modal split according to household poverty (%)*

Whether considering female or male practices, poverty results in an even greater share of travel by walking, to the detriment of public transport for women (-11 points), and personal transport (-8 points) as well as public transport (-4 points) for men. These modal splits confirm that, despite a variety of forms of public transport, access to it on a daily basis is not guaranteed. Several structural elements contribute to reducing the poor population's use of public transport. Levels of service vary very widely between neighborhoods depending on their remoteness and quality of roads. Fares rise with increasing distances, which affects poor residents, often located on the outskirts, when they have to go into town, even if they avoid the most expensive modes, such as taxis. The importance of the latter element is further strengthened by the severe economic constraints to which households living in poverty are subjected.

Daily mobility is a significant expenditure item for Dakar households. Already accounting for nearly 11% of the income of non-poor households, it increases to 15% for poor households, and among these, it increases to 16.5% for deprived households (Table 3.4). Among poor households, three-quarters of the mobility budget goes to public transport expenditure (almost the totality, among deprived households), while among non-poor households, which are slightly more motorized, personal modes capture more than half of mobility expenses. However, the gap in absolute levels of expenditure on public transport is to the detriment of poor households, who spend one-third less on average. Already substantial when measured at the household level, this gap increases even further when measured at the individual level, regardless of activity status and gender. Poor working women spend nearly half as much as non-poor working women, despite the need for mobility required by professional activity (Table 3.5). Among schoolchildren, public transport expenditure is 60% lower than that of non-poor schoolchildren, 50% lower among wives without professional activity, nearly 40% among the unemployed and retired and 30% among other inactive people.

	Non-poor	Poor	*of which* Deprived
All modes	10.7	14.8	16.5
including **Public transport**	5.3	11.2	15.8

Table 3.4. *Share of mobility expenditure in total income, according to household poverty (%)*

	Non-poor	Poor	*of which* Deprived
All individuals	49.1	77.7	98.5
Working men	30.9	63.3	95.8
Working women	67.3	91.7	100.0

Table 3.5. *Share of public transport expenditure in total mobility expenditure, according to household poverty (%)*

While the economic constraint affects the modal choices and practices of non-poor individuals, it appears particularly significant for the mobility behavior of poor individuals. It virtually "condemns" poor households that do not have vehicles and thus makes their members dependent on public transport, but public transport is not always affordable either. High shares of mobility expenditure and simultaneously limited incomes show that greater public transport use is not feasible, as in many other African cities (Diaz Olvera et al. 2013). While it is not possible to assess the extent of unmet mobility needs, comparison between poor and non-poor by gender and activity status, levels of public transport mobility and related expenditure shows that this consumption is generally rationed among the poor, more or less significantly depending on individual financial capacities.

3.3.3. *Local mobility*

The spatial scope of travel is affected by this impeded access to motorized modes of transport and in particular to public transport. Categorizing trips according to the distance away from home distinguishes three types: internal to the neighborhood of residence; leaving the neighborhood while remaining in the department of residence;

beyond the limits of the department of residence. Confirming analyses carried out in Ouagadougou (Boyer et al. 2016), this classification shows that poverty is accompanied by a greater frequency of trips within the neighborhood (10 points more and even 17 points more for the deprived), and fewer exchanges with the rest of the department of residence and the rest of the metropolis (Figure 3.3).

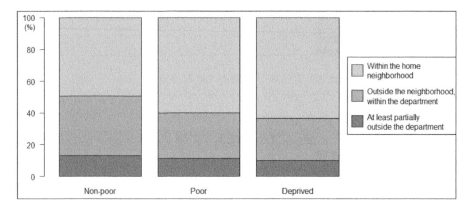

Figure 3.3. *Spatial distribution of trips according to household poverty. For a color version of this figure, see www.iste.co.uk/lesteven/urban.zip*

The spatial pattern among the poor, typically more restricted to spaces closest to the home, potentially relies on differences in the composition of the two groups, that is, activity statuses and related social roles. The effect of poverty is equally strong for women and men (Table 3.6). Consideration of activity status confirms the spatially restrictive effect of poverty on mobility. However, among working men, the effects of poverty appear to be attenuated, the distance from their workplace moving them further away from home than in the other categories. The increased polarization of travel around the home is confirmed by the analysis of spatial configurations of mobility: 61% of the non-poor made only round trips from home, compared to 65% of poor individuals and 69% of the deprived.

Travel within the neighborhood allows the maintenance of neighborly solidarity and the development of local informal resources, thus contributing to the life of neighborhoods and peripheral areas. But it enables only a limited spectrum of urban opportunities and resources to be activated, given the marked lack of resources in many peripheral areas. Examination of three structuring activities of daily life, that is, studying, shopping and working, shows various facets of the conditions of access to urban resources which are differentiated according to the level of poverty.

	Non-poor	Poor	*of which* Deprived
Men	44.1	53.9	58.5
of which Workers	37.1	42.4	44.4
of which Schoolchildren, students	58.6	69.2	74.6
Women	55.5	65.7	68.0
of which Workers	49.2	59.0	58.0
of which Schoolchildren, students	59.8	63.3	67.0

Table 3.6. *Share of trips within the neighborhood of residence, according to gender, individual activity status and household poverty (%)*

3.4. Going to study: degraded conditions of access to institutions

While a professional activity provides an income in the present, schooling is a part of current household expenditure, but also determines future access to incomes and their amount. However, household poverty has a negative impact on access to education.

In the Dakar metropolis, as in other cities of the Global South, children from poor households are less educated than others and their share in the school system decreases as the level of education increases (Table 3.7). The share of children from poor and deprived households in middle school is equivalent to their share in the whole population. But they are proportionally slightly more numerous in primary school and significantly less numerous in high school. The higher proportion of poor and deprived children in primary school is related to a greater occurrence of low achievement.

	Non-poor	Poor	*of which* Deprived
Primary	42	58	14
Middle school	49	51	12
High school	59	41	6
Higher education	71	29	3

Table 3.7. *Share of non-poor, poor and deprived among all schoolchildren and student groups, according to level of schooling (young people aged 6–24)*

Thus, among the 12–16 age group, which covers roughly the theoretical time of middle school attendance, 41% of poor children are still in primary school. In contrast, this situation applies to only 27% of children from non-poor households. Finally, even if private education does not necessarily mean better learning conditions, recourse to the public system is often the sign of a more limited world of choice for parents. However, among middle school children, 76% of poor children attend public school, 20 points more than among children from more affluent households.

School participation and success depend on multiple factors. Its major determinants include, on the side of demand for education, parents' attitudes toward school and study conditions at home, and on the side of supply of education, the availability of schools within neighborhoods and class sizes. Conditions of physical access to educational establishments are also contributing factors (Diaz Olvera et al. 2010). Travel practices appear less favorable to poor children, as shown by distances to the establishments, and even more so the modes of transport used to access middle school.

The distance to public middle schools, 1.2 km on average, is not related to the economic status of the household. This is not the case for private middle schools: 1.8 km for children from non-poor households, 1.9 km for those from poor households and 2.7 km for those from deprived households. The difference in travel practices is accentuated between non-poor and poor, and a fortiori the deprived, once the modes used are taken into account (Table 3.8). In the public system, walking is omnipresent, although public transport is used for one in five trips among the non-poor – twice as many as among the poor. In the private sector, which is generally more distant, the share of walking is significantly lower than for the public schools among the non-poor, but only slightly reduced among the poor and still equally high among the deprived. Due to public transport only being used for the longest trips, the result is greater walking distances between home and private middle schools. They thus differ between non-poor and poor at a ratio of 1 to 1.6 (2.3 for the deprived). To access public middle school as well, the walking distance is slightly longer for children from poor households, +12% (+20% for the deprived).

Trips to middle school are more burdensome for children from poor households. They are hampered by the reduced supply of public middle schools in the neighborhoods where these populations live in large numbers. When they attend private education, travel is made even more difficult because of the search for less expensive and often more distant schools. The cost of public transport forces them to depend on walking, even for long distances. The effects of increased distance are all the more significant because the concrete conditions of walking are difficult. In the city center, people need to dodge around on sidewalks crowded by street activities or car parking, and even take risks by walking on the roadway. In peripheral areas, the absence of footpaths and uneven and sometimes unstable ground, which becomes even more degraded in the rainy season, make it very difficult to walk. A greater walking distance therefore not only means increased time "wasted" on travel, but also greater fatigue and therefore more fragile attention in class and whilst doing any homework.

	Public			Private		
	NP	P	D	NP	P	D
Walking	80	91	90	60	84	91
Public transport	19	9	10	30	13	9
Personal vehicle	1	0	0	10	3	0

NP: non-poor. P: poor. D: *of which* deprived.

Table 3.8. *Modal split of home-middle school trips, according to household poverty and type of school (public or private)*

This makes it more difficult for children from poor households to get to school. Alongside other factors, this increased difficulty contributes to limiting their chances of academic success (Diaz Olvera et al. 2010). Indirectly, it leads to the intergenerational reproduction of situations of poverty.

3.5. Shopping for food: a little further, a little less easy

The number of daily trips made for food purchases is similar regardless of household poverty: 0.6 daily trips. It is however closely linked to gender, with only 0.3 trips for men but 0.8 for women and up to 1.2 for wives without professional activity.

Food purchases are, even more than basic education, a local activity (Boyer and Delaunay 2017): the average distance to the point of sale is 700 m. However, one purchase trip out of 12 is longer than 1.5 km. Nevertheless, the poor, and even more so the deprived, travel further for this activity than the non-poor (Table 3.9). Between the two extreme groups, the average distance increases by 15% while travel times increase by 20%. This imbalance is due to the use of different modes.

	Non-poor	Poor	*of which* Deprived
<0.5 km	75	66	60
0.5–1.5 km	17	25	30
> 1.5 km	8	9	10

Table 3.9. *Breakdown by distance category of trips for food purchases, according to household poverty*

The modal split is overall insensitive to household poverty. At 90%, walking dominates, and this share increases only very slightly for the poor. But, while the use of personal modes remains the prerogative of a few trips by the non-poor, the modal split, disaggregated by distance classes, shows for the poor a much lower level of use of public transport within 2 km (Figure 3.4). The use of public transport is however far from widespread, even over long distances: for the poor and deprived, one in five trips over 3.5 km still relies on walking.

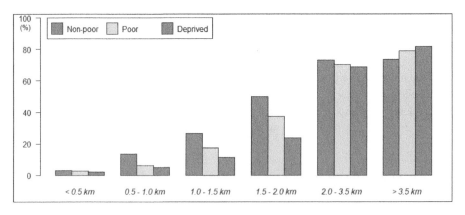

Figure 3.4. *Use of public transport for food purchases, according to distance and household poverty. For a color version of this figure, see www.iste.co.uk/lesteven/urban.zip*

Traveling for food purchases is thus more difficult for the urban poor and even more difficult for the urban deprived. Walking over long distances is the norm, access to public transport is less frequent. In addition, it takes place in worse conditions, with more frequent successive use of several vehicles and/or the use of the most crowded modes. Added to this is the virtual absence of taxis, even though the non-poor use them for 10% of their trips in public transport for food purchases. Although taxis are more comfortable and more spacious – useful for any bulky purchases – they are five times more expensive on average than other forms of public transport. The economic constraint, as in the case of access to education, is always present, given that housewives as well as middle school students do not have individual incomes.

3.6. Living in the outskirts, working in the neighborhood instead of downtown Dakar

Jobs are unevenly distributed over the urban area. The department of Dakar accommodates 45% of households, but 55% of jobs and 75% of public employment. Professional incomes depend on the occupation and the place where it is practiced. All activities combined, they vary by a factor of two between the three peripheral departments and the department of Dakar. But these income gaps are not only explained by the nature of the jobs. For example, we find the same ratio of 1–2 between the three peripheral departments, on the one hand, and the central city, on the other hand, for the "petty trades" of the informal economy, retail trade or other services (salesperson, hairdresser, tailor, carpenter, etc.), which are more often occupied by the urban poor. Being a street vendor in Dakar rather than in the rest of the region, or a trader in a neighborhood market rather than in the city center, has an impact on potential income levels. As a result, a mobility of relative proximity gives hope of higher incomes to a resident of Dakar than to one of Rufisque, and the latter will have to agree to travel a longer way to access a higher paying job. Mobility for work is therefore a priori different depending on where the workers live (Bertrand 2010). To better understand the distinctive features of the mobility patterns of workers from poor populations, we focus here on inhabitants of specific peripheral areas.

We selected three municipalities in the department of Pikine, Keur Massar, Malika and Yeumbeul Nord (Figure 3.1), which comprise 10% of the metropolitan population and have the particularity of having a high proportion of poor (64% of households against the average of 40%) and deprived (23% against 9%) populations. The jobs to be found there are generally low paying. Thus, the income from the "petty trades" mentioned above corresponds, when located in these three municipalities, to 80% of that obtained in the rest of the department of Pikine and 40% of that obtained in Dakar. Our analysis will focus on these "petty trades": retail trade, crafts and other services.

In the rest of this section, when we talk about workers, it will therefore only be workers residing in these three municipalities of Pikine and engaging in "petty trades". We thus control the effect of place of residence as well as the effect of type of activity in order to better perceive the influence of poverty on mobility practices.

In terms of gender and age, the three categories of workers (non-poor, poor and deprived) are close, mainly distinguished by a significantly lower level of education in less favorable household situations. The same is true of job characteristics. Seniority in the activity, the number of months worked in the last year, or the number of days worked in the last month differ little, although these indicators are systematically lower among deprived workers. It is in terms of spatial characteristics that the differences are most marked.

When the workplace is fixed, it is closer to home for workers from poor households, or is home-based, predominantly for the deprived (Table 3.10). For these low-income Pikine residents, working in nearby areas is not equivalent to distant jobs, and especially to those located in Dakar, which are significantly more remunerative. The non-poor travel greater distances than the poor to reach their place of work, but do so more quickly (Table 3.11).

	Non-poor	Poor	*of which* Deprived
In their own home	28	28	37
Near home	39	43	36
Elsewhere in the periphery	14	16	16
In Dakar	19	13	11
Total	100	100	100

Table 3.10. *Location of workplace in relation to home, for certain workers ("petty trades", inhabiting three municipalities of Pikine, with a fixed workplace), according to household poverty*

	Non-poor	Poor	*of which* Deprived
Distance (km)	5.2	4.6	4.4
Duration (min)	29	31	33
Speed (km/h)	10.7	8.8	8.0

Table 3.11. *Characteristics of home-to-work trips of certain workers ("petty trades", living in three municipalities of Pikine, having a fixed workplace), according to household poverty*

This is due to a partially differentiated use of modes (Figure 3.5). While the gaps between working poor and non-poor are small, deprived workers make a greater use of walking. The breakdown by categories of distance shows that the non-poor workers use public transport even for short distances and personal modes for the longer ones. Poor workers, and even more so deprived workers, reserve public transport for the longest distances, and use it in worse conditions, as in the case of food purchases, which implies successively taking several vehicles and an increased use of Tatas.

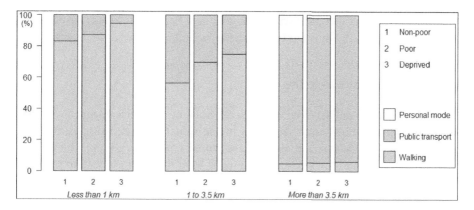

Figure 3.5. *Modal split of home-to-work trips of certain workers ("petty trades", living in three municipalities of Pikine, having a fixed workplace) for different categories of distance, according to household poverty. For a color version of this figure, see www.iste.co.uk/lesteven/urban.zip*

Three contrasting ways in which public transport is used to access the workplace appear (Table 3.12). Compared to the non-poor, poor workers travel similar distances, spending less money but taking more time. Deprived workers, whose workplace is half as far away from home, spend less time on these trips, but the cost of travel, equivalent to that paid by the non-poor, is high given the distances they travel.

	Non-poor	**Poor**	*of which* **Deprived**
Distance (km)	8.4	8.2	4.4
Duration (min)	43	52	33
Cost (CFA francs)	280	220	277

Table 3.12. *Characteristics of home-to-work trips using public transport by certain workers ("petty trades", living in three municipalities of Pikine, having a fixed workplace), according to household poverty*

The similarities in the modal split between the three categories of workers can thus be better understood. As the distance to the workplace increases, the use of public transport is less and less avoidable (Andreasen and Møller-Jensen 2017). The poor and a fortiori the deprived are thus forced to make a trade-off between time and money spent on travel. This trade-off appears clearly if we consider the share of professional income that workers devote to commuting: 11% among the non-poor, 16% among the poor and 28% among the deprived. For poor workers, use of public transport is a reality, but it is costly in monetary spending as well as in time budgets.

3.7. Restricted access to the city

Non-poor, poor and deprived urban dwellers are of course heterogeneous groups within which situations vary according to individual characteristics, particularly gender and activity status, and also diverse mobility practices coexist. But beyond this diversity, the daily mobilities of the poor have the common feature of being similar in volume to those of the non-poor, while remaining different in the way in which they are performed. In this respect, the case of Dakar confirms previous results (Diaz Olvera et al. 2007, 2013). City life is punctuated by the regular performance of a set of compulsory activities: earning a living, attending school, shopping for food, caring for children, etc. This set of activities largely determines the amount of travel to be made. In contrast, whether you are a man or a woman, an informal worker, a middle school student, or an inactive person in charge of household activities, the travel patterns are very different depending on the poverty situation of the household. The poor are excluded from personal modes due to monetary constraints and only have limited access to public transport, which they reserve for the longest distances. Moreover, among the poor, access to public transport is really widespread only for working people, who may obtain an income thanks to the ability to get to their workplace. But, as shown in the case study of workers from the informal sector in three peripheral municipalities, the patterns of public transport use appear much less favorable for the poor (costly and time-consuming intermodality, use of public transport modes with low service quality), further complicating their access to "the city".

The focus on three municipalities of Pikine is particularly enlightening as to the impact of the availability of financial means. This availability makes it possible to improve mobility conditions and, if necessary, to go beyond the home neighborhood. Whether working people, schoolchildren or housewives, the economic constraint appears to be decisive in the differences highlighted. Despite restrictions on access to motorized modes, compared to non-poor households, effort rates for mobility are much higher among poor households and, a fortiori, among deprived households. Their low income is the root cause. Transport expenditures by workers in poor households are primarily directed toward financing their own mobility, leaving little margin for facilitating the mobility of other household members, young people having to go to middle school or high school, inactive people who need to travel as part of "household management" (food purchases, etc.). The latter are then most often reliant on very frequent and sometimes long journeys on foot to carry out their activities outside the home.

The difficulties encountered in achieving mobility in turn contribute to perpetuating situations of poverty in the short as well as in the longer term. In the short term, given the remoteness and under-provision of many residential areas, walking does not allow access to all urban amenities. Willingly or not, the poor have to restrict their field of activity to their own neighborhood, with fewer earning opportunities and, presumably, higher expenses due to more expensive purchases at neighborhood markets or retailers. In the medium and long term, the more restricted access of children from poor households to the supply of schools has an impact, among other factors, on continuation in school and possible access to more remunerative jobs. This contributes to the intergenerational reproduction of situations of poverty. If leaving home is undoubtedly a necessary condition for households to implement strategies to exit poverty, it is by no means a sufficient condition.

3.8. Conclusion

A city of significant size and surface area, with strongly separated residential and economic functions and a multifaceted transport system, Dakar is particularly illustrative of the multiple links between daily mobility and poverty in the large cities of Sub-Saharan Africa, and more broadly in the metropolises of the "Global South". The analyses of the 2015 Dakar Survey of Mobility, Transport and Access to Urban Services thus make it possible to provide unambiguous answers to our two initial questions. The mobility of the urban poor has specific characteristics that make it a difficult part of everyday life. This difficulty is likely to hamper efforts to emerge from situations of poverty in the medium or long term, and is likely to mitigate their effects in the short term. At the heart of these mechanisms is the economic constraint characterizing the daily lives of poor households. Two lessons emerge with regard to the implementation of pro-poor urban policies.

First of all, at the level of the urban transport sector, the ambitions for modernization pursued in many countries, including Senegal, can only be counterproductive with regard to the urban poor if limited to the implementation of one or two BRT lines or the "formalization" of the sector. Indeed, such measures most often result in a de facto increase in the cost of transport and thus drive the poor a little further away from using motorized modes, further increasing their dependence on walking. A transport policy that effectively takes into account the needs of the urban poor should therefore be organized around two complementary axes: improving walking conditions and access to public transport. The first involves the construction and improvement of pedestrian infrastructures according to the local environment: maintenance or creation of sidewalks, restrictions on their use (car parking, street businesses), street lighting, etc. The second depends on controlling public transport expenditure, that is, the fare of each mode of transport and the total cost resulting from successive use of several vehicles during a trip. This requires better control of the production costs of transport services and, above all, real fare integration of all modes of public transport.

More broadly, improving the living conditions of the poor requires in-depth reflection and action on the balance of functions within the city in order to reduce the need for long journeys. Better facilities for peripheral districts (basic services, jobs, etc.) of course promote access to urban amenities, but an improvement in provision in the immediate vicinity will not be sufficient to meet all one's needs. These interventions should be integrated into a more global reflection aimed at creating opportunities on an intermediate scale between the neighborhood and the metropolis at the level of municipalities, or groups of municipalities if we take the example of Dakar. Wider access to urban amenities, at an acceptable cost for households, probably requires a renewal of urban planning, aimed at the emergence of secondary polarities within existing urbanization zones.

3.9. References

Agence Nationale de la Statistique et de la Démographie (2014). Rapport définitif – Recensement général de la population et de l'habitat 2013. Report, ANSD – Ministère de l'Économie, des Finances et du Plan, Dakar.

Alkire, S., Foster, J., Seth, S., Santos, M.E., Roche, J.M., Ballon, P. (2015). *Multidimensional Poverty Measurement and Analysis*. Oxford University Press, Oxford.

Andreasen, M.H. and Møller-Jensen, L. (2017). Access to the city: Mobility patterns, transport and accessibility in peripheral settlements of Dar es Salaam. *Journal of Transport Geography*, 62, 20–29.

Bertrand, M. (2010). De l'accès au logement à la relation domicile-travail : enjeux sociaux et spatiaux des mobilités dans la région du grand Accra (Ghana). *Revue tiers monde*, 201, 87–106.

Boyer, F. and Delaunay, D. (2017). Se déplacer dans Ouagadougou au quotidien, moyens, contraintes et pratiques de la mobilité. Monograph, Monographies Sud-Nord, Université Paris 1 Panthéon Sorbonne.

Boyer, F., Gouëset, V., Delaunay, D. (2016). Les mobilités quotidiennes, un révélateur des inégalités sociospatiales à Ouagadougou. *Autrepart – Revue de sciences sociales au Sud*, 80, 47–68.

Bryceson, D.F., Mbara, T.C., Maunder, D. (2003). Livelihoods, daily mobility and poverty in Sub-Saharan Africa. *Transport Reviews*, 23(2), 177–196.

Damon, J. (2014). Chiffres, approches et paradoxes de la pauvreté urbaine [Online]. Available at: http://journals.openedition.org/questionsdecommunication/8989 [Accessed 30 April 2019]

Deaton, A. (1997). *The Analysis of Household Surveys: A Microeconometric Approach to Development Policy*. World Bank Publications, Washington, DC.

Diaz Olvera, L., Plat, D., Pochet, P. (2007). Mobilité quotidienne en temps de crise. *Belgeo – Revue belge de géographie*, 2, 173–188.

Diaz Olvera, L., Plat, D., Pochet, P. (2010). A l'écart de l'école ? Pauvreté, accessibilité et scolarisation à Conakry. *Revue tiers monde*, 202, 167–183.

Diaz Olvera, L., Plat, D., Pochet, P. (2013). The puzzle of mobility and access to the city in Sub-Saharan Africa. *Journal of Transport Geography*, 32, 56–64.

Diaz Olvera, L., Plat, D., Pochet, P. (2015). Assessment of mobility inequalities and income data collection. Methodological issues and a case study (Douala, Cameroon). *Journal of Transport Geography*, 46, 180–188.

Godard, X., Diaz Olvera, L., Dieng, A., Kane, C., Adolehoumé, A.P. (2001). Guide méthodologique d'enquête-ménages de mobilité dans les villes en développement. Guide, Sitrass, Lyon.

Grieco, M., Apt, N., Turner, J. (1996). *At Christmas and on Rainy Days: Transport, Travel and the Female Traders of Accra*. Avebury, Aldershot.

Herpin, N. and Verger, D. (1997). La pauvreté une et multiple. *Economie et Statistique*, 308/309/310, 3–22.

Lombard, J. (2015). *Le monde des transports sénégalais. Ancrage local et développement international*. IRD Editions, Marseille.

Lombard, J., Bruez, F., Diakho, A. (2006). Les transports sénégalais à l'aune du système-monde. In *La mondialisation côté Sud. Acteurs et territoires*, Lombard, J., Mesclier, E., Velut, S. (eds). IRD Editions – ENS, Paris.

Mandel, J.L. (2004). Mobility matters: Women's livelihood strategies in Porto Novo, Benin. *Gender, Place and Culture*, 11(2), 257–287.

Paugam, S. (2005). *Les formes élémentaires de la pauvreté*. PUF, Paris.

Razafindrakoto, M. and Roubaud, F. (2005). Les multiples facettes de la pauvreté dans un pays en développement. Le cas de la capitale malgache. *Economie et Statistique*, 383–385, 131–155.

Sakho, P. (2002). U comme urbain ou développement urbain et transport à Dakar. In *Les transports et la ville en Afrique au sud du Sahara*, Godard, X. (ed.). Karthala-Inrets, Paris-Arcueil.

Sakho, P. (2014). La production de la ville au Sénégal : entre mobilités urbaines, migrations internes et internationales. PhD thesis, Université Cheikh Anta Diop, Dakar.

Salon, D. and Aligula, E.M. (2012). Urban travel in Nairobi, Kenya: Analysis, insights, and opportunities. *Journal of Transport Geography*, 22, 65–76.

Salon, D. and Gulyani, S. (2010). Mobility, poverty, and gender: Travel "choices" of slum residents in Nairobi, Kenya. *Transport Reviews*, 30(5), 641–657.

Sietchiping, R., Permezel, M.J., Ngomsi, C. (2012). Transport and mobility in Sub-Saharan African cities: An overview of practices, lessons and options for improvements. *Cities*, 29(3), 183–189.

Sitrass-Curem (2016). Enquête ménages sur la mobilité, le transport et l'accès aux services urbains dans l'agglomération de Dakar. Report, Conseil Exécutif des Transports Urbains de Dakar sur crédits IDA-Banque Mondiale, Sitrass-Curem, Lyon-Dakar.

4

Children's Mobility: Comparative Perspectives Between France and Quebec

Sylvanie GODILLON[1,2]

[1] UMR Géographie-cités, Université Paris 1 Panthéon-Sorbonne, Paris-Aubervilliers, France
[2] INRS, Montreal, Canada

4.1. Introduction

There are not many analytical studies concerning children in the French-speaking social sciences (Lehman-Frisch and Vivet 2011). The transport and mobility fields are not an exception. Researchers often consider children as "an organizational constraint" for their parents. At best, they observe children's travel, and sometimes consider children's representations and perceptions as such. Travel methods and services are conceived and designed to meet the needs, habits and resources of adults, in particular motorized adults (Sutton and Kemp 2002). For example, crossing times for traffic lights are often poorly suited to a young child's walking speed. Yet these mobility systems play an important role in children's mobility practices, learning and health.

Before discussing the specificities of child mobility, it is worth considering its definition. What is a child? When does childhood begin? When does it end? The notion of "child" in the academic literature is strongly polysemic. There is no scientific consensus on the age at which childhood ends. This chapter specifically discusses children, rather than adolescents who may be more autonomous in their mobility.

The concept of childhood was updated in the 1990s through reflections that showed how it is a social construction that changes depending on the society and historical period (Jenks 1996). The reconsideration of the definition of the child as universal has led to discussion of children's social and spatial differences in order to understand the complexity of their daily lives and their relationship to space (Holloway and Valentine 2004). In the 1970s, some research projects on young people and children were initiated in France, focusing on children's perceptions and their relationship to space. Thus, studies in sociology showed the unsuitability of the urban environment for children's perceptions, particularly in old neighborhoods that did not offer leisure spaces (Chombart de Lauwe 1979). This work has remained marginal in the French social sciences. Beginning in the 1990s in English-speaking environments, the discipline of Children's Studies has taken shape. The influence of English-language research in Quebec has contributed to the emergence of this theme in Quebecois scientific literature, with a particular focus on children's mobility and their relationship to public spaces (Cloutier and Torres 2010). Research on the urban practices of children and young people tends to show a decline in the presence of children in public spaces. Indeed, society's growing concern for children's safety has led to the confinement of children and the privatization, institutionalization and fragmentation of their territories in the cities of developed countries (Holloway and Valentine 2004; Karsten and Van Vilet 2006; Rivière 2016).

This chapter discusses the mobility of children in two different contexts through examples in France in Europe and Quebec in North America. Comparing them makes it possible to analyze possible effects related to geographical organization, with urban density being much lower in North America than in Europe, while being similar in economic and cultural contexts. This comparison allows us to highlight the similarities and specificities of child mobility in northern countries. The diversity of modal practices for getting to school will be presented, before describing the effects of these modal characteristics on health, safety and the environment. Examples of public policies implemented in France and Quebec to promote walking and cycling among children will help to shed light on current initiatives.

4.2. Children as mainly passengers in individual motorized modes

4.2.1. *School as structuring family organization*

The main reason for children's travel relates to school activity. School plays an important role because it creates a rhythm for family activities by generating a large number of trips related to children being accompanied by the adults responsible for them. School, as a social marker and a guarantee of education, is so important that it may be a decisive factor in the choice of place of residence (Viard 2006). The trend, in France as in Quebec, is to select the school when children enter middle or high school. This choice tends to increase the kilometers traveled. For example, in the Montreal metropolitan area, the direct distance between school and home increased by 7% between 1998 and 2008 (according to travel surveys). At the same time, school closures in rural areas may also contribute to an increase in the kilometers traveled to school.

Although the presence of children increases parents' environmental awareness, it also tends to increase the use of cars, especially when traveling to school (Polk 2003). Thus, families tend to settle in the urban peripheries, especially for financial and educational reasons (greenery, space, physical and social safety). This residential choice results in individual motorized trips to escort children and adolescents who do not have access to a car.

4.2.2. *The predominance of motorized modes for getting to school*

Little is known about the mobility characteristics of children under 12 in either France or Quebec. Mobility surveys in France (National Transport and Travel Survey of 2008 in France, renamed National Mobility Survey in 2019, and household travel surveys at local community level) or in Quebec (Origin-Destination Survey in the major cities which include three-quarters of the Quebec population) interview individuals over the age of 5 or 6, but very few analyses target children directly. Trends show a strong use of individual motorized modes among children, which has a tendency to increase.

In 2008 in France, 38% of trips for study purposes were made by car, whereas they represented only 15% of trips in 1982. The car was the main mode of transport for getting to school in 2008 in France (according to the National Transport and Travel Survey). Trends are similar on the other side of the Atlantic. In the Montreal area, the share of cars for taking children aged 6–12 to school increased from 22% to 31% between 1998 and 2003 (Lewis and Torres 2010). Between 1991 and 2006, the modal share of car trips for children in the Quebec City region increased from 9% to 32%. In 2013, the trend was for an increase compared to 2008 in the number of motorized trips by children, and an increase in trips dropping off or picking up someone (Figure 4.1).

Daily use of the car varies according to the age of the children with a significant decrease around 11 years, the year of entry to middle school (Olm et al. 2005). It varies greatly between areas, with a greater use of the car among rural children than among urban children. Parents take their children on car trips because they consider this mode of transport to be more practical, especially in a context where parents themselves go to their workplace by car. Traveling by car saves time in constrained schedules, especially when both parents work (Motte-Baumvol et al. 2011). Urban sprawl and dependence on the automobile largely explain this upward trend in children's motorized travel. The car is also the main mode for getting to leisure activities.

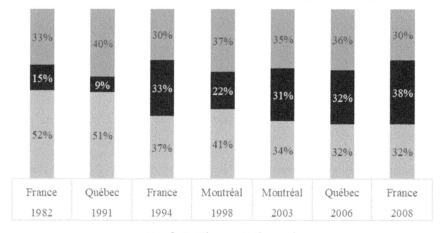

Figure 4.1. *A decrease in travel by foot to places of study since 1980 in France and Quebec. For a color version of this figure, see www.iste.co.uk/lesteven/urban.zip*

When parents do not take children to school by car, children may travel by bus, especially high school students in France and Quebec. In France, the share of public transport to get to the place of study grew from 19% in 1982 to 25% in 2008. In Quebec's urban peripheries, school buses transport young teenagers from their homes to public secondary schools in their area (Bachiri and Després 2008).

This increase in the use of individual and collective motorized modes in children's daily mobility occurs at the expense of the use of active modes such as walking and cycling.

4.2.3. *Walking and cycling, modes used less and less*

Since the 1980s, the trend in France, as in Quebec, is that there has been a decline in active transportation for getting to school in favor of the automobile and public transportation. In 2003 in the Montreal area, 34% of children aged 6–12 walked to school, compared to 41% in 1998 (Lewis and Torres 2010). In the Quebec City region, the modal share of walking among elementary school students going between home and school decreased from 51% in 1991 to 32% in 2006. In France, in 2008, walking accounted for 32% of trips between home and study and has decreased by 20 points since 1982. While walking was the main mode of getting to school until the 1990s, the car replaced it in the early 2000s. Distance between the place of residence and school allows us to understand the use of active modes. For example, in France in 2008, for distances of less than 1 km, 57% of children went to school on foot or by bicycle.

Some urban environments are more conducive to walking than others. Thus, children walk to school more often in urban areas than in rural areas, both in France and Quebec. Young people in central Quebec City travel more often on foot and by public transport than those in urban peripheries and rural areas (Vandersmissen 2008). In France, findings also differ between traditional neighborhoods and new cities (Depeau 2008), as well as among young people in large housing estates who mostly get around by walking (Ramadier et al. 2008). Economic and social characteristics are superimposed on urban characteristics. For less affluent families, walking remains a less costly mode of transport. Thus, to better understand children's modes of travel, it is also necessary to look closely at the rate of motorization of households, the employment rate of parents, public transport (route and schedule), the choice of schools and, more broadly, the influence of social and cultural values.

This erosion of the use of active modes for school mobility, but also for leisure mobility (visiting friends, going to extracurricular activities, etc.), has repercussions in terms of health due to the lack of physical activity. These trends also have impacts on insecurity and the environment.

4.3. Important health, safety and environmental issues

4.3.1. *Physical inactivity impacts children's health*

The motorization of school trips has a strong impact on the mobility of children, and more particularly on their health. The greater the amount of time spent physically inactive, the higher the prevalence of overweight and obesity, in a context where the consumption of processed food products requires an increase in physical activity.

As a result of an imbalance between energy intake and expenditure, obesity and being overweight promote the onset of type 2 diabetes (44% of cases attributable to being overweight/obesity according to the World Health Organization (WHO)), heart disease (23% of cases attributable) and cancer (between 7% and 41% of cases attributable to being overweight/obesity, depending on the location). At a global level, WHO recognizes being overweight and obesity as the fifth leading cause of death, leading to the death of at least 2.8 million people each year. In France, figures from the National Institute of Health and Medical Research (INSERM) indicate that being overweight and obesity affect 16% of boys and 18% of girls among children and adolescents aged 5–17. These figures have been stable over the last 10 years. In Quebec, according to the National Institute of Public Health of Quebec (INSPQ) for the period from 2009 to 2013, being overweight and obesity affected 25% of young people aged 6–17, a sharp increase since the beginning of the 1980s, but this has remained stable since 2004. Food and physical activity in children may explain the differences between the two contexts.

Walking to school could be an effective physical activity for achieving the periods of activity that WHO recommends. Children who walk to school burn more calories than those who travel by car (Tudor-Locke et al. 2001). The number of calories they burn during these trips is said to be equivalent to 2 hours per week of physical education (Mackett et al. 2005). However, other research has relativized the importance of walking to school, as travel between home and school is often too short to have a significant impact on the total physical activity of schoolchildren (Landsberg et al. 2008).

Even though there is debate about the effectiveness of the impact of walking and cycling on the level of physical activity, several studies note its positive impact on general health. Indeed, walking to school is associated with unstructured and spontaneous activities, such as playing on the street or in parks (Mackett et al. 2005). In addition, walking and cycling allow for direct contact with the urban environment and gaining experience of local public spaces (Prezza et al. 2005). The autonomous mobility of children, without direct adult supervision, involves active transportation, allowing the acquisition of skills essential to development (Davis and Jones 1996; Dixey 1998; Fotel and Thomsen 2003). Thus, the motorization of travel erodes children's ability to develop an in-depth urban and social experience.

4.3.2. *Parental fears of accidents and assaults*

It is precisely children's mobility without adult supervision that seems to be in decline, in connection with the problem of road safety thanks to high levels of car traffic in public spaces, not to mention parental fears of kidnappings and assaults, especially sexual assaults. The safety of children is thus sometimes preferred to their autonomous mobility.

In France, in 2017, transport accidents accounted for 8% of the causes of death of children aged 1–4 years and 9% of those aged 5–14 years, and were the leading cause of death of 15–24 year olds (24%), according to INSERM-CepiDc data. With more cars around schools due to more children being taken to school by car, parents do not want to let their child walk there, which then increases traffic around schools. Children's pedestrian mobility has changed in recent decades, which has impacted their behavior in public spaces and their risk of accident as pedestrians. Children are increasingly late to begin to travel autonomously. In the early 2000s, only 12% of French people aged 6–11 walked between home and school without being accompanied (Olm et al. 2005). In Quebec, even elementary school students who live close to their school are increasingly traveling by car, their travel being combined with those of their parents who go to work (Lewis and Torres 2010). The motorization of trips to school has thus had an impact on the acquisition of pedestrian skills in children, with an increase in the age of autonomous travel.

This phenomenon has resulted in the appearance of a second peak of accidents for child pedestrians. This finding has been observed since 1970 (Hillman et al. 1990) in most industrialized countries. In France (Observatoire National Interministériel de Sécurité Routière 2008) as in Quebec (Cloutier 2008), there are two peaks of accidental pedestrian morbidity in children: the first at age 7, which is explained by the child's level of psychological development, and the second at 11–12 years old, which is explained by entering a new school cycle, and which corresponds to entering secondary education, which is often further away from home than primary school. This second peak corresponds to the moment when parents let their children move around on their own for the first time, when they had not previously been used to walking. Indeed, street experience is necessary for the child to acquire skills to guarantee their safety, for example, checking for the presence of a vehicle before crossing the road (Demetre 1997; Granié 2004).

The decline in active transportation has a strong impact on children's development, not only of their mobility, but also their autonomy (Torres 2007). Pedestrian travel produces knowledge and shapes attitudes about the rules of travel spaces: safety rules, rules of interaction with others and rules of respect for the public good. Young pedestrians must learn to manage their presence and movement while learning to share space with other users (Granié 2010). The paradoxical challenge for parents is to look after the well-being of their children while contributing to their development of autonomy (Schapiro 1999). In this sense, understanding the role of parents is necessary for understanding children's mobility characteristics (Rivière 2016); the presence of unaccompanied children in public spaces has gradually become a marker of neglect or even parental irresponsibility (Pain 2006). In addition, gender stereotypes influence parents' educational practices. Parents supervise girls more than boys, increasing restrictions and controls (Granié 2008). Parents tend to encourage boys and help girls (Morrongiello and Hogg 2004; Hagan and Kuebli 2007). In the event of an accident, a boy's behavior is perceived as a violation of rules, while that of a girl is considered as a poor consideration of risks (Morrongiello and Hogg 2004). Beyond the fear of accidents, parents fear sexual assault, to which girls are perceived to be more vulnerable than boys.

4.3.3. *A difficult but necessary change faced with climate issues*

There is another paradox among parents between the desire, for their children's sake, to have a garden, a good school and the means to travel by car, and worries about climate issues, especially for the future of their child. This gap between residential choices and individual values produces cognitive dissonance, in other words, an internal contradiction within individuals (Festinger 1957). Behind the lifestyles associated with the spread-out city, the effects on health and air pollution are real.

In France, in September 2020, the High Council for Climate published a report on France's carbon neutrality, recalling that transport contributes to 31% of greenhouse gas emissions, mainly because of road travel. Leading the sectors with highest emissions, transport exceeded the objectives set by the Climate Plan in 2015 by 8%. In Quebec, also committed as a Canadian province to the Paris Agreements of 2015, 43% of emissions are attributable to transport, according to the 2014 Quebec Inventory of GHG Emissions. Greenhouse gas emissions from the transportation sectors are trending upwards.

To reduce greenhouse gas emissions related to travel, the question arises of rationalizing car travel. School trips are not a major factor, compared to the number of car trips to the workplace. Thus, in 2008 in metropolitan France, the number of commuting trips was 16.5 million with 73% made by car, while trips between home and school represented 9.1 million with 36% by car (ENTD 2008). However, reducing the number of car trips to school would both reduce pollution and increase the safety and health of children and their parents.

4.4. Actions to encourage modal change for daily mobility

Faced with these observations of the decline in walking and cycling and the rise in health problems related to physical inactivity, the public authorities in France and

Quebec are promoting programs to encourage a change in mobility behavior for going to school.

4.4.1. *Organizing accompaniment of children on foot*

Actions to encourage walking to school have multiplied over the past 20 years. To promote walking, parent volunteers have developed "walking school buses", locally called *Pédibuses*, since the end of the 1990s. A Pédibus is a pedestrian school pick-up system operated on foot by volunteers and functioning as a bus with routes, schedules and stops (Figure 4.2). In France, the promoters of Pédibuses use several arguments related to physical activity, the fight against obesity, lack of road safety, air quality or even autonomous travel (Pigalle 2019).

Figure 4.2. *A Pédibus in Paris, France (photo credit: G. Lesteven, 2021)*

In Quebec, since 2010, the Canadian Cancer Society has promoted the implementation of walking school bus projects in Quebec schools, the "Trottibus". According to the Canadian Cancer Society, the four benefits of this system are as follows: a greener neighborhood, more daily physical activity, better concentration in the classroom and the opportunity to become a good pedestrian. Compared to

France, the arguments put forward in Quebec are more concrete on the issues of health and safety, and less linked to climate issues.

Initiated more than two decades ago, these activities have not stemmed the decline in walking trips to school. The major difficulties are the lack of volunteers and also the lack of continuity in projects, left to parental initiatives (Cloutier et al. 2018; Pigalle 2019). Although local authorities promote walking school buses, it is extremely rare for them to be organizers of this system, in France or Quebec.

4.4.2. Pedestrianizing the streets around schools

Adapting the public spaces around schools is an action that local authorities can carry out. The principle is to close the streets around the schools to car traffic permanently or temporarily at drop-off and pick-up times. In France, the city of Paris has adapted the surroundings of about 120 schools in 2021 and 49 in 2022, thanks to its "Streets to Schools" project. During the Covid-19 health crisis, which required significant interpersonal distancing, the Paris municipality tested temporary adaptations such as flower boxes, plots, signage and ground painting. Residents and schoolchildren had to test these inexpensive and temporary developments before they were made permanent.

Figure 4.3. *Pedestrianization of a street near a school in Lyon (photo credit: S. Godillon, 2022)*

Other local authorities in France have also set up temporary or permanent closures of streets around schools, such as in Lyon where seven schools were involved at the start of the 2020 school year. For example, a local street with little traffic was closed to traffic next to the Joannes Masset school in the ninth arrondissement of Lyon (Figure 4.3). The street was closed with bollards. The goal was for children and adults to appropriate public spaces. There is therefore a strong interaction between policies for speed reduction and for promotion of active modes.

Quebec has not tested this type of action. In addition to incentives for walking, local authorities in both Quebec and France have implemented actions to encourage the use of bicycles to travel to school.

4.4.3. *Developing children's cycling skills*

In 2005, Quebec implemented a program aimed at encouraging students to use bicycles to travel to school. The program "Mon école à pied, à vélo !" (My school on foot, by bike!) promotes active transport among students and their parents through class activities and newsletters. It works to create settings more favorable to these modes of travel by analyzing obstacles to cycling near schools. In 5 years, the program has benefited more than 40 schools, involving more than 12,000 students. But during the 2010 review, many actors in the education and health sector expressed their worries about the health and safety of primary school students. In addition, an INSPQ study in 2010 showed that it was dangerous to come to school by bicycle: in the Montreal region, the risk of injury is 4.7 times higher among pedestrians and 18.1 times higher among cyclists than among children traveling by car (Burigusa et al. 2011). Since the end of this initiative, the "Cycliste averti" (Aware Cyclist) program has continued to promote cycling for Quebecois school children. In France, initiatives are more recent with the launch of the "Savoir Rouler à Vélo" (How to Ride by Bike) program in April 2019, which aims to generalize learning to cycle and autonomy on public roads for children between 6 and 11 years old, before entering middle school.

These programs have the potential to improve children's safety when they ride a bicycle. Indeed, theoretical cycling education, given in class, is effective especially if lessons are combined with theoretical and practical sessions (Rubio et al. 2018). For children to be able to travel by bike, it is also important that their parents have confidence in the safety of the routes they take, which requires adaptations.

4.5. Conclusion

For the past 20 years, trends show that children have become less likely to be pedestrian and less autonomous in their mobility, and escorted more often in cars by adults. Less walking has health consequences related to physical inactivity, cognitive consequences related to the relationship to public spaces and autonomy, and environmental consequences due to the kilometers traveled by car to get to school or to extra-curricular activities. Faced with the observation of less active mobility by children, public authorities in France and Quebec are implementing programs to encourage walking or cycling and are redeveloping public spaces near schools to make them safer. If these initiatives contribute to reducing the role of the automobile in cities, there is a challenge to reverse the effects of automotive mobility which has been promoted for several decades and suburban sprawl has reinforced.

The decline in the presence of children in public spaces also contributes to changes in urban environments, with cities designed for adults, especially for motorized ones (Sutton and Kemp 2002). In recent years, initiatives have begun to give children a place in the streets. For example, in Paris, adaptation and animation projects aim to give space for games and children, like painting games on the ground or setting up mobile barriers to close off the streets at certain times. To make room for children in public spaces and in their mobility, our relationship with children will have to change to conceive the child as a full user with specific needs, including safety and autonomy.

4.6. References

Bachiri, N. and Després, C. (2008). Mobilité quotidienne dans la communauté métropolitaine de Québec d'adolescents résidant en territoires rurbains. *Enfances, familles, générations*, 8, 9. doi: 10.7202/018490ar.

Burigusa, G., Lavoie, M., Maurice, P. (2011). Sécurité des élèves du primaire lors des déplacements à pied et à vélo entre la maison et l'école au Québec. Scientific advice report, Institut national de santé publique du Québec.

Chombart de Lauwe, M.-J. (1979). *Un monde autre, l'enfance : de ses représentations à son mythe*. Payothèque, Paris.

Cloutier, M.-S. and Apparicio, P. (2008). L'environnement autour des écoles a-t-il un impact sur le risque routier impliquant des enfants piétons à Montréal ? Apport de la régression de Poisson géographiquement pondérée. *Territoire en mouvement*, 1, 25–38.

Cloutier, M.-S. and Torres, J. (2010). L'enfant et la ville : notes introductoires. *Enfances, familles, générations*, 12, i–xv.

Cloutier, M.-S., Charbonneau, J., Godillon S. (2018). Évaluation du programme Trottibus au Québec. Final report, INRS-Centre Urbanisation Culture Société, Montreal.

Davis, A. and Jones, L. (1996). Children in the urban environment: An issue for the new public health agenda. *Health & Place*, 2, 107–113.

Demetre, J. (1997). Applying developmental psychology to children's road safety: Problems and prospects. *Journal of Applied Developmental Psychology*, 18(2), 263–270.

Depeau, D. (2008). Radioscopie des territoires de la mobilité des enfants en milieu urbain. Comparaison entre Paris intra-muros et banlieue parisienne. *Enfances, familles, générations*, 8, 7. doi: 10.7202/018489ar.

Dixey, R. (1998). Improvements in child pedestrian safety: Have they been gained at the expense of other health goals? *Health Education Journal*, 57, 60–69.

ENTD (2008). National transport and travel survey. Survey, Insee, SESP, Paris.

Festinger, L. (1957). *A Theory of Cognitive Dissonance*. Stanford University Press.

Fotel, T. and Thomsen, T. (2003). The surveillance of children's mobility. *Surveillance & Society*, 1, 535–554.

Granié, M.-A. (2004). La construction des règles comportementales sur le port de la ceinture chez l'enfant : analyse du contenu d'entretiens auprès d'enfants de 5 et 8 ans. *Recherche – Transports – Sécurité*, 83, 99–114.

Granié, M.-A. (2008). Influence de l'adhésion aux stéréotypes de sexe sur la perception des comportements piétons chez l'adulte. *Recherche – Transports – Sécurité*, 101, 253–264.

Granié, M.-A. (2010). Socialisation au risque et construction sociale des comportements de l'enfant piéton : éléments de réflexion pour l'éducation routière. *Enfances, familles, générations*, 12, 88–110.

Hagan, L.K. and Kuebli, J. (2007). Mothers' and fathers' socialization of preschoolers' physical risk taking. *Journal of Applied Developmental Psychology*, 28(1), 2–14.

Hillman, M., Adams, J., Whitelegg, J. (1990). *One False Move: A Study of Children's Independent Mobility*. Policy Studies Institute, London.

Holloway, S.L. and Valentine, G. (2000). Children's geographies and the new social studies of childhood. *Children's Geographies: Playing, Living, Learning*, 1, 1–26.

Jenks, C. (1996). *Childhood*. Routledge, London.

Karsten, L. and Van Vliet, W. (2006). Children in the city: Reclaiming the street. *Children Youth and Environments*, 16(1), 151–164.

Lehman-Frisch, S. and Vivet, J. (2011). Géographies des enfants et des jeunes. *Carnets de géographes*, 3, 3. doi: 10.4000/cdg.2074.

Lewis, P. and Torres, J. (2010). Les parents et les déplacements entre la maison et l'école primaire : quelle place pour l'enfant dans la ville ? *Enfances, familles, générations*, 12, 44–64.

Mackett, R., Lucas, L., Paskins, J., Turbin, J. (2005). The therapeutic value of children's everyday travel. *Transportation Research*, 39(2–3), 205–219.

Morrongiello, B. and Hogg, K. (2004). Mothers' reactions to children misbehaving in ways that can lead to injury: Implications for gender differences in children's risk taking and injuries. *Sex Roles*, 50(1), 103–118.

Motte-Baumvol, B., Belton-Chevallier, L., Shearmur, R.-G. (2011). Différences de genre et formes de dépendances des conjoints biactifs dans l'accompagnement des enfants. *Géographie, économie, société*, 13(2), 189–206.

Observatoire National Interministériel de Sécurité Routière (2008). La sécurité routière en France. Bilan de l'année 2004. Report, La Documentation française, Paris.

Olm, C., Chauffaut, D., David, E. (2005). L'éducation au risque routier : rapport d'analyse de la phase quantitative auprès des parents et des jeunes. Report, CREDOC/Prévention routière et de la Fédération française des sociétés d'assurances, Paris.

Pain, R. (2006). Paranoid parenting? Rematerializing risk and fear for children. *Social & Cultural Geography*, 7(2), 221–243.

Pigalle, E. (2019). Déplacements en Pédibus à l'épreuve des modes d'habiter. *Espaces et sociétés*, 4, 93–110.

Polk, M. (2003). Are women potentially more accommodating than men to a sustainable transportation system in Sweden? *Transportation Research Part D: Transport and Environment*, 8(2), 75–95.

Prezza, M., Alparone, F.R., Cristallo, C., Luigi, S. (2005). Parental perception of social risk and of positive potentiality of outdoor autonomy for children: The development of two instruments. *Journal of Environmental Psychology*, 25, 437–453.

Ramadier, T., Petropoulou, C., Bronner, A.-C. (2008). Quelle mobilité quotidienne intra-urbaine sans la voiture ? Le cas des adolescents d'une banlieue de Strasbourg. *Enfances, familles, générations*, 8, 8. doi: 10.7202/018492ar.

Rivière, C. (2016). Les temps ont changé. Le déclin de la présence des enfants dans les espaces publics au prisme des souvenirs des parents d'aujourd'hui. *Les annales de la recherche urbaine*, 111, 6–14.

Rubio, B., Cestac, J., Assailly, J.-P. (2018). Sécurité routière des enfants, développement, compétences et efficacité des mesures d'éducation. *Recherche, transports, sécurité*, 3, 17.

Schapiro, T. (1999). What is a child? *Ethics*, 109, 715–738.

Sutton, S.E. and Kemp, S.P. (2002). Children as partners in neighborhood placemaking: Lessons from intergenerational design charrettes. *Journal of Environmental Psychology*, 22(1–2), 171–189.

Torres, J. (2007). La recherche par le projet d'aménagement : comprendre le vélo chez les enfants à travers les projets "Grandir en ville" de Montréal et de Guadalajara. Thesis, Université de Montréal.

Tudor-Locke, C., Ainsworth, B., Popkin, B. (2001). Active commuting to school. *Sports Medicine*, 31(5), 309–313.

Vandersmissen, M.-H. (2008). Modes de transport et territoires pratiqués en solo par les adolescents de la région urbaine de Québec. *Enfances, familles, générations*, 8, 8. doi: 10.7202/018491ar.

Viard, J. (2006). *Éloge de la mobilité : essai sur le capital temps libre et la valeur travail.* Éditions de l'Aube, La Tour d'Aigues.

PART 2
Urban Public Transport

5

Mobility, Public Transportation and Super-Aging in Japan

Sophie BUHNIK
*Graduate School of Environmental and Information Studies,
Faculty of Urban Life Studies, Tokyo City University, Japan*

5.1. Introduction: Japan or the efficiency of urban transport faced with super-aging

As the demographic transition progresses, relationships between transport, mobility and aging become a major source of concern for stakeholders in planning. Over the course of the 20th century, migration to cities reinforced the depopulation trends of many rural and landlocked regions, despite recurrent waves of popularity for a "return to the countryside" that the Covid-19 pandemic has brought back on the agenda[1]. But the history of these migratory waves, combined with longer life expectancy, is in turn leading to an increase in the number of elderly inhabitants in large urban areas at rates that public authorities and transport operators rarely anticipated. The aging of societies therefore highlights a gap between, on the one hand, a conception of the city which invokes speed and fluidity – where the ability to move around is essential as a central norm of capitalism (Boltanski and Chiapello 1999; Bauman 2000) and, on the other hand, the slowness, breaks and pauses or

---

1 On rural-to-urban migration in contemporary Japan, see Klien (2020). Japanese media often publish lively portraits of individuals or families moving temporarily or permanently to the rural world, in reaction to the constraints imposed by measures to combat the spread of the Covid-19 pandemic (see: https://www.japantimes.co.jp/news/2020/07/18/national/social-issues/rural-migration-japanese-countryside/).

Urban Mobility Systems in the World,
coordinated by Gaële LESTEVEN. © ISTE Ltd 2023.

palliatives, which the elderly rely on to complete their journeys. Influenced by physiological changes, urban dwellers entering old age spend less on travel, although wide variations between individuals can be observed, depending on their life course and the environmental factors surrounding them (Marcilhac et al. 2021).

In response to the challenge of maintaining attractive and accessible urban settings despite a steady increase in the number of elderly residents, an important body of research has focused on the challenges of adapting travel systems and their efficiency to the needs of seniors (inter alia; Lord and Piché 2018; Raulin et al. 2020). A sociotechnical approach is essential to assess barriers to transport as they are perceived by seniors; but it generally consists of discussing the constraints encountered by individuals who have been physically weakened by age, as part of a larger group of users. In the French context in particular, most prospective studies combining issues around aging and sustainable transport are based around a "gerontogrowth" paradigm (Dumont 2013): they project an increase in the number of seniors within more general demographic projections for urban regions. But the implications of the elderly becoming the largest age group are rarely addressed, especially in metropolitan areas where the most complex transport systems are located. While the practices of aging households in urban areas that are stagnating or even shrinking rather than growing are beginning to attract attention, case studies remain limited to small and medium-sized towns.[2]

At the same time, trends toward economic slowdown or even degrowth are promoted by many ecologist movements as a lever to reduce the global environmental footprint of our lifestyles (inter alia; Boutaud and Gondran 2020). The call for frugality manifests itself in the promotion of non-motorized travel, urban agriculture or forms of exchange combining solidarity and proximity. But in spite of its breadth, the literature on ecological transition hardly mentions how homebound seniors accommodate themselves to the promotion of "soft" modes of transport (Imerzoukene Driad et al. 2014). All in all, the idea that shifts in urban production and management models will have to adapt to an uncertain world at a time when the over 60s will outnumber the under 30s on a global scale, which finds little echo in western-centric urban studies.

---

2 In 2011, 283 of the 771 urban areas in metropolitan France had a lower resident population than in 1990, with mostly small and medium-sized areas suffering from low to negative migratory and natural net changes, which accelerates their aging. The attention paid to declining cities, however, has encouraged work in France on the strategies of network operators faced with a decrease in consumption flows and on the commercial devitalization that strikes the heart of cities. These themes incidentally address the practices of residents in areas near these devitalized infrastructures (see Béal et al. 2021).

In this regard, Japanese research on transport and mobility in the city offers a striking contrast here, as Japan's demographic transition has, for several decades, required joined-up thinking about technological innovations, socioeconomic reconfigurations, ecological transition and care for seniors at all levels of territorial development. The country has indeed, since the 2000s, entered into an unprecedented era of super-aging[3], although North-East Asia (South Korea, Taiwan, China) is following the same path. The term refers to the combination of increased life expectancy and declining fertility rates, resulting in a rise in the proportion of people over 65 years of age to more than 21% of a given population – or even more, depending on the region. Generations born up until the 1960s live longer and are not sufficiently replaced by those born after 1980. In the East Asian context, this situation also arises from birth control policies framed by state apparatuses that have made the fight against perceived overpopulation a condition for their development (Attané 2016). Not only does it heavily impact the socioeconomic redistribution of wealth across generations, it also leads into an abrupt transition – sometimes over barely two decades – from rapid, seemingly uncontrolled trends of urban growth to processes of urban decline that look virtually irreversible. The reactive capacities of institutions designed in the 20th century to govern huge conurbations are challenged.

Thus, this chapter is meant to provide an overview of transportation issues in super-aging Japanese metropolitan areas, compared to their counterparts in other continents. How do mobility systems, designed to serve global cities of several million inhabitants, evolve in the face of continuous and absolute demographic decline? Their case is all the more enlightening in that Japan is still considered a model of efficiency in urban transit, a leading country for daily train trips per person[4]. The extensive body of reports published by ministries, companies, design offices and associations every year in Japan represents a unique source of information about the reconfigurations of multimodal networks known for their exceptional scope. Based on this vernacular documentation and data from population and traffic censuses, key elements of the geography of Japan's demographic transition will first be presented; then we will see how super-aging affects urban dynamics and in turn, mobility behaviors according to mode, age groups, motives for travel and the average built density of inhabited spaces. Then, we will look at the reactions of local actors to a contradictory development affecting aging suburban areas: the decline in commuting by train and the high motorization of households up to around 75 years old contribute to a devitalization of station neighborhoods, which older people continue to depend on for their access to

---

3 From *chō-kōreika*, a term commonly used in Japan.
4 With approximately 3,400 km traveled in 2016 (Statistical Handbook of Japan 2018), compared to 2,526 in Switzerland, 1,442 in France and 1,237 in Germany in 2019, according to available Eurostat data.

day-to-day services. Finally, we will discuss the negotiations conducted between central administrations, businesses, local authorities and users to maintain services to urban areas in decline.

5.2. Geographies of super-aging in Japan and their influence on public transport networks and daily mobilities

Punctuality, speed, comfort, integration into residential fabrics despite the sometimes gigantic size of infrastructures, a commercial diversity and vibrancy enabled by shopping arcades connecting different lines, repair works following disasters. By all accounts, Japanese urban transport elicits admiration, justifying its reputation as the "feet of the nation" (*kokumin no ashi*). Such reliability is largely due to private rail operators: at the turn of the 20th century, they had already formed conglomerates whose transportation activities blended with nascent expertise in urban planning. Land value capture strategies were accordingly implemented to enhance revenues derived from passenger and freight traffic. This then prompted companies to submit residential development projects to municipalities, starting in the early 1920s (Aveline 2003). Their success was such that urban centers, organized around castles and temples during the Edo period (1603–1868), moved to train stations from the 1890s onwards. Rail also constitutes a key element of national policies aimed at overcoming the isolation of regional marginal areas and improving the carriage of raw materials from zones of extraction to zones of consumption. However, this image of outstanding rail accessibility does not cover the whole country: first and foremost, it concerns global cities or attractive localities from a touristic perspective, which are concomitantly the most sought after by foreign visitors. But today and even in these areas, network and rolling stock operators are suffering from the repercussions of Japan's depopulation. It is relevant to briefly explain the latter's geography in order to understand the problems of downsizing that await mobility service providers.

5.2.1. *The deepening depopulation of Japan's peripheries*

Since 2010, the annual number of deaths in Japan has exceeded that of births, and these negative natural trends are not balanced by positive migration rates, despite recent measures facilitating labor immigration[5]. In 2020, the population of the archipelago stands at 126.2 million and could drop to less than 100 million by 2040; while the proportion of people over 65 has reached 29.1% nationally (just

---

5 Which the Covid-19 crisis has brought to a halt. In 2018, 7 million work visas were issued, an all-time high and an increase of 18.5% compared to 2017. Source: Ministry of Foreign Affairs, 2015 statistics.

over 36 million inhabitants), compared to 12.5% (14 million) for those under 15 and 58.6 for the 15–64 (75.5 million) age group. The 15–64 age group, which makes up the bulk of the employed population, could drop to less than 60 million by 2040.

With the increase in life expectancy (more than 81 years for men and 87 years for women), the over 65 category includes at least two groups: "young seniors" who retain their autonomy and "older seniors" who, experiencing a disengagement[6] from their environment, are forced to reduce the spatial perimeter of their daily activities. Besides, the socioeconomic consequences of this transition have long been unevenly distributed, with the deepening decline of peripheral and rural regions during the 20th century, despite public investments in infrastructure and public facilities or programs encouraging young adults to settle in the countryside (Figure 5.1).

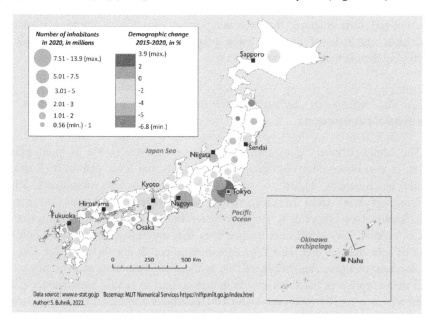

Figure 5.1. *Number of inhabitants per prefecture (todōfuken) in 2020 and demographic trends from 2015–2020. For a color version of this figure, see www.iste.co.uk/lesteven/urban.zip*

---

6 Coined by sociologists and gerontologists, the concept of disengagement defines an individual process of self-reorganization of daily life and activities, in reaction to the physical and relational changes brought on by aging over the years, in interaction with the sociocultural context (Meidani and Cavalli 2018, p. 9). It aims to better explain why and how the phenomena of social withdrawal or loss of engagement with the environment occurs among senior adults.

Since the 2000s, however, depopulation has also reached the fringes of metropolitan areas (Buhnik 2016). The results of the 2015 census, and the ongoing tallying of those from 2020, confirm that only the cores of metropolitan areas are recording population gains or at least demographic stability, particularly within their central districts, which partly mitigates the rise in the percentage of inhabitants over 65 years old. However, because of their size, these areas include up to hundreds of thousands of seniors.

The rest of the territory is experiencing a sharp decline: between 2010 and 2015, the change in the number of inhabitants fluctuated between −1 and −10% in a majority of the 718 municipalities recorded on January 1, 2015. As municipal mergers have led to the incorporation of depopulated villages and boroughs into large municipalities, all local authorities find themselves struggling with the environmental, legal or financial problems caused, inter alia, by the maintenance of underutilized infrastructure, the increasing areas of residential and agricultural wastelands, the risks of death at home of isolated inhabitants, or difficulties in identifying the heirs of abandoned property.

5.2.2. *An aging of suburban fringes reinforced by changes in residential preferences*

The center-periphery geography of territorial decline, visible at interregional scales, is also observed at the inter- and intramunicipal level. However, it shows greater heterogeneity linked to land fragmentation, which complicates urban planning services' tasks of categorizing buildings and operations to support revitalization (see Figure 5.3). An unoccupied house, slowly deteriorating due to lack of repairs, may stand next to dwellings that are still inhabited, on adjoining plots of less than 80 m². There is, moreover, a correlation between the date of development of a given neighborhood, the aging of its inhabitants and vacancy rates. With the exception of listed heritage buildings subject to careful maintenance (such as temples or works by renowned architects), buildings built since 1945 have a short lifespan, 45 years on average. Urban renewal is performed more through destruction/reconstruction than rehabilitation, and the second-hand real estate market remains very residual (Buhnik and Koyanagi 2020). Consequently, in housing developments for first-home buyers, the transition of the original buyers to retirement[7] and then to old age, may lead to a rapid increase in vacancy rates in a short period of time. Few households are interested in taking over "old" properties that are inexpensive to buy but expensive to modernize and adapt to changes in

---

7 In Japan, the retirement age has been set at 65 for private companies, but many retirees still work to complement a low pension income and avoid falling into poverty. In 2021, the government approved a reform encouraging companies to let their employees work until the age of 70.

certain standards, including anti-seismic standards. Several authors have come up with the notion of *double aging* to describe material obsolescence (facades, interiors, public spaces) fueled by the lack of generational renewal (Yui et al. 2017).

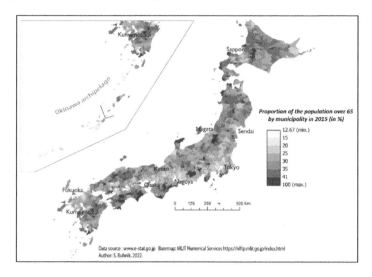

Figures 5.2. *Share of inhabitants over 65 by municipality in Japan in 2015. For a color version of this figure, see www.iste.co.uk/lesteven/urban.zip*

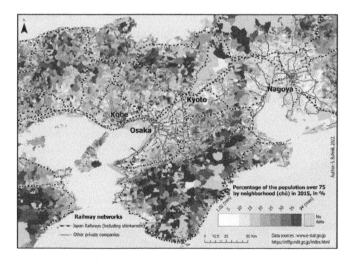

Figures 5.3. *Share of inhabitants over 75 by neighborhood in the Osaka-Kyoto-Kobe (Kansai) region. For a color version of this figure, see www.iste.co.uk/lesteven/urban.zip*

Double aging processes are in progress in the suburban fringes, starting with neighborhoods near train stations, which are chronologically the first to have been developed. These were major places for households to move to during the post-war era of recovery (1955–1973) and the peak of Japan's economic prosperity (1975–1990). Suburbs became an integral and higher stage of the housing ladder, a pathway toward family-size home ownership shaped by central and local governments, as well as the real estate partners of railway companies (Aveline 2003). The bursting of the bubble in 1990, causing a fall in land prices throughout the archipelago, followed by the revival of high-rise condominium housing developments in city centers in the 2000s, calls into question the relevance of the purchase of land and a house far from employment centers[8]. The prospects of earning an income from renting or reselling this type of property are dwindling, and more and more rights-holders are trying to avoid the burdens linked to inheriting their parents' house (Buhnik and Koyanagi 2020). By contrast, areas located around rail transportation hubs have experienced a significant "rejuvenation" over the past 20 years, linked to inflows of working-age populations, which is particularly true in the metropolitan cores of Tokyo, Nagoya and Osaka (Figure 5.3).

It is also from the 1990s, in the context of an increased labor market segmentation[9], that the number of households of one to two people began to grow: the unmarried, two-income couples, retired couples or single people whose residential backgrounds diverge from those of the *male single earner* household[10]. Many preferred apartment housing closer to their place of employment, close to a station hub and a wide range of services (Kubo and Yui 2011). Aware of these changes, and committed to promoting the attractiveness of metropolises through a revival of urban production (Forrest and Hirayama 2009), the Japanese government has supported major renovation projects under the banner of *transit-oriented development*. The skylines of Tokyo, Osaka or Kyoto have been transformed by the proliferation of apartment buildings (condominiums), which may target specific customer bases according to their specific features. Faced with the decline in the number of candidates for single-family housing, suburban communities which rely on their residential attractiveness have remained on the lookout for innovative projects (Buhnik 2016). This has led, for example, to the erection of housing

---

8 This is a characteristic that must be accounted for in the comparative approach to Japanese urban dynamics: the boom in real estate prices in the 1980s pushed the middle classes out of city centers, but service jobs (particularly in companies) were not widely relocated to the suburbs (see Yui et al. 2017).
9 Marked by the deepening of wage inequalities and employment conditions according to gender, age and level of qualification (Lechevalier 2010).
10 This means a parents-plus-child household whose income is based on the husband's professional career, while domestic tasks are delegated to the wife.

developments which promote their integration of digital technologies in order to reduce residents' carbon footprint: car parks for hybrid vehicles, sensors measuring individual energy consumption (see Granier 2019). Business interests seeking new markets thus meet the public challenges of compact city goals and adapting housing to the expectations of a declining and aging population. In this respect, the devitalization of many suburbs is not exclusive of continuing construction projects, more often than not on unbuilt land.

5.3. The influence of passengers' sociodemographic characteristics and location on transportation reconfigurations

Influenced by the urban dynamics and social changes described above, mobility behaviors of Japan's residents vary according to the positioning and density level of the territories where they live. On the one hand, the revival of housing construction in the heart of metropolises favors a modal shift toward non-motorized travel; on the other hand, the use of cars predominates in aging suburban areas and small and medium-sized agglomerations in non-metropolitan regions. Within major urban areas, these developments have recomposed the use of the multimodal railway networks that have radiated out from major stations in central cities: they form territories that are considered the *domains* (*ensen*) of the companies managing them (Aveline 2003). With the retirement of the cohorts born from the 1940s to the 1960s, commuter travel between suburbs and employment centers is giving way, in share and in number, to the more local mobility of elderly and/or childless households. They are moving toward active modes (cycling, walking) or, conversely, toward using individual vehicles, depending on the supply of shops and services and the level of public transport services around their home. However, train lines leading to employment, commercial and leisure districts of major cities remained, until 2019, extremely busy during rush hours.

5.3.1. *Changes in rail traffic: key figures and explanations*

The depopulation of Japan is reducing the total number of trips and passengers recorded each year on the archipelago. However, the preference for certain modes of transport and associated facilities is impacted differently according to territory types and age groups. Despite the continued employment of a growing proportion of inhabitants aged 60–75, demographic decline is reducing the total number of trips using collective transport or private vehicles. First, by train, in 1992, the number of trips made for (so-called regular) home-work commuting on all private lines[11] reached a record 8.6 billion and 5.7 billion for lines belonging to the six companies resulting from the privatization of Japan National Railways in 1987. In 2011, these figures were 7.7 (−10%) and 5.5 (−3%) billion. However, the number of non-regular passengers[12] increased by 15% over the same period (Table 5.1).

	Private companies		JR companies	
Date	1992	2011	1992	2011
Annual number of trips (billion)	13.96	13.87	8.98	8.83
Commuters (regular)	8.64	7.67	5.70	5.48
Non-commuters (non-regular)	5.32	6.19	3.30	3.35

Table 5.1. *Number of trips made on private railway lines and Japan Railways (JR), in 1992 and 2011 (source: Ichikawa 2017)*

In the three metropolitan areas of Greater Tokyo, Osaka-Kyoto-Kobe and Nagoya (*sandaitoshiken*), the share of rail for professional travel exceeds 60%[13] and accounts for almost half of all trips. The train also prevails for interregional journeys[14] through the *shinkansen* high-speed lines operated by the regional JR companies (Figure 5.4). In 2019, rail thus attracted more than 25 billion public transport journeys, out of a total of 31.2 billion compared to 5.8 billion by bus and taxi (SBJ 2021). However, this represents a decrease of about 1% compared to 2015. Since 2020, protective measures against the spread of Covid-19 have reduced home-work traffic by up to 80%[15], while border closures have also put a halt to

---

11 Ichikawa's (2017) survey includes the Tokyo subway: it is operated by a joint-stock company jointly owned by the Government of Japan and the Tokyo Metropolitan Government. Municipally operated subway lines (like Kyoto's) are not, however, counted in these figures.

12 That is, taking the train for non-professional motives. This common categorization reveals that the desynchronization of mobilities, related to the diversification of working schedules, has long been less significant in Japan than in the rest of the OECD (Aveline 2003).

13 Percentages are higher in Tokyo and Osaka, but lower in Nagoya: the latter is known as the birthplace of the Toyota firm and subsequently, of car culture in Japan.

14 Except in Hokkaidō to the north, where it is equally shared with flight travel, and the Okinawa archipelago to the south. The extent of Japan's land in latitude (excluding maritime territories) is 3500 km.

15 Even when states of emergency were enforced in response to spikes in contamination, the Constitution does not allow the confinement of residents to their homes, and collective transport has thus not been suspended. Companies have nevertheless been encouraged to massively resort to teleworking.

tourist travel. Bus transport, which oscillated around 10 billion trips per year in the early 1970s, stabilized at 4 billion in the 2000s. It has experienced a slight increase since the 2010s, often as a substitute for rail in the event of line closure.

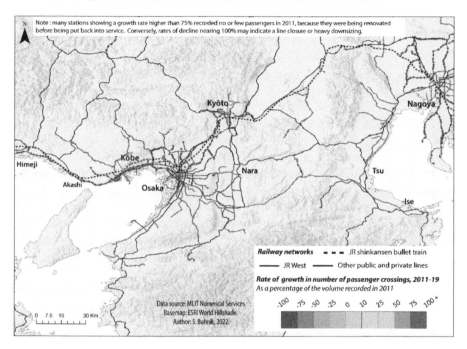

Figure 5.4. *Changes in the average daily number of crossings (entrances/exits) at stations in the Osaka region, from 2011 to 2019. Note: points represent the percentage of passengers gained or lost compared to traffic measured in 2011, but they are not proportional to the volume of passengers passing through these stations. For a color version of this figure, see www.iste.co.uk/lesteven/urban.zip*

These general developments in public transport also vary according to the areas served. In the Osaka (Kansai) region, the Hankyū, Hanshin and Keihan companies linking the city of Kyoto to the business and leisure districts in the north of Osaka city were able, until 2020, to offset the decline in revenue from center-suburb traffic by relying on the increase in tourist travel. This leads to an increase in the daily number of entries/exits at the stations of these lines (Figure 5.4). But even on the Umeda-Sannomiya line (owned by Hankyū), the busiest in Kansai, the number of annual passengers decreased from 224 to 206 million between 1992 and 2011

(Ichikawa 2017). The future of the Nankai and Kintetsu companies, which serve the Osaka region to Wakayama in the south and Nara in the east, is more compromised due to the depopulation of these more rural prefectures (Figure 5.2). Kintetsu recorded a 20–30% drop in passenger traffic on 13 of its 14 lines between 1992 and 2011 (Ichikawa 2017), which has continued since (Figure 5.4).

5.3.2. Unpacking the factors behind the rise in motorization rates in aging and shrinking Japan

The individual vehicle is the dominant mode of transport outside urban centers, as well as for freight. The number of vehicles registered in Japan remained stable between 2005 and 2015, at about 82 million, or 640 cars owned per 1,000 inhabitants, plus a fleet of 58 million buses and taxis. According to data from the National Police Agency, the number of holders of driver's licenses in Japan is stagnating at 82–83 million. More than 5.5 million holders are 70 years of age or older: this represents about 12.2% of licensed women and 17.8% of licensed men. The 16–29 age group represents just over 13% of the women and men with a driving license in 2020, a decline over the past 10 years (NPA 2020).

Whether active or inactive, young or old people living in densely urbanized areas give up owning a car for similar reasons: avoiding the costs of renting a parking space, insurance, gas and relying on renting a vehicle for long distance trips. Bicycles and mopeds, which account for a significant proportion of business travel in Japanese cities (up to 30–40% in certain districts of municipalities with populations greater than 400,000 inhabitants), are enjoying renewed popularity thanks to the success of condominium housing, the spread of electric bicycles, and the rise of home food deliveries, mainly performed by two-wheeled drivers (MLIT 2013).

On the other hand, shifting back to the car for commuting, shopping, friendly or medical visits is very common among residents of medium-sized towns, and is essential among suburban households over 50 years old, especially after retirement, even when the average density of their residential environment fluctuates between 1,000 and 3,000 inhabitants/km^2 (Iwama et al. 2021). This is explained first of all by the topography of the Japanese territory: urbanization is concentrated on narrow coastal plains, quickly reaching hills, resulting in steep slopes despite the levelling that accompanied the development of new cities or port areas such as Kobe and Kitakyūshū. Second, the participation of housewives over 50 years of age and pensioners in local economic and social life (return to part-time employment after children have entered middle school, volunteering, participation in election campaigns, etc.) is a powerful factor in increasing the number of daily trips by car.

Recent white papers on traffic estimated that 63% of women and 94% of men aged 69–74 drive several times a week (Cabinet Office 2018).

On the other hand, the rate of motorization drops quickly after the age of 80 for physiological and budget reasons (cost of insurance and the need to undergo regular examinations to keep your license). There is also a generational effect: older individuals have lived in less motorized cities and used to do their shopping in independent shops or small markets on shopping streets, the majority of which were around train stations.

5.4. Seniors' exposure to urban decline and the changing role of station neighborhoods in aging agglomerations

Consequently, differences in mobility practices between centers and peripheries are greater than during the period of rapid growth of Japanese cities (1950–1990). The continued motorization of senior suburban households is linked to their relative emancipation from commuting and accompanies a process of commercial decentering caused by the rise of shopping malls. The transfer of the purchasing practices of many households to these malls has harmed small independent businesses. The resulting commercial devitalization has hit the shopping streets adjacent to suburban or "secondary" stations in the hierarchy of rail networks. However, older seniors who have lost their autonomy, and who travel more on foot or by walker to do their errands (MLIT 2013), remain attached to "traditional" services and shops that were concentrated in shopping arcades near stations.

5.4.1. *Attachment to station neighborhoods tested by the decline in rail traffic and commercial devitalization*

Local authorities and operators are thus faced with the following dilemma. Relatively young and older senior adults use the transport function of rail infrastructure on a more occasional basis, even though efforts have been made to make stations more accessible or less expensive for them, through coupons or discount cards. But, at least as much as working users, they demand the maintenance of a regular service on lines affected by a decline in the number of passengers, because the station hubs are still a focus point of their sociabilities. In the suburbs and in particular, satellite towns (Nakamura 2005) laid out according to the theories of C.A. Perry (Aveline-Dubach 2015), stations accessible through pedestrian pathways still serve as neighborhood centers, thus concentrating small businesses, supermarkets, medical and educational services, as well as premises rented to non-profit associations. The latter developed in the wake of a 1998 law facilitating their creation and registration. In addition, going out for shopping determines an increasing share of the mobility of isolated elderly people. Between 1970 and 2015, the average size of Japanese households fell from 3.4 to 2.3 individuals. Of the 53.3 million households registered in 2015, there were 1.9 million men and 4 million women over the age of 65 living alone. Taking into account the temporalities of urban sprawl described above, these seniors are overrepresented in older housing developments, generally closer to stations.

The gap is thus widening between the decline in interurban rail flows and the recomposition of flows of non-commuters around stations. Along a network, station neighborhoods may follow opposite trajectories. The communication nodes in the heart of the metropolises (such as Shinjuku, Shibuya, Shinagawa or Ueno in Tokyo, Umeda and Namba in Osaka) benefit from regeneration plans and architectural overhaul, which reinforce their commercial, cultural and residential centrality (Tiry-Ono 2018). In Tokyo, the vacancy rate on shopping streets remains below 9%, compared to a national average of 15% in 2015. On the other hand, this average is largely reached or exceeded in the station districts of outlying suburban municipalities and medium-sized towns, which are less connected to metropolitan economies.

After reaching their peak in 1982 with 1.72 million units, there were only 990,000 independent stores in 2016 across the national territory, which did not prevent an increase in the total retail surface. From 1997 to 2017, stores dedicated to the sale of food products fell from 526,000 to 390,000 units. In an essay for ESRI Japan, T. Takahashi and T. Yakushiji calculated that in 2010, almost 44 million Japanese people (35% of the population) lived more than 500 m from retail businesses, of whom almost 10 million are over 65 years of age[16]. The highest proportion of inhabitants without pedestrian access to local services is found in mountainous and less densely populated areas, which coincides with the above-mentioned geography of aging. In suburban localities where employment had been predominantly manufacturing, such as around Osaka and Nagoya, the replacement of disused industrial sites with malls of more than 30,000 m^2 has led to an increase in the number of store clerks and turnover of the local commercial sector. Meanwhile, the number of store managers fell by 15–20% in the 1990s alone (Nakamura 2005).

---

16 Source: https://www.esrij.com/industries/case-studies/13825/ (in Japanese).

5.4.2. Between automobile dependence and new places of sociability for senior suburban households

Under these conditions, public authorities are observing a rise in the number of residents struggling to access the services and businesses they need on a daily basis. From 2000 to 2012, the percentage of those over 60 years of age interviewed by the Secretariat for Social Cohesion Policies (Prime Minister's Office) who complained of a deterioration in their mobility for purchases rose from 11.5% to over 17% (Kudo et al. 2012). The term "people with low purchasing capacity" (*kaimono jakusha*) refers to elderly, disabled and/or low-income people who have to travel more than 800 m to find basic necessities or food staples (Figure 5.5). In residential areas in demographic decline, the automobile dependence of seniors is worrying, although the geography of *kaimono jakusha* only incompletely reflects that of the shrinkage of businesses and services (see section 5.5). Their figure has become emblematic of a society affected by its aging and by the deepening of social and territorial disparities, attributable to the effects of the liberalization and decentralization measures of the 1990s and 2000s (Lechevalier 2010). The differentiated vulnerability of the elderly to the closure of shops and services reflects shifts in Japanese urban policies since the end of the bubble.

Influenced by the early emphasis that Japan's modern state put on physical education and sports for all ages, many Japanese seniors are used to walking long distances and may carry light shopping bags or baskets if they use a walker or a bicycle (Iwama et al. 2021). However, in declining urban areas with shopping streets undergoing processes of devitalization, elderly residents who can move easily on foot or on two wheels will turn to the car for their errands, not only to reach more thriving shopping areas, but also to avoid passing through spaces with many empty or unoccupied buildings, which make them feel anxious (Kudo et al. 2012; Iwama et al. 2021).

The lack of human presence may indeed aggravate the consequences of a fall on the street (delay in first aid treatment). In order to reduce the risk of seniors colliding with cars or bicycles, municipalities first worked on improving their signage and roads. Better guidance for visually impaired and hearing impaired people at crossroads, or creation of zones with stringent speed limits (no more than 30 km/h), are implemented thanks to the quantities of information transmitted in particular by the regional divisions of the Ministry of Land, Infrastructure, Transport and Tourism (MLIT). Since 2004, public data indicate a considerable decline in road accidents: of the 472,000 recorded in 2017, nearly 3,700 had a fatal outcome. Accidents involving seniors have decreased in number, although the over 65s are victims of around 55% of fatal road accidents, of which 24.3% involved the over 80s. Seniors are five times more likely to die from a road accident than other age groups. The road accident mortality rate, a national average of 0.63% in 2017, peaked at 3.7% for those over 75 years old.

Figure 5.5. *An elderly person leaning on a walker on a street in northwestern Kyoto (at a gradient of about 6%). Buhnik, November 2012. For a color version of this figure, see www.iste.co.uk/lesteven/urban.zip*

Media coverage of accidents caused by motorists over the age of 85 has led to stricter monitoring of driving by older seniors. In 2019, nearly 600,000 Japanese agreed to surrender their license in exchange for a certificate authorizing them to benefit from reduced bus and taxi fares (NPA 2020). The automobile remains the main, if not the only means of access to shopping centers appreciated by aging households. Apart from the fact that individuals born after 1945 were more accustomed than previous generations to frequenting shopping malls, the latter provide a safe and comfortable environment, including light, escalators, clean toilets, food courts and reception staff. In addition, discount prices or promotional offers adjusted to the erosion of post-retirement incomes are easier to find inside malls. Despite their historical and aesthetical value, many traditional streets seem dilapidated by comparison. The merchants' associations in charge of their maintenance respond by organizing neighborhood fairs, sometimes flea markets, by affirming their place in local political life or by developing a personalized and friendlier relationship with customers.

5.4.3. *Questioning the present and future strategies of railway companies*

It is interesting to remember that automobility in Japan established itself later, albeit at a faster pace, than in Europe and North America. Beginning in the 1980s, it strengthened in connection with *productivist welfare capitalism* (Holliday 2000): that is, the way in which arrangements between ministries, companies and political leaders encouraged the middle-class quest for home ownership in post-war Japan.

During the 1980s, the explosion of land prices pushed back the frontiers of urbanization in a way that neither central and local governments nor companies resolutely tried to slow down until the 2000s (Yui et al. 2017). The appreciation of the yen, by stimulating the relocation of manufacturing or assembly activities to South Asia, weakened territories where manufacturing employment was important. The recovery efforts of the 1990s de facto increased the importance of the construction and public works sector in the labor market: in medium-sized towns, it is not uncommon for 15–20% of jobs to depend on construction projects, including those of shopping malls. Their growth was encouraged by the deregulation in 1994 of the Large-Scale Retail Store Law (*Daikibo kōritenpo ricchi hō*), which restricted their volume and controlled their competition with smaller retailers.

Railway companies have accommodated urban sprawl as they frame their strategies in terms of the land they own around their lines. They can encourage the implementation of activities managed by subsidiaries or partners in order to increase land rents, but also to attract residents likely to use their networks. Most companies also operate bus lines that connect their stations to more remote areas. As landlords, they are therefore interested in setting up activities for educational or leisure purposes (Aveline 2003). The arrival of university campuses was sought after early on, with some companies not hesitating to grant land to universities for their campuses or to build stations serving them.

Faced with a collapse in the number of commuters passing through the gates of suburban stations every day, many operators can no longer envisage development based on the widening of train carriages or increases in frequency during peak hours.

From 1980 to 2000, companies were competing to improve the speed of intercity journeys, resulting in a multiplication of train services named *Super* or *Express*. Noting the aging of their customers in the suburbs, they are turning more toward integrated development around their "flagship" stations, in the wake of the Urban Renaissance Special Measures Law of 2002 (Kubo and Yui 2011; Aveline-Dubach 2015). In addition to the construction of housing towers and commercial and leisure areas, premises near the stations accommodate more school or health and care services catering to seniors or young parents[17].

The rise of tourism has also convinced railway companies to make train travel a leisure product in itself, providing berths with panoramic views and meal trays featuring locally grown products from the areas being traveled through. This requires thoughtful investment, suitable for lines passing through rural rather than suburban landscapes. This is the case for the Nanatsuboshi, a train traveling through the Kyūshū region, whose demand for sleeping cars is 10 times greater than its capacity, despite a fixed price of at least 3,500 euros for five days. It is nonetheless a barely profitable service which the JR Kyūshū company operates mainly for prestige, knowing how Japan's society remains highly perceptive to the beauty of its trains and railway infrastructures. Meanwhile, more and more companies like JR West allow passengers with bicycles to board their carriages in light of the growing popularity of hiking and trails.

Thus, gains in non-regular passengers partially offset the decline in commuters: the latter still account for the majority of passenger-kilometers, in a country where the price of tickets is proportional to the distance traveled during a journey. Each company sets its prices, there is no zonal subscription valid for all lines in an agglomeration, even though different private and public operators have no problem sharing the space of a station when their lines intersect there and interpenetrating their volumes (Tiry-Ono 2018). Since the 2000s, only five companies have seen their turnover increase: JR East, JR Tokai, JR Kyūshū, Tokyo Metro (public subway), as well as the private company Tōkyū, which serves the west and southwest of the capital (Ichikawa 2017) (Figure 5.6). Having longer networks no longer benefits operators.

---

17 The surroundings of renovated stations particularly attract investments from listed healthcare properties (Healthcare REITs), and thus form points of fixation for financialized retirement homes and nursing homes (see Aveline-Dubach 2022).

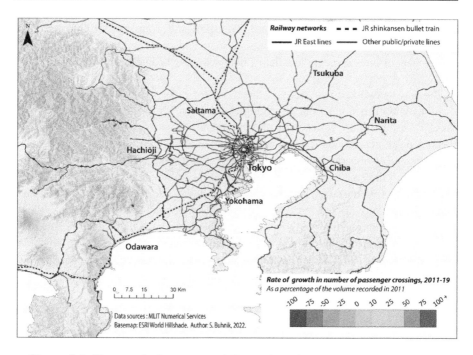

Figure 5.6. *Changes in the average daily number of crossings (entrances/exits) at stations in the Tokyo region, from 2011 to 2019. For a color version of this figure, see www.iste.co.uk/lesteven/urban.zip*

5.5. Maintaining accessibility in aging cities and regions: transport policies at the crossroads of care and local autonomy

While the possibility of closing unprofitable lines has long been postponed at the request of central and local governments, the widening of deficits and the entry of foreign investors[18] into the capital of transport companies may encourage them to separate from their most loss-making segments or streamline the management of stations. As early as 1968, an advisory board of Japan National Railways recommended the removal of 83 rural lines carrying less than 3,000 passengers or 600 tons of freight per day; 11 of them ceased to operate in the following years (Ichikawa 2017). Since the beginning of the Covid-19 pandemic, and with the support

---

18 The investment fund Cerberus entered the capital of Seibu in 2013 before selling its shares, faced with the reluctance of the executive committee to abandon five rail segments and its baseball team. See: https://asia.nikkei.com/Business/With-US-backer-parting-ways-Seibu-set-for-new-era-of-growth.

of the Ministry of Land, Infrastructure, Transport and Tourism (MLIT), meetings have been held between mayors, business leaders and civil servants to anticipate the replacement of lines carrying less than 2,000 passengers per kilometer by buses.

Railway network downsizing is therefore not new, but now affects suburban localities within medium to large agglomerations, which did not expect to face the risk of losing their connection to interregional networks and the resulting phenomena of accelerated devitalization. Municipalities and residents' associations are particularly concerned about the transformation of stations into "ghost stations" working with the smallest possible staff due to the automation of ticket offices and gates. Seniors find unstaffed stations dangerous, and dislike replacement bus stations whose shelters provide less protection from the sun or rain, and which expose them to a higher risk of collision with passing cars. Seniors may thus lose an incentive to move around their neighborhoods. Local authorities and the population as a whole feel the isolation symbolized by the closure of a station, hence the fact that its sustainability represents as much a socioeconomic issue as a political priority.

5.5.1. *Integration of public and private actors in compact city policies*

Faced with these developments, communities wishing to maintain a rail connection have often negotiated a style of public–private management known as the third sector: municipalities or departments agree to use part of their budgets to operate with a limited but regular service (one train per hour on average). This is the formula chosen by the municipality of Toyama, on the Sea of Japan, which inaugurated a joint company to manage the replacement of JR railway lines with a tram service that has become famous, overcoming the initial fears of residents regarding a rise in local taxes. Moreover, according to a survey by the Ministry of Agriculture conducted among 1,244 municipalities in 2019, around 73.5% of them have, with or without state support, implemented programs aimed at reducing the number of people who suffer from the devitalization of their neighborhood (MAFF 2021). The conclusion is unanimous: to promote active aging and delay the emergence of neurodegenerative diseases, incentives for the elderly to leave their homes are essential. This means removing physical barriers to mobility and ensuring the dissemination of services and activities that make them want to go out around their homes.

The virtues attributed to active aging mean that the value of a station, in the eyes of seniors, is based less on the speed of the trains that serve it than on its stability and comfort, as well as its punctuality compared to road traffic, which is often congested (Koike 2014; Ichikawa 2017). The fall in the number of users on certain lines has a positive effect on the perception of their comfort by increasing the probability of finding free seats, instead of fearing that the seats reserved for disabled people will be occupied: it greatly contrasts with the congestion issues that frequently reached an unbearable point level in the 1980s[19]. Stations have retained their status as landmark and their proportions, and concourses have been an ideal location for the installation of temporary stalls selling directly distributed agricultural products. The joint involvement of transport operators, agricultural cooperatives and/or local businesses contributes to the success of roadside rest areas based on the architectural codes of the railway station (*michi no eki*), which may receive grants from the Ministry of Land or the Japan Tourism Agency as part of regional revitalization schemes. Municipalities with tourist sites accessible by rail will make their stations a gateway to their local economy and the backbone of their territorial branding: in addition to the sale of locally crafted products, free pediluves may be provided so that visitors may bathe their feet in spring water. The vitality of non-metropolitan transport hubs is thus increasingly linked to their ability to satisfy needs for rest or discovery while customers await their next departure.

The success of revitalization strategies focused on the renovation of stations, especially outside metropolitan areas, requires synergies between the types of routes and patterns of use. This reduction of distances between the remaining resources of aging and declining cities in order to maximize their use, as Japanese urban planning documents put it, legitimizes support for compact cities. They have been the dominant focus point for sustainable urban development in post-growth Japan: since the late 1990s, compact city discourses and models have been included in all ministerial guides and municipal master plans. Behind this all-encompassing and rather fuzzy term, defenders of the compact city hope, on the one hand, to encourage the establishment of firms near urban and suburban stations. They expect, on the other hand, to regulate inter-municipal competition to attract jobs and households. Selecting "hot spots" for redevelopment at the municipal level, based on the nodes of existing networks (Figure 5.7), represents an easy-to-understand mechanism for the governance of urban decline. This scheme supposedly benefits from the long-term decline in land values in Japan, which facilitates the relocation of hospitals and schools to downtown areas.

---

19 In his study of the city of Takatsuki, Nakamura (2005) indicates that the daily rate of train overcrowding there fell from 243% in 1965 (a rate which he describes as "murderous") to 143% in 2003, 100% corresponding to occupancy of all seats.

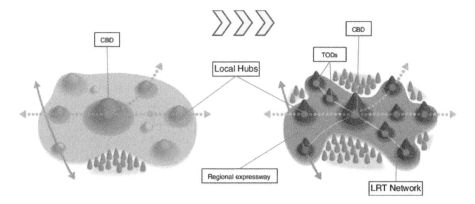

Figure 5.7. *The ideal compact city form: A diagram for the municipality of Utsunomiya, cited as a model in the guides of the Ministry of Land (MLIT). Source: Koike (2014), reproduced with permission. For a color version of this figure, see www.iste.co.uk/lesteven/urban.zip*

Nevertheless, it is difficult to materialize this ideal of planned shrinkage, despite constant political and administrative support. Besides the conflicts caused by more selective issuance of building permits, pro-compact city policies stumble on their ability to strengthen the sociospatial cohesion of the municipalities concerned and the well-being of their elderly residents. In Japan, studies of food deserts criticize a reductionist approach to constraints on access to urban resources: to better align the distribution of shops and services with the habitat of the elderly is a commendable goal, but it underestimates the influence of social capital on the food habits of the elderly. The accumulation of surveys conducted in variously urbanized spaces (Tokyo, regional capitals, medium-sized cities) tends to show that "people with low purchasing mobility" are over-represented among workers' and employees' households in large cities: they often live alone since their children have left home and may rarely communicate with their neighbors. In contrast, residents in suburban residential areas interviewed in the 2010s by several university teams maintained more ties with their neighbors and complained less about the distance, however high, from shops (Iwama et al. 2021, pp. 4–12 and 49–59). Preventive rehousing of isolated seniors in more dynamic neighborhoods is therefore no guarantee of improving their social participation, insofar as a denser, pedestrianized residential environment does not guarantee that these seniors will leave their accommodation more often.

5.5.2. Institutionalization of volunteering to curb the shrinkage of transport

In suburban spaces that have grown rapidly before entering an early decline, the sustainability of a quality transport network is not only hampered by the erosion of the customer base; its logistics are also challenged by labor shortages. It is in the most declining regions that driver job vacancies are the highest, in part because operators are unable or unwilling to raise driver salaries (Fujinami 2019).

These considerations have been conducive to several legislative reforms, including the Basic Law on Transport Policies (*kōtsū seisaku kihon hō*) of 2013. Under this reform, individual drivers are now allowed to participate in operating community transport systems if they demonstrate adequate skills. Vehicles belonging to non-profit associations or even volunteers themselves, or loaned by municipalities, may transport residents at a fare equal to the operating costs of the service. Municipal social services may use this so-called "white" license to negotiate with associations the establishment of *welfare taxis*: local governments contribute to the purchase of vehicles, equipment or software needed to manage fleets and schedules. In some cases, supermarkets offer a car service for senior customers or create mobile grocery stores, in partnership with other private or civil society actors.

In order to prevent these deregulations from leading to the rise of "real-fake taxis", non-professional community transport is necessarily limited to declining areas poorly served by public transport and lacking local services. Local authorities must ensure its coordination with conventional public transport actors and confine it as much as possible to the "last mile", that is, the distance between the homes of people with limited mobility and nearby train or bus stations (Fujinami 2019). This calls for travel plans centered on the logic of *Mobility as a Service* (MaaS). This expression, now ubiquitously referred to among transport stakeholders in Japan, depicts advances in the individualization of the use of networks based on the digitization of urban environments, more specifically on automation, platformization and open data. MaaS appears to be a major avenue for consolidating decentralized and hybrid governance of public transport in areas which are isolated and/or threatened by the withdrawal of incumbent operators.

Nevertheless, the democratic dimension of these devices is questionable (see Fujinami 2019). While the 2013 law introduced a "right to move freely" (*jiyū ni idōsuru kenri*), its text says little on the duty of the public authorities to enforce this right[20]. In a situation where municipalities are indebted but endowed with greater regulatory autonomy, some of them sometimes pressure residents to invest as volunteers in the maintenance of unprofitable infrastructure (Takamura 2009). However, many experts fear the weariness that gradually overtakes volunteers and advocates of social entrepreneurship in charge of these well-intentioned initiatives. The latter were able to enthusiastically launch alternative car or grocery truck services, before giving up due to lack of time, low funding or even lower gratification (Iwama et al. 2021). Moreover, the intervention of authority figures in neighborhood communities to convince isolated seniors to seek help often proves to be as efficient as volunteer commitment. Despite institutional recognition, volunteerism and civic autonomy alone cannot, therefore, replace conventional transport systems, especially when a volunteer leaves and the issue of their succession arises.

The possibility of supporting citizen initiatives through robotics or smartphone applications is fueling enthusiasm for MaaS. But the challenge of the digital divide is thus becoming more acute, between households that are equipped and informed of the existence of useful sites, and those suffering from digital illiteracy. In 2017, about 51% of 70–79 year olds living in Japan reported connecting to the Internet at least once a day, and various measures have been taken to increase this rate, such as the organization of workshops by the volunteer programmer movement *Code for Japan*. As illustrated by the testimonials of nurses in charge of setting up Zoom sessions in retirement homes at the start of the Covid-19 pandemic, seniors can derive cognitive benefits from their interactions with advanced communication technologies, without eliminating the feeling of loneliness. In order for seniors to take advantage of these tools to move around better, professionals need to familiarize them with these innovations. MaaS therefore does not replace the need to recruit, under decent salary conditions, a labor force working at the intersection of transport and *care* to meet the needs of a very aged society.

5.6. Conclusion

Contemporary urban Japan is characterized by impressive contrasts between very dense areas, whose wealth and commercial diversity strikes visitors, and territories, whose sustainability is threatened by their decline. It is there that local communities struggle with a combination of commercial devitalization, increase in housing vacancies, aging of the remaining residents and budget austerity. This situation does

---

20 If the Japanese government were seriously enforcing this right, coverage of areas underserved by local buses would cost 120 billion yen (about 914 million euros) annually (Fujinami 2019).

not, at first glance, present a fundamental difference with the problems pertaining to rural areas or small and medium-sized towns in other countries in demographic transition. However, the aging of Japanese society is such that it now hinders the maintenance of territorial organizations where older seniors can benefit from mutual aid networks or services run by adults who are often already in their sixties or seventies.

In contexts of super-aging, scenarios of urbanization based on the extension of transport infrastructure and the race for performance, become obsolete. Examples of unprofitable railway lines are increasing, especially in suburbs where older residents are insufficiently replaced by the arrival of younger newcomers. However, the number of closures remains limited, given the decline in recorded commuter flows: this preservation owes as much to socioeconomic and logistical considerations as to ideological aspects. It indeed relates to the "emotional" attachment (*jōchoteki na miryoku*; Ichikawa 2017) of Japan's society to its own history with railway infrastructures: their expansion is closely associated with Japan's transformation into an economic powerhouse (Fujinami 2019), especially among decision-makers and company executives who were trained in engineering schools and marked by the symbolism of efficient train transit in the post-war period.

Under such circumstances, the autonomy of the elderly, which is seen as a key to successful aging in official discourses, favors the relocation of seniors to well-connected neighborhoods. Projects to resize Japanese cities have clearly given priority to concentrating urban revitalization operations around stations in order to combine ecological transition issues with solutions to overcome the isolation of seniors. But in addition to their rather complex implementation, compact city scenarios reinforce the concentration of Japan's inhabitants in the country's most dynamic cities and territories. Moreover, it cannot be ignored that the causes of loneliness in elderly and/or disabled residents do not depend only on the livability of the territories to which they are recommended to move.

5.7. References

Attané, I. (2016). La fin de l'enfant unique en Chine ? *Population & Sociétés*, 7(535), 1–4.

Aveline, N. (2003). *La ville et le rail au Japon*. CNRS Éditions, Paris.

Aveline-Dubach, N. (2015). *Vieillissement et déprise urbaine au Japon. Les nouveaux défis de l'aménagement*. La Documentation française, Paris.

Aveline-Dubach, N. (2022). Financializing nursing homes? The uneven development of health care REITs in France, the United Kingdom and Japan. *Environment and Planning A: Economy and Space*, 1–21.

Bauman, Z. (2000). *Liquid Modernity*. Polity Press, Cambridge.

Béal, V., Cauchi-Duval, N., Rousseau, M. (2021). *Déclin urbain. La France dans une perspective internationale*. Éditions du Croquant, Paris.

Boltanski, L. and Chiapello, E. (1999). *Le nouvel esprit du capitalisme*. Gallimard, Paris.

Boutaud, A. and Gondran, N. (2020). *Les limites planétaires*. La Découverte, Paris.

Buhnik, S. (2016). Une mobilité amoindrie ? Décroissance démographique et évolution des mobilités quotidiennes dans la conurbation Ôsaka-Kyôto-Kôbe. *Espaces, Populations, Sociétés* [Online]. Available at: https://journals.openedition.org/eps/6150 [Accessed 29 October 2021].

Buhnik, S. and Koyanagi, S. (2020). La vacance résidentielle au Japon : d'un problème d'accès au sol au souci d'y échapper. In *La ville inoccupée. Enjeux et défis des espaces urbains vacants*, Arab, N. and Miot, Y. (eds). Presses des Ponts, Paris.

Forrest, R. and Hirayama, Y. (2009). The uneven impact of neoliberalism on housing opportunities. *International Journal of Urban and Regional Research*, 33, 998–1013.

Fujinami, T. (2019). Jinkō genshō-ka no jizoku kanōna komyuniti kōtsū [Sustainable community transport in the context of demographic decline]. *JRI Rebyū*, 6(67), 77–96.

Granier, B. (2019). Gouverner la consommation d'énergie des ménages. Renouvellement des enjeux et des instruments d'intervention (1973–2017). *Ebisu. Études japonaises*, 56, 223–252.

Holliday, I. (2000). Productivist welfare capitalism: Social policy in East Asia. *Political Studies*, 48(4), 706–723.

Ichikawa, H. (2017). Jinkō genshō jidai e no tetsudōgaisha no bijinesu-moderu no mosaku [The quest for an economic model for railway companies in a time of demographic decline]. *Toshi jūtaku-gaku*, 97, 15–20.

Imerzoukene Driad, H., Hamman, P., Freytag, T. (2014). La mobilité des personnes âgées dans le "quartier durable" de Rieselfeld à Fribourg-en-Brisgau. *Revue géographique de l'Est*, 54(3–4) [Online]. Available at: https://journals.openedition.org/rge/5224 [Accessed 2 January 2022].

Iwama, N., Asakawa, T., Tanaka, K., Sasaki, M., Komaki, N., Ikeda, M. (2021). *Urban Food Deserts in Japan*. Springer, Singapore.

Jentzsch, H. (2019). La revitalisation régionale et ses contestations locales. Le cas de la promotion de l'oenotourisme à Yamanashi. *Ebisu. Études japonaises*, 56, 191–221.

Klien, S. (2020). *Urban Migrants in Rural Japan: Between Agency and Anomie in a Post-growth Society*. SUNY Press, New York.

Koike, H. (2014). Mobility perspective for a local city in Japan. *IATTS Research*, 38(1), 32–38.

Kubo, T. and Yui, Y. (2011). Transformation of the housing market in Tokyo since the late 1990s: Housing purchases by single-person households. *Asian and African Studies*, XV(3), 3–21.

Kudo, K., Kimura, A., Nozaki, H., Ueda, K. (2012). Suggestion for continuous cooperation derived from cases of services supporting people with limited access to shopping facilities. NRI Papers, 170, Nomura Research Institute, Tokyo.

Lechevalier, S. (2010). *La grande transformation du capitalisme japonais*. Presses de Sciences Po, Paris.

Lord, S. and Piché, D. (2018). *Vieillissement et aménagement : perspectives plurielles*. Les Presses de l'Université de Montréal.

MAFF (2021). 'Shokuryōhin akusesu mondai' ni kansuru zenkoku shichōson ankēto chōsa kekka [Results of a national survey of municipalities on access problems to food]. Report, Ministry of Agriculture, Forestry and Fisheries [Nōrinsuisanshō], Tokyo.

Marcilhac, A. (2021). *Environnement et vieillissement : partenaires ou adversaires ?* UGA Éditions, Grenoble.

Meidani, A. and Cavalli, S. (2018). Vivre le vieillir : autour du concept de déprise. *Gérontologie et société*, 40(155), 9–23.

MLIT (2013). Heisei nijūyon-nendo kokudo kōtsū hakusho [2012 white paper on transport and territory]. White paper, Ministry of Land, Infrastructure, Transport and Tourism [Kokudo kōtsūshō], Tokyo.

Nakamura, T. (2005). The issues of satellite city in the era of declining population: From the study of Takatsuki City, Osaka. *The Journal of Economic Studies, Nihon Fukushi University*, 31, 55–82 [In Japanese].

Nishihara, J. (2015). Spatial government system of newly merged municipalities and population changes within municipalities impacted by those government systems. In *Urban Geography of Post-Growth Society*, Hino, M. and Tsutsumi, J. (eds). Tohoku University Press, Sendai.

NPA (2020). Unten menkyo tōkei [Driving licence statistics]. Report, National Police Agency, Traffic Bureau [Keisatsuchō kōtsū kyoku], Tokyo.

Raulin, F., Butzbach, C., Negron-Poblete, P., Poldma, T., Lord, S. (2020). Vers l'amélioration de la marchabilité de la ville pour tous. Retour d'expérience sur l'aménagement de l'accessibilité autour d'un centre commercial à Montréal. *Géocarrefour*, 94(4) [Online]. Available at: https://journals.openedition.org/geocarrefour/13323 [Accessed 3 January 2022].

Rausch, A. (2006). The Heisei Dai Gappei: A case study for understanding the municipal mergers of the Heisei era. *Japan Forum*, 18(1), 133–156.

SBJ (2021). *Statistical Handbook of Japan 2021*. Statistics Bureau of Japan [Sōmushō tōkei kyoku], Tokyo.

Takamura, G. (2009). Japon : participation des habitants… au service public. In *La république antiparticipative. Les obstacles à la participation des citoyens à la démocratie locale*, Tournon, J. (ed.). L'Harmattan, Paris.

Tiry-Ono, C. (2018). *L'architecture des déplacements. Gares ferroviaires du Japon*. Infolio, Paris.

Yui, Y., Kubo, T., Miyazawa, H. (2017). Shrinking and super-aging suburbs in Japanese metropolis. *Sociology Study*, 7(4), 195–204.

6

From Calcutta to Delhi and Hyderabad: Genealogy of Indian Metros

Bérénice BON
IRD-Cessma (French National Research Institute for Sustainable Development), Paris, France

6.1. Introduction

On February 17, 2021, the engineer E. Sreedharan announced his candidacy for the post of prime minister of Kerala, one of the southern states of India. He was, at this time, 89 years old and retired from the Indian Railways. This engineer spent the last 17 years of his career running Delhi's metro agency. He has had a lasting impact on the way metros are designed in India, but also, more broadly, on their governance structures and on national urban transport policies. He now enjoys a high level of notoriety and credibility, thus pushing him to become a candidate, in 2021, for the highest political office. He has succeeded in extending his field of competence far beyond the realm of public transport alone.

This engineer, called the "metro man", has been one of the pillars in India of the "metro industry" (Tiwari 2007) which began to operate from the mid-2000s: more than 15 projects are underway, with strong social and spatial implications and requiring considerable financial investment. In 2021, 10 metros were operational in the Indian metropolises of Kolkata (Calcutta), Delhi, Bangalore, Gurgaon, Mumbai (Bombay), Chennai, Kochi, Lucknow, Hyderabad and Pune. In 2020, the Delhi metro represented more than 400 km of lines, at a total cost of about 13 billion euros. It carries more than 3 million passengers daily, and more lines are under construction. By way of comparison, the whole London Underground network is estimated at 403 km and that of Paris at 220 km. The Delhi metro can therefore boast of being one of the longest intra-urban networks.

We propose to use the professional background of engineer Sreedharan to trace the genealogy of Indian metros and their governance models[1]. This entails following the early work of engineer Sreedharan for the Calcutta metro in the 1970s, his ascent as director of the Delhi metro agency in the middle of the 1990s, then finally as general consultant from 2010 for all metro projects in India. Through his life story, we highlight certain political, financial and technical issues with these major transport projects. How have their governance structures developed toward greater integration of the private sector and decision-making within the Indian state? Have these projects always relied on capital provided by international donors?

By focusing on the biography of Sreedharan, we show in the first part how the political and technological experience of the Calcutta metro contributed to shaping a financial and institutional model for the Delhi metro in a context of multiple political and urban reforms in India. In a second part, we study more precisely the institutional, technical, but also human components of the Delhi metro, through examination of the professional knowledge of the engineers who would lead the implementation of the metro. Finally, in a third part, we show how the governments of various Indian cities have chosen (or have not chosen) to follow or distance themselves from this model of the Delhi metro, and thus from the recommendations of engineer Sreedharan.

6.2. The first metro in Calcutta: jewel for rail engineers, burden for urban policies

Sreedharan was born on June 12, 1932 in a district of southern India, at that time under the rule of the British Empire. The son of a wealthy owner of agricultural land, he was able to devote himself fully until his adolescence to his studies and sports activities. He began his career as a teacher at the Polytechnic School of Kozhikode not far from his childhood home before entering, in 1953, the very selective national competition for the corps of railway engineers, in which he

---

1 This research is based on field surveys carried out in Delhi between 2011 and 2014 as part of a thesis funded by the European project FP7 Chance2Sustain and hosted at the Center for Human Sciences in New Delhi. The surveys have been updated to 2019 as part of the ANR ENGIND on the engineering profession in India.

succeeded brilliantly. His first achievement as an Indian railway engineer was the reconstruction of a bridge that had collapsed in the open sea following a cyclone on the east coast of India. The reconstruction of this bridge in 1964 is considered an engineering feat because the reconstruction was carried out in only a few months in the open sea, introducing technical innovations. This project accelerated Sreedharan's career. In 1971, as then deputy chief engineer of the Railways, he was posted to the city of Calcutta (now Kolkata in the state of West Bengal) to work on the first Indian metro project. The Railways entrusted him with this responsibility because of his credibility gained during the reconstruction of the bridge.

We will show that this first Indian metro was a very important learning moment for railway engineers, but also for political authorities, who would draw institutional and financial lessons from it.

6.2.1. The birth of the Calcutta metro: emerging urban transport policies across India

In 1951, five Indian cities exceeded 1 million inhabitants. Calcutta, capital of the state of West Bengal[2], was then the most populous city with 4.67 million inhabitants[3]. The Indian Constitution promulgated in January 1950 does not include urban transport as a specific sector. Responsibility for urban development and for urban transport is part of the prerogative of the regional states. Before 1986, at national level, urban transport was not assigned to a particular ministry and depended on several ministries: for rail transport, it was the Ministry of Railways, and for road transport, the Ministry of Surface Transport. For example, for the city of Calcutta, the regional government, via its transport department, is in charge of roads, the trams and the buses that predate the metro (Bhaduri and Dey 2012). As for rail transport, the backbone of India-wide transport, it is at the center of the recommendations of the national commissions for servicing new urban developments on the urban periphery and between cities. The Railways were then a powerful, quasi-autonomous institution with several hundred thousand employees who had the technical and financial capabilities to realize these projects. In Calcutta, the construction of the metro thus brought a new dimension to rail transport by considering not only suburban developments, but also travel within the city.

---

2 Calcutta, renamed Kolkata in 2001, was until 1911 the capital of British India. Following an attempt to partition Bengal, the capital was transferred to Delhi.
3 In 1951: Bombay (2.97 million), Madras (1.54 million), Delhi (1.43 million) and Hyderabad (1.13 million). Urban population growth post-independence was strengthened by the influx of refugees from Pakistan (especially in cities in northern India).

As early as the 1950s, three metro projects in India were being studied: Delhi, Bombay and Calcutta. In 1949, as part of a project of cooperation, a committee of French experts were appointed by the head of the government of West Bengal for the city of Calcutta. Two metro lines, East–West and North–South, were then considered. In 1969, the Ministry of Railways also created a structure responsible for developing a master plan for the Calcutta metro: the Metropolitan Transport Project (MTP-R). Five corridors were then defined, including a priority corridor crossing the city from North to South. However, these initial studies and network plans did not lead to a green light for the construction of the metros. The green light would come from two other factors: first, the political context in the state of West Bengal in the early 1970s, and, second, the proliferation of planning projects in the 1960s in Calcutta, including the development of a planning document relating specifically to transport.

In 1967, the government of the state of West Bengal passed from the Congress Party to a left-wing coalition[4]. Four years of regional state-wide political instability followed, culminating in the establishment of President's Rule in the early 1970s. The elected state assembly was dissolved and the authority of the central government, dominated by the Congress Party, was imposed at state level in West Bengal[5]. This authoritarian political shift accelerated decision-making for the construction of major projects. The political decision to build the Calcutta metro project was announced during the visit of Indian Prime Minister Indira Gandhi in April 1972 (Kharbanda and Pinto 1996).

Political control by the central government also led to an ambitious urban development program in Calcutta, and several projects were approved. In 1977, a metropolitan agency (the CMDA[6]) was created in Calcutta for the specific management of urban planning and urban policies. It should be noted that the metro did not depend on this authority, which was therefore involved neither in its decision-making, nor, importantly, in coordinating with other modes of transport and with urban development plans. This decision-making, in an exceptional context of central government and the involvement of railways controlled at national level, would not be challenged.

The governance structure for the metro was debated at the national level in 1972 around the crucial issue of financing. The Ministry of Railways, which carried out the latest studies on the metro project and which had a central role in major transport

---

4 Alliance of the Communist Party of India and the Revolutionary Socialist Party.

5 The imposition of President's Rule is justified by the deterioration of the state of "law and order", as provided for in the 1950 Constitution.

6 Calcutta Metropolitan Development.

policy directions, was then appointed as project manager, responsible for the construction and management of the major project, but not as the sole agency responsible for financing. It was decided that the central government would finance most of the capital cost for the project. This therefore implied a strong dependence on the Railways[7] by the central government for this project, which was treated separately from the budget debated annually for all the other activities of the Railways.

The construction of the Calcutta metro experienced significant delays mainly due to financial difficulties and late payments from the central government, which would profoundly influence the policy choices of the Delhi metro 30 years later. Indeed, the decision-makers of the Calcutta metro planned in 1972 the construction of a 16.5 km line from the south of the city to the north, with 15 underground stations and 2 elevated stations; construction time was then estimated at 7 years. But the work ended in 1995, following the initial plan but after 23 years of construction. The total cost of the project in 1995 represented more than 10 times the original estimated cost (Kharbanda and Pinto 1996). The Calcutta metro became the target of many controversies and criticisms in Indian political debate.

In fact, from 1972 to 1979, the funds allocated were not sufficient to purchase the equipment and raw materials necessary for the construction of the metro and, between 1974 and 1975, the oil crisis resulted in a very significant increase in the cost of the project; the central government then took the decision to stop it. The project was finally relaunched with the intervention of pro-metro lobbies, who underlined the positive effects of long-term investments in densely populated cities. During the 1970s and 1980s, the colossal investments represented by the metros and the political decisions on these investment choices made entirely by the public authorities were at the heart of debate on the metros for other Indian cities (Dalvi 1986). Moreover, since 1950, the World Bank has fueled strong criticisms of these choices by recommending that governments invest in renewing bus fleets, and exercise great caution for metro projects deemed as too expensive.

Finally, the financing difficulties encountered during the implementation of the Calcutta metro and the position of international institutions such as the World Bank delayed the green light for the other metro projects studied in the 1950s. The Calcutta metro was a first step of experimentation in the mode of financing, the inclusion of technical engineering knowledge and major railway works in an urban environment for the central government. It retained significant decision-making powers, shared with the Ministry of Railways. This metro was built without

---

7 By "Railways", we mean the national company of Indian Railways under the authority of the Ministry of Railways.

coordination with the local urban authorities, and without the support of a master development plan decided by the urban authorities. The state of West Bengal considered the metro to be a Central State Project and refused to participate in its financing.

But, despite these difficulties, the Calcutta metro represented for the Ministry of Railways important technological innovations and a situational change for rail engineers: they were operating in an urban context, giving rise to new technical and political constraints.

6.2.2. *The Calcutta metro, jewel of railway engineers*

From 1972 to 1977, Sreedharan worked on the construction site of the Calcutta metro. He devoted himself to the construction of 16 km of tunnels and stations, and to this end received training in Japan at the Tokyo metro agency. For these railway engineers, the Calcutta metro represented the opportunity to confront the problems of a large project in an urban environment, not, as we have seen, through discussions with the competent urban authorities, but by integrating within its corporation of engineers new reflections on the choice of lines, construction methods and technologies. These innovations were shaped within the train sector, and not in view of a new metro-type sector, even less so in the urban context specific to Calcutta. The governance structure around the project effectively excluded other urban actors: there was no time for debates with actors who would bring in questions around urban issues specific to Calcutta.

During the work on the Calcutta metro, several engineers increased their credibility and their positions within the Indian railways. These are the same engineers who would, a few years later, occupy the highest decision-making positions for the Delhi metro. Engineer Sreedharan thus directed the agency in charge of the Delhi metro from 1996 to 2011, after being deputy chief engineer of the Calcutta metro, while Mangu Singh, appointed director of the Delhi metro agency in from 2012, was an engineer from 1989 to 1996 on the Calcutta metro project. The Calcutta metro was for these railway engineers a moment of innovation, creation and acquisition of experience around new equipment and new ways of operating. Most of the necessary materials and equipment were designed and produced in India, while opening up the project to transfers of expertise and equipment. While the preliminary studies were mainly carried out in the 1940s and 1950s by the French expertise of the Paris metro and the English expertise of the London Transport Board, the Ministry of Railways subsequently called on the expertise of the Soviet Union in the context of the Cold War, then on that of Japan and Hungary. The technical difficulties posed by the Calcutta metro for these engineers were associated with the construction of tunnels and their signaling and ventilation. In addition, the fact that the majority of the project was underground, justified mainly by the density of the built-up area, implies that it had very little influence on the city's buildings in the sense that it did not lead to major demolitions and remains discreet within the urban landscape. This is not the case for the mainly elevated Delhi metro. The main argument put forward by the Delhi authorities was the lower cost of elevated rather than underground structures.

Around this first Indian metro, criticisms were therefore not directed toward the engineering but toward the institutional arrangements around the project, and especially on its financing structure, which would lead to the rethinking of governance structures for this type of project. While the knowledge of railway engineers is legitimate, financial difficulties and delays attributed to budget problems and political conflicts weighed upon the success of the project, and its ability to set a model for other metros across India.

In the end, the criticisms of engineers or government experts led to the shared observation that this project "does not have a framework of its own" (Singh 2005). The idea then became that of creating a specific authority for the metro, also outside the bureaucratic structure of the railways. The Calcutta metro, as a source of innovation and learning, ultimately lends weight to the arguments of engineers and experts defending an exceptional legal and regulatory framework, that is, the creation of a specific entity for major metro projects.

To conclude, the first Indian metro shows, at both city and national level, a long learning process for structures of governance among public authorities specialized in the construction and management of railway infrastructure and competent authorities in the field of urban planning. This project announced the emergence of urban policies in India and the advent of an urban transport policy, but also, for major projects, the creation of specific authorities and new models of liberalization under state control with the participation of private actors.

6.3. Construction of a political and technical model around the Delhi metro

Sreedharan retired from the railways in June 1990, which in no way hindered his career ambitions. With the halo of his status as a brilliant engineer, fully devoted to his work, he was appointed director of the Konkan Project, where 760 km of train lines were to be built on a very steep coast of western India. Recalling the experience of the Calcutta metro, Sreedharan asked to have a "blank check" guaranteeing his autonomy of action:

While I had been retired from the Railways since June 30, Mr. George Fernandes [then Minister of Railways] asked me to take over the project. I told him that I had no hesitation if I had a "blank check" for the design and execution of the project; I wanted no interference either from politicians or bureaucrats [...] I drew from my thirty-six years of professional life in the Railways, full of good ideas. However, I could not put them into practice because of the straitjacket of the government's way of working and the strict procedures that had to be followed (Sreedharan, 2004, pp. 163–175).

For both the Konkan project and the second Indian metro, that of Delhi, railway engineers would impose their way of doing things, and be directly supported by the Indian central government and not the local political authorities. In this second part, we show the political and technical power of the agency in charge of the Delhi metro, which succeeded in asserting itself as a central player for the other Indian metro projects. We also highlight the weight of the expertise of engineers as a vector of transformations and reforms that go beyond the mere technical framework and possibly overdetermine the action of governments.

6.3.1. *Delhi, capital of India and center of experimentation for major urban projects*

After independence in 1947, the Indian capital experienced very strong urban growth, and its population doubled to reach nearly 1.4 million inhabitants in 1951 (Dupont 2015). In 2010, the population of the Delhi metropolitan area (i.e. the Territory of Delhi and the outlying urban centers) was estimated at around 24 million, making it the largest metropolitan area in India, ahead of Mumbai (21 million). A 2014 UN report predicts that the population will approach 36 million by 2030. The growth of the urban built-up area followed the main roads and railway lines, connecting the heart of the city with peripheral satellite cities in the neighboring states of Uttar Pradesh, Haryana and Rajasthan, which are now major economic hubs. These demographic and economic dynamics, but also the political desire to attain the rank of world city, take material form in the urban space: fast roads and flyovers, large shopping centers, new real estate projects near the international airport, economic projects for the high-tech sector at the very heart of the city's boundaries and no longer pushed to the periphery. These dynamics are accentuated with the economic orientations given to the capital region, in particular the construction of the Delhi–Mumbai industrial corridor, or the delineation of priority investment zones to attract private capital a few tens of kilometers from the center of Delhi. In 2014, the city of Delhi was designated by WHO as being the world's most polluted with fine particles (Dupont 2015). It continues to frequently make national and international headlines for having some of the highest levels of air pollution in the world. In the urgent need to respond to peaks in pollution, the rapid pace of urban sprawl, and strong socioeconomic inequalities, political decisions regarding public transport are complex. These projects enable the mobility of millions of inhabitants, but this does not necessarily mean there has been a significant drop in the number of private cars. For the upper and affluent middle classes, trips are still usually made by car, with their driver.

Source: Delhi, author, 2016

Figure 6.1. *Public and private transport in the north of Delhi. For a color version of this figure, see www.iste.co.uk/lesteven/urban.zip*

The capital city is also characterized by the very strong presence of the central state in all the workings of the city, equally in terms of land, urban planning and public services. Unlike the other major cities, Delhi has no metropolitan authority and the Delhi government controls neither the acquisition nor the development plans of land, which are in the hands of a parastatal agency administered by the central state (under the name of the Delhi Development Authority, DDA). Municipal authorities, meanwhile, have the smallest portfolio. In the end, Delhi occupies a special place in urban reforms, which are often initiated and applied first in this city before being deployed in other Indian cities, as was the case for the very specific model of the Delhi metro.

6.3.2. *National sectoral reforms, a favorable context for metros at local level*

In 1985, a National Commission on Urbanization (NCU) was established. This recognized the link between urban infrastructures and economic development by initiating reflection on the levels of planning, and by differentiating issues specific to urban centers from those of regional development. A report by this commission dating from 1988[8] thus points to the lack of consideration of cities, the insufficiency of resources available to local urban authorities, but also the lack of investment from the central government and regional governments. Making explicit reference to the experience of the Calcutta metro, this report insists on the need to generate internal resources and to rethink the financing models of these projects. It is the way of managing state spending for these projects, whose legitimacy is not called into question, that is therefore raised but not made explicit. In the broader context of economic reforms in India in the late 1980s (Ruet and Tawa Lama-Rewal 2009), new sources of credit and investment are targeting large cities, which themselves attract more private capital in the context of a gradual strengthening of a policy favoring urban India. These reforms are accelerating significant changes in the trajectory of governance of major Indian cities. In 1986, the central government transferred responsibility for planning and coordinating urban transport systems to the Ministry of Urban Development. Since 1986, this ministry has defined the broad policy guidelines relating to metros across India, and decided on the legislative and regulatory framework, with the nodal role played by the agency in charge of the Delhi metro.

In the 1980s, the position of this ministry in the metro sector was asserted in parallel with the weakening of the role of the Ministry of Railways, faced with financial difficulties and significant delays in the completion of the Calcutta metro. In these years of reform, the Railways were heavily criticized at the highest levels of government and by influential international organizations such as the World Bank. The financial management but also the governance structure of the Railways and their slow adaptation to technological innovations were the targets of criticism. Engineers took a stand not for the privatization of Indian Railways, but for a restructuring and a necessary overhaul of investments, managerial practices, or even operational procedures (Dalvi 1995). It is in the context of major transport projects, notably the Konkan train project mentioned above, that these internal reforms would take place and subsequently be applied to major metro projects.

---

8 Report of the National Commission on Urbanisation, New Delhi: Govt. of India Publication, Vol. II, 1988.

The Konkan train project in fact became a real technical feat for the Railways (Kerr 2007) and it strongly consolidated the credibility of Sreedharan as an engineer. For Sreedharan, two steps were necessary for the success of the project: a new financing structure, and the creation of an agency specifically in charge of contracting and implementation for the project, thus creating a distance from the bureaucratic space of the Ministry of Railways, contrary to what had been decided for the Calcutta metro. Sreedharan thus introduced working directly with large private Indian firms such as Larsen & Toubro and Gammon India, which are today at the forefront for the construction of metros. He also initiated a new process of contracting with foreign firms, importing materials from Europe, such as hydraulic machines for tunnel construction.

It is in this particular context of major economic and urban management reforms, critiques of the Railways as an institution, and the strong credibility of some railway engineers, that the public agency in charge of the Delhi metro was created.

6.3.3. *Building a metro but also a political and technical model*

In 1989, the Delhi government commissioned the public consulting firm RITES, specializing in the field of transport, particularly rail, for the feasibility study of the Delhi metro, that is, to analyze the technical and financial viability of the metro. In 1994, the central government approved "in principle" the metro project, on the basis of the feasibility study, and authorized the preparation of the detailed project report, on the one hand, and economic and financial analyses, on the other hand, as well as an initial environmental impact assessment. These analyses and evaluations were again conducted by the consultants RITES. The detailed project report was submitted in May 1995.

The year 1995 saw the establishment of the Delhi Metro Rail Corporation Ltd (DMRC), in charge of the design, execution, operations and maintenance of the Delhi metro. The DMRC is an administration of the Delhi government and the central government (via the Ministry of Urban Development, not the Ministry of Railways like the Calcutta metro), who hold the same amount of shares in its capital and appoint the same number of representatives to its board of directors. But, on the legislative level, as detailed below, the DMRC is in fact closely dependent on the central government and not on the Delhi government, allowing it particularly to benefit from numerous tax exemptions, as well as an accelerated decision-making process freed from the obligation to obtain permission from local authorities. In addition, we show that within the DMRC institution, the decision-making space is totally centralized around the power of its director general, and the Ministry of

Urban Development under the authority of the central state. The metro law of 2002, which would later become a national law, reinforces the powers of the DMRC.

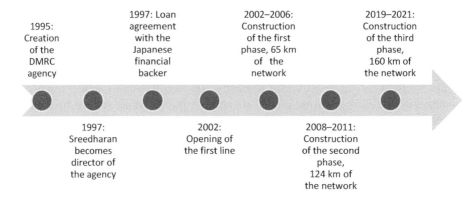

Made by the author.

Figure 6.2. *Chronology of the Delhi metro*

In October 1997, Sreedharan had been officially retired from the Railways for 7 years, since 1990. His strong credibility as an engineer, and notoriety among the public and all political authorities, explains why he was appointed Director General of the DMRC by the Delhi government. He therefore left the Konkan train project agency and moved to Delhi.

Two other levels of decision-making for the metro were set up at the highest summit of the central state: a committee chaired by the Council of Ministers of India and a designated group of ministers. These two levels of decision-making at central government level are important because they helped to significantly accelerate the decision-making process, a modality justified by the Ministry of Urban Development as avoiding additional costs due to delays caused by a complex institutional structure. This favored the establishment of an exceptional legislative and regulatory framework for metros, and limiting the decision-making space for the major project at the central state level. In 2002, a Delhi metro law was approved to allow a legislative framework for metro operations, which like the Calcutta metro could no longer rely solely on the regulations specific to train projects. Analysis of this 2002 law makes it possible to affirm that it confers much greater power on the DMRC agency, through its director general, by granting it greater autonomy for decisions relating to the management of the project and the choice of technology. On the other hand, it places the DMRC under the sole supervision of the Ministry of

Urban Development, not the Delhi government. Finally, it is stipulated that for all operational infrastructure, the DMRC is exempt from local authority authorizations and building permits. The framework for action of the major project is thus voluntarily restricted to this parastatal agency and its director general, who are now supervised only by the central government. This process is reinforced by the agency's financing structure, which relies on external financing, a strong difference here too from the Calcutta metro.

In fact, on February 25, 1997, Japan's Overseas Economic Cooperation Fund (now JICA, the Japan International Cooperation Agency) granted the central government a loan for the first phase of metro construction. India had every interest that the loans should pass through the central government, thus also justifying the latter's weight in the governance structure of the project. When loans are made directly to the central government by international bodies with repayment periods on average of 50 years and grace periods of 10 years, this helps justify the participation of the central government. The loan was passed on to the DMRC on the same terms as those obtained by the central government. The first metro line opened in 2002, an exceptional success at national and international level, as it was completed without delay, and even before the scheduled date.

The DMRC, and more broadly the metro sector in India, have been strongly influenced by the personality and expertise of Sreedharan. In terms of day-to-day management of the agency, Sreedharan directed upon taking office in 1997 that all other decision-making positions be occupied exclusively by railway engineers. In addition, the recommendations it issued between 2003 and 2013 for metros have all been implemented, particularly in terms of financing, privileging control by public authorities and keeping private actors at a distance. In Delhi, although many subcontractors and large private engineering companies are involved in the operational phase of the metro (more than a hundred), they are in fact kept away from decision-making structures, as with the municipal authorities who are marginalized. The DMRC thus delegates certain civil engineering works, but especially signaling works and the supply of rolling stock. The agency retains direct control over all of the so-called "central" areas such as management, security and consultancy. In the rail industry, several major competitors with a global presence participate in the Delhi metro, for example, Bombardier (Germany), Alstom (France), Rotem (Korea), Siemens (Germany), Thales (France) and Mitsubishi (Japan). The year 2004 was marked by the production of the first two metro trains in India by Bharat Earth Movers Ltd (BEML), based in Bangalore in the state of Karnataka.

Sreedharan also targeted the institutional structure for metros at the national level, arguing for greater centralization of decisions in the hands of public authorities, and the establishment of criteria to indicate when a city can (or must) invest in a metro. The DMRC is presented as a model from the point of view of its governance structure, but also of expertise and technological capital. In 2003, Sreedharan announced to the press that other metros would be built in cities with more than 3 million inhabitants, and that the DMRC was the nodal agency for financial, technical and political advice. The final stage of the project for disseminating a national model was reached in 2009 with the amendment of the Delhi metro law of 2002 to provide legal coverage for metro operations, not only in Delhi but in all Indian cities. The Delhi metro agency then became the main consultant for the preparation of detailed project reports – the first stage of project design – for metros in 15 Indian cities[9]. In 2001, the DMRC took the decision to market its consultancy services nationally and internationally for other metro or engineering projects, and the first contract was signed with the Jakarta metro in Indonesia in 2008. In 2007, the DMRC became a member of Nova, a benchmarking group for metro operators (14 in total) worldwide, an important step in building the DMRC's international legitimacy and its ability to mobilize international certifications for local issues related to the environment and town planning.

Indian railway engineers, supported by the concentration of the agency's governance structure in their hands and those of the central government, have thus proved their technical and political capacity to carry out a project of this magnitude. But this is not without criticism, especially in the face of a lack of consultation with local urban authorities, in particular with municipal authorities who struggle to obtain the necessary funding for the maintenance of bus fleets, and a lack of consideration of environmental, urban and socioeconomic factors specific to certain areas of the city (Ramachandraiah 2008; Bon 2015).

In 2012, Sreedharan left his position and retired to his native village, while retaining expert status with Indian railways and metro agencies, and with the UN on the Transport Commission.

6.4. Private firms and regional states: counterweights to the Delhi metro model

Metros in other major Indian cities, which were operational in 2021 (Mumbai, Chennai, Kochi, Hyderabad, Bangalore, Ahmedabad, Jaipur) are far from being

---

9 Kochi, Kolkata, Bangalore, Pune, Mumbai, Ahmedabad, Jaipur, Chennai, Lucknow, Chandigarh, Ludhiana, Greater Noida, Nagpur, Hyderabad and Navi Mumbai.

modeled based on Delhi, despite the fact that for most of them, the DMRC remains one of their main consultants. Various factors have influenced the design and implementation stages of metros: the funding and governance structures chosen; integration into urban plans; the weight of certain personalities (elected officials, employees of international donors, urban planners); the size of the cities and their political status (Kochi, for example, is a city of less than 1 million inhabitants where the municipal authorities have managed to enter the negotiation space of the major project and hold discussions with the donors, unlike Delhi).

It is also important to place all of these major transport projects in the broader context of the development of urban and mobility policies. These include, for example, affirmation from 2015 onwards of the TOD model, which advocates the integration of lines into urban buildings, or the national Smart Cities program, which includes projects for multimodal stations reshaping the link between metro lines and bus corridors; but also political changes and contemporary economic and health crises that have in the short term shaken up the schedules for completing the work, and the availability of financial capital for this type of large project.

The genealogical tree of Indian metros therefore is still to be completed by taking each metro project as a case study. We focus here solely on the Hyderabad and Mumbai metros, due to their position as metropolises and their political weight at national level, and their differences in governance structure compared to the Delhi metro. In fact, many metros follow the Delhi model with a partnership agreement between a regional state and the central government and loans from international donors. Contrary to this governance structure, the Hyderabad metro offers a public–private partnership, and the Mumbai metro a hybrid model, in which some lines are built under public–private partnerships and others by public authorities alone.

6.4.1. *The controversial arrangements of the Hyderabad metro*

In 2008, Sreedharan repeatedly spoke up in the national press to criticize the ongoing political negotiations in the large metropolis of Hyderabad in southern India (then the state of Andhra Pradesh) in the context of the construction of the metro:

> The DMRC prepares detailed project reports for all metros in the country, including Hyderabad. For none of the cities was the BOT (public–private partnership) model recommended, except for the Hyderabad metro. We reaffirm this recommendation. There were specific reasons that suggested that the BOT model (public–private partnership) would be a success in Hyderabad: the low cost of construction because there is no tunnel, and the very high projections

of demand [...] What was later revealed was that the government of Andhra Pradesh offered 150 ha of very attractive city land to the concessionaire, enabling it to benefit from over 300 ha of commercial area. DMRC never recommended this [...] I have no hesitation in firmly defending the fact that all other metros in the country must be built following only the successful model of the DMRC (Sreedharan, October 31, 2008, Indian Express).

Sreedharan focuses in this press article on the particular structure of the Hyderabad metro that led to controversial economic tradeoffs between the private concessionaire and the regional state of Andhra Pradesh. Denouncing abuses around land deals between the government of Andhra Pradesh and the private concessionaire, Sreedharan took the opportunity to reaffirm the DMRC model for all metros in India, a model that he believes also allows significant reductions in project costs. One of the issues around the Hyderabad metro is in fact the significant transfer of land by the regional government to the private concessionaire in a nontransparent manner, also strongly denounced by civil society (Ramachandraiah 2010).

In the case of Hyderabad, it is not the central state, but the regional government that occupies the role of prime contractor. Unlike other Indian metros, the autonomy of this project is reinforced by the fact that it is governed by a regional law, previously applied to the city's tram system. Hyderabad Metro Rail Limited (HMR), the agency responsible for the construction, operation and maintenance of the metro, was born out of a concession agreement in September 2010 between the government of Andhra Pradesh and a major engineering firm, Larsen & Toubro (L&T), creating on this occasion a new branch of its business (L&T Metro Rail). The concessionaire L&T is responsible for the construction, management and maintenance of the metro during the 35-year concession period. The regional government provided 40% of the total cost of the project and the private partner 60%.

Although elected officials from the municipality are represented on the board of directors of the HMR metro agency, we note that the key positions have all been allocated to bureaucrats and technical experts from the government of Andhra Pradesh, in particular representatives of the Hyderabad metropolitan authority. This therefore makes it possible to combine a strong entrepreneurial model, with major experts from the private sector involved in the financing structure and in the execution of the project, with an administrative and political entity controlled in its majority by the government of Andhra Pradesh. This governance structure has strong implications for control over urban land.

Indeed, our analysis of the concession contract reveals that the regional government has four main obligations: to grant land to the private partner to ensure the construction of metro infrastructure, but also as a return on investment; to provide the private partner with construction rights and permits; to coordinate actions with other authorities; and to ensure "that no local taxes, tolls, charges are levied or imposed on the metro system". Thus, in the name of return on investment, hundreds of hectares for real estate projects are granted to the private concessionaire. These lands thus benefit from the regional government's privilege to create land reserves in the name of the transport project. Estimates of revenue from ticket sales and real estate are of equal value. In 2013, 108 hectares were transferred to L&T by the regional government to build shopping centers, office buildings and some residential condominiums for the upper middle classes on the largest land holdings.

Behind these major transport projects, therefore, there remain difficult trade-offs: the Hyderabad metro in 2021 is the second longest metro in terms of kilometers of lines after Delhi, and it has undoubtedly enabled improved mobility for millions of inhabitants, and thus contributed to reductions in air pollution. However, economic models of return on investment are contributing de facto to strengthening the privatization of certain urban spaces and the urbanization of wastelands or sensitive ecological spaces along the new metro corridors. In 2021, the commercial real estate provided by the private concessionaire L&T continues to promote the construction of business parks dedicated to high technologies.

6.4.2. *Mumbai's hybrid model*

The first lines of the Mumbai metro on the west coast of India in the state of Maharashtra were built on the part of the city located on a peninsula, thus in an extremely dense urban environment where the roads are at all hours of the day saturated with cars. The metro is a breath of fresh air for those who can afford a ticket, allowing them to cross the peninsula much more quickly, and to reach the outlying districts to the north and east of the city. It carries an average of 500,000 passengers per day. In 2015, public transport, mostly buses, carried more than 70% of the population, but the use of private vehicles increased by more than 400% between 2008 and 2015 (Saxena 2019).

In 2003, following several studies commissioned by the Mumbai metropolitan authority, the government of Maharashtra entrusted the Delhi metro agency, the DMRC, with preparing a master plan for the Mumbai metro project. Analysis of this document reveals that the DMRC not only defines the phases of network construction, the number of corridors and the East–West corridor considered a priority, but also recommends a governance structure based on the same model as the DMRC. However, the government of Maharashtra would noticeably distance itself from the Delhi metro by opting for a public–private partnership model for the first two metro corridors. Phase 1 of the works was planned for between 2006 and 2011 and Phase 2 between 2011 and 2016. In 2006, a consortium of private companies (the large Indian conglomerate Reliance and the French company Veolia) won the tender launched by the government of Maharashtra for a period of 35 years. The regional government via the development agency of the metropolitan region of Mumbai thus formed a partnership with this private concessionaire. The metropolitan region's development agency, the MMRDA,[10] under the supervision of the government of Maharashtra, has a strong financial capacity and controls other key projects in the form of public–private partnerships, such as the Bandra-Worli bridge, the elevated monorail[11] and the second airport at Navi Mumbai, under the supervision of the Chief Minister of the State of Maharashtra (Zérah 2009).

As to the agency in charge of the metro, the board of directors is composed of seven members appointed by the private concessionaire Reliance and three members appointed by the MMRDA. While the MMRDA owns a lot of land that it resells in plots for major operations, particularly commercial, for the metro these intra-urban plots of land were not available. The MMRDA then began negotiations in very dense areas of the city, building by building[12]. The absence of an exceptional framework for the acquisition of land is put forward to explain a significant delay in the construction of the metro: the MMRDA was to provide private partners with all the land in 2008, but this would only be done at the beginning of 2013. The political dimension intervened at all stages, around control over land in a climate of strong rivalry between the municipality and the government of Maharashtra, which were from different political parties.

---

10 Mumbai Metropolitan Regional Development Authority. The MMRDA was created in 1975 with the task of formulating master plans for the Mumbai metropolitan region, providing financial assistance for projects with a regional dimension, assisting local authorities in implementing infrastructure projects and coordinating the implementation of projects or programmes in the metropolitan area. The Mumbai metropolitan region is divided and subdivided into multiple jurisdictions governed by different levels of government (districts, municipalities, town panchayats, census towns, villages). The first phase of the metro (the Versova to Andheri corridor) is in the island part of the region (18 km from the south to the north of the peninsula), that is, the geographical area formed by the districts of Mumbai and Mumbai Suburban which constitute the Municipal Corporation of Greater Mumbai.
11 With the Indian company Larsen & Toubro and the Malaysian company Scomi Engineering.
12 And where land use differs: precarious informal settlements, residential buildings, shops, public structures, etc.

Following these difficulties, between 2016 and 2021, for the design and construction of the third corridor of the Mumbai metro, the institutional structure adopted was the same as that of the DMRC, that is, a partnership agreement between the central government and the government of Maharashtra and a loan from the Japanese Cooperation Agency. The Mumbai metro has thus returned to a form of centralization of decisions to facilitate these controls over land and the obtaining of permits and building rights due to strong political rivalries and the specificities of the urban environment. The Mumbai metro project also led to recommendations in political circles for a necessary affirmation of local urban authorities by calling for a redefinition, for example, of the role of the metropolitan authority MMRDA in major public transport projects and by stepping away from the sole embrace of the DMRC. In 2003, the detailed project report for the Mumbai metro was in fact prepared by the DMRC without an independent commission, and without a process of consultation with local urban stakeholders. The political choices focused on opening up the action framework to private operators, and then returning to the Delhi model. The major project thus still remains outside the competence of local authorities, especially municipal authorities, even though they also have a right to develop land.

6.5. Conclusion

Tracing the genealogy of Indian metros leads us through the history of transport policies and urban policies in India. This genealogy is linked to the multi-scalar government of India and the adjustment of competences between the central government and the regional states, but also to the difficult emergence of sectoral policies for urban transport, as well as the political role played by railway engineers. These questions are common to other territories in the Global South.

India, a major emerging country, has the technical and financial means to implement and support metro projects. We have shown the very important role played by the Delhi metro and its agency in imposing a model of governance controlled by the highest political levels: the central government and regional states assisted by foreign donors. This major project also involves many foreign engineering and consulting firms. Their role in large Indian cities is part of a more general movement of opening up to globalization and metropolization. As for local urban authorities (municipalities, urban planning agencies), they are unable to assert themselves in decision-making. This model of governance is rooted, on the one hand, in the political and technical experiments around the Calcutta metro in the 1970s, and, on the other hand, in the affirmation of the collective identity of railway engineers. These engineers maintain ways of working and a relationship to the hierarchy around the common framework of Indian Railways, while opening up to and drawing upon economic liberalization reforms and transfers of expertise. The Delhi metro agency, due to the personality and political weight of these engineers, as well as the support provided by the central government, has disseminated a model of a regulatory and legal framework and technical engineering under the control of public actors. The predominance of engineers in the transport sector at urban level and "siloed" governance, centered around national authorities, are characteristic features in many African cities, as well as in some European and French metropolises.

At national level in India, the most visible variations around this governance model are related to the political powers of some regional states. We have thus highlighted, in the city of Hyderabad, a very strong alliance between the regional state and a large private engineering firm. At national level in India, major metro projects have only opened up since the end of the 2010s to new considerations around the importance of soft mobility (thinking about multimodal transport platforms, for example) and the integration of urban buildings. In some cities where metro construction has also required massive investments, the number of daily passengers has not reached the projections made by public authorities. For example, in the city of Lucknow, the number of daily passengers in 2019 represented less than 20% of government projections (Srivastava 2019). Criticism is leveled at investments that prioritize metro projects over buses in secondary cities. It is difficult for public authorities to tradeoff between a decrease in ticket prices that may increase supply and expectations in terms of economic benefits. At the end of the 2010s, the highest number of new cars was recorded in Delhi compared to other Indian cities. Private vehicles (cars and motorcycles) are the most common on the roads. Thus, in 2019, 64% of vehicles registered in 2019 were motorcycles, 30% cars and 1% autorickshaws (Planning Department 2019). While the number of passengers per day in 2019 for the metro fluctuated between 2.5 and 3 million, it remained half of that for public buses. Note that 4.3 million people take the bus each day in Delhi (Planning Department 2019). These buses are controlled by the Delhi municipality. However, the fleet remains old with limited investment compared to those granted for the metro.

6.6. References

Bhaduri, S. and Dey, T. (2012). Changing profile of State transport undertakings in mass transport services: A case of Kolkata City. *Researchers World – Journal of Arts, Science & Commerce*, 3(2), 45–56.

Bon, B. (2015). A new megaproject model and a new funding model. Travelling concepts and local adaptations around the Delhi metro. *Habitat International*, 45(3), 223–230.

Dalvi, M.Q. (1995). Should Indian railways be privatised? *Economic and Political Weekly*, 30(2), 103–112.

Dupont, V. (2015). Delhi : les défis d'une métropole en expansion. *Urbanités* [Online]. Available at: https://www.revue-urbanites.fr/entretien-delhi-les-defis-dune-metropole-en-expansion-avec-veronique-dupont/.

Kerr, I.J. (2007). *Engines of Change: The Railroads that Made India*. Praeger Publishers, Westport.

Kharbanda, O.P. and Pinto, J.K. (1996). *What Made Gertie Gallop? Learning from Project Failures*. Van Nostrand Reinhold, New York.

Planning Department (2019). Economic survey of Delhi 2018–19. Survey, Government of NCT of Delhi.

Ramachandraiah, C. (2008). On metro rail systems. *Economic and Political Weekly*, 43(11), 2150–2158.

Ramachandraiah, C. (2010). Hyderabad's elevated metro rail. The undoing of the city and its public transport. Report, Citizens for a Better Public Transportation in Hyderabad.

Ruet, J. and Tawa Lama-Rewal, S. (eds) (2009). *Governing India's Metropolises*. Routledge, New Delhi.

Saxena, S. (2019). Moving millions with Mumbai metro. ADB Briefs, 114, South Asian Development.

Singh, S.K. (2005). Review of urban transportation in India. *Journal of Public Transportation*, 8(1), 80–97.

Sreedharan, E. (2004). Konkan Railway: Right on track. In *Ideas That Have Worked*, India Department of Administrative Reforms and Public Grievances (ed.). Viking Penguin Books, Gurgaon.

Tiwari, G. (2007). Urban transport in Indian cities. In *LSE Cities Conference Newspaper*, London.

Zérah, M.-H. (2009). Une "Vision Mumbai" pour transformer la ville ou la difficulté à (re)penser la gouvernance métropolitaine. *Echogéo.*, 10, 2–14.

7

Non-Centralized Urban Transport: An Illustration Based on the Case of Jakarta

Rémi DESMOULIÈRE
ACP (Comparative Analysis of Powers), Gustave Eiffel University, Marne-la-Vallée, France

7.1. Introduction

Thai *tuk-tuk*s, Beninese *zemidjan*, Peruvian *combis*, but also post-Soviet *marshrutkas* or US *dollar vans* are some examples of transport services that, without being planned and often without public funding, contribute to daily travel in a wide variety of urban contexts in the Global South as well as, though to a lesser extent, in some of the Global North. These minibuses, collective taxis, three-wheeled cargo vehicles and other motorcycle taxis appear as paradoxical objects in several respects. Well known to their users, a common part of the urban landscape in the cities where they operate, they nevertheless hold many puzzles for urban planning and for the social sciences, with regard to their economy, the genesis of their routes and their service areas, or their modalities of control. Scientific and political discourse concerning them also reveal a set of contradictory representations: to the same extent, they are celebrated as the spearheads of a resourceful and inventive popular economy supporting urban transformations while mitigating some of their perverse effects, and castigated as factors of congestion and disorder in the streets. The chronic lack of legitimacy they suffer in the eyes of public authorities reflects a lack of trust in a strategic urban service that is not controlled directly by the state, which is reflected in the category of "informal transport" that is most frequently used to designate them, despite its ambiguity.

This chapter presents the specificities of these forms of transport and the place that they hold in constantly changing mobility systems. It also highlights the interest they present for the geography and economics of transport as well as for urban planning. They in fact demonstrate transport services produced "from below", originating from investments and socioprofessional relations that are dispersed in space, but organized at the level of urban areas of several million inhabitants. To grasp the different dimensions – operational and socioeconomic dimensions but also political ones – of this subject and to hold together the different theoretical paradigms that contributed to its construction, as a key to understanding it, we will here adopt the notion of non-centralization, understood as the absence of a network operated and managed in a unified way.

The reflections developed here are mainly sustained by case analyses from the Indonesian capital, Jakarta, studied during the second part of the 2010s as part of thesis work on the territorialities of minibus operators (Desmoulière 2019). This work combined three complementary methodological approaches: documentation work based on a corpus of press archives, official statistics and cartographic data; daily observation of transport locations and vehicles, which allowed the keeping of field diaries; as well as a set of 59 semi-structured interviews conducted between September 2014 and June 2017 with four categories of actors (drivers, vehicle owners, heads of organizations and civil servants from the various municipal transport services in the metropolitan area).

The case of Jakarta may be considered representative of the current dynamics of non-centralized transport on a global scale due to several characteristics. The Jakarta metropolitan region, which has nearly 30 million inhabitants, presents in the first place a wide range of non-centralized transport, including almost all the forms that can be observed in the world. It is also marked by major transformations linked, on the one hand, to metropolization and, on the other hand, to the development of new mass transit networks since the beginning of the 2000s – bus rapid transit (BRT), then the metro – which have raised questions about the place of non-centralized transport in the city. However, analyses from the case of Jakarta will be compared with other examples or synthetic studies, to highlight the diversity of situations and practices from one city to another while focusing on invariant elements.

The first part of this chapter reviews the different currents of research that have taken an interest in non-centralized transport, with distinct theoretical and practical objectives, and the vocabulary that each of them has produced, before explaining the terminological option of non-centralization that has been used here. With this notional framework established, the second part examines the socioeconomic and political structures involved in the operation and governance of this form of transport at several levels, from systems that allow for the daily rental of vehicles to public policies aiming, more or less explicitly, to guide and control the development of the sector. It is the understanding of these relations of power and the territories they produce that finally allow us to examine, in the third part, the place occupied by non-centralized transport in contemporary metropolises through analyzing their adaptability and the possibility of coexistence with more centralized transport systems.

7.2. Words and things: terminological issues

Paratransit, intermediate transport, artisanal transport, popular transport, informal transport: there is no shortage of words to designate a category that has been constituted above all by exclusion, bringing together everything that diverges from the classic, mainly European, model of transport planned and operated by the public sector. The profusion of terminology certainly reflects a latent uncertainty as to what might constitute the common factor for all these forms of transport, but each of these terms is also indicative of a particular angle of approach, theoretical and practical objectives, and even value judgments regarding them.

7.2.1. *Paratransit, a functional approach*

The first research on non-centralized urban transport services was carried out not in the Global South, but in the United States in the early 1970s. The federal Department of Transport was in fact the first to introduce a specific term, paratransit, to designate them in 1972. The construction of the term suggests the idea of services operating alongside, or in complementarity with, mass transit networks. Two years later, the urban planner R. F. Kirby gave an initial definition – very broad and still largely based on exclusion – of the notion, assimilated to "forms of intraurban passenger transportation which are available to the public, are distinct from conventional transit (scheduled bus and rail), and can operate over the highway and street system" (Kirby et al. 1974, p. 9). This definition opens up the paratransit category to a wide variety of vehicles, fitting "somewhere between private passenger transport and conventional public transport in terms of cost and quality of service" (Rimmer 1980, p. 937): intermediate buses or midibuses (approximately 25 seats), vans (between 6 and 14 seats depending on model and configuration), shared taxis, motorcycle taxis or even, more specifically in cities in the Global South, motorized tricycles and pedicabs.

Figure 7.1. *Intermediate buses (in the background) and vans (an* angkot, *in the foreground on the right) in a Jakarta terminal (R. Desmoulière, April 2017)*

Figure 7.2. *Motorcycle taxis affiliated with the Grab platform (in the foreground) and vans with tinted windows (in the background) in Jakarta (R. Desmoulière, November 2018)*

Figure 7.3. *Gas-powered (left) and gasoline-powered (right) three-wheeled vehicles on a Jakarta street (R. Desmoulière, July 2016)*

The advent of paratransit in the US research agenda on urban transport thus responds to very concrete issues: these services, seen as flexible and adaptable, must be able to support the large companies operating transport networks, which are experiencing a crisis linked to the growing use of cars. They also allow provision of services to the sprawling and sparsely populated suburbs of North American cities, where the dispersion of demand undermines the profitability of large public transit infrastructures (Orski 1975). This research on paratransit is devoted to two main objects. On the one hand, paratransit scholars rehabilitate *jitneys*, collective taxis that spread throughout the cities of the United States because of the economic crisis caused by the beginning of the First World War, before disappearing at the beginning of the 1920s due to new legislation which attacked their comparative advantages and closed the market to smaller operators (Eckert and Hilton 1972). On the other hand, they are searching in the cities of the Global South, where non-centralized transport has continued to consolidate its presence throughout the 20th century, for models to inspire public policies. This approach was still significant, at the end of the 1990s, in the work of the urban planner R. Cervero, who published *Paratransit in America: Redefining Mass Transportation* (1997), which combines research contributions on non-centralized transportation in the United States, Latin America and Southeast Asia to examine the relevance and feasibility of large-scale redevelopment of the sector in US cities, particularly in terms of regulations.

At the turn of the 21st century, the paratransit field saw renewed interest in the context of new research conducted on the notion of transport on demand (TOD). The challenge is to curb the spread of private cars and the automobile dependence of cities by envisaging transport services that are more flexible in terms of schedules and spatial reach, and able to adapt to the complexity and singularity of daily mobility practices. In France, collective research has been conducted in this direction, mainly by sociologists, urban planners and legal scholars, as part of the Programme de recherche et d'innovation dans les transports terrestres (Program of Research and Innovation in Land Transport – PREDIT) of the Ministry of Equipment, Housing and Transport (Le Breton et al. 2000). This work has primarily dealt with on-demand transport experiments launched by local authorities or companies in Europe, in particular minibuses and collective taxis whose journeys can adapt in response to reservations made online or via telephone platforms, in rural areas or in sparse urban peripheries (Le Breton 2001). However, they are also open to the contributions of fields of research conducted in the Global South, in particular the work of Goldblum (2001) which links the development of paratransit to the process of metropolization in Southeast Asia. The idea of a transfer of models from the Global South to the Global North remains valid, though some authors like Orfeuil (2008) point out that the socioeconomic conditions and methods of organizing operations, which have allowed the success of paratransit in the cities of the Global South (unregulated labor, strong competition among operators and drivers, absence or non-compliance with safety standards, absence or weakness of tax levies), cannot be transposed to the global level, nor be held up as a model. During the 2010s, the considerable spread of the use of smartphones and mobile Internet provided a new technological basis for the deployment of on-demand transport services, as illustrated by the success of platforms linked to apps such as Uber and Lyft. However, the relationship between the latter and paratransit remains ambiguous: while all of these services share flexibility and the ability to adapt to demand, platforms are private actors that are difficult to manage and regulate, and may be at cross purposes with pre-existing segments of paratransit supply (Mulley and Nelson 2016). The two debates mentioned here – on the transfer of experience from the Global South to the Global North and on the contribution of platforms to paratransit – testify to the need to go beyond a functional approach to non-centralized transport to understand the systems of socioeconomic and political relations that they are embedded in.

7.2.2. Informal transport and artisanal transport: from the socioeconomic to the political

As the main competitors with the concept of paratransit, the informal transport and artisanal transport categories reflect an approach that places greater emphasis on the modalities of operation and management of transport services.

Informal transport, the oldest form of transport, appeared as early as the 1970s (Godard 1987), in line with the work of the International Labour Organization (1972) and Hart (1973) on the informal sector, defined as all activities outside the administrative and statistical frameworks usually used by economists, and referring more specifically to subsistence activities undertaken in the cities of developing countries by migrants of rural origin, poorly integrated into urban circuits of employment. Initially, the notion was used as a substitute for paratransit in works aimed at repositioning non-centralized forms of transport within the urban economic structures that have led to their emergence. However, it was only much later, at the turn of the 2000s, that use of this term became widespread in works dealing with paratransit in the cities of the Global South. This diffusion of the concept happened at the cost of a semantic shift, from the economic toward the legal and political registers. This is evidenced, for example, by the definition given by R. Cervero, introducing a report prepared for the UN Habitat program:

> The term adopted in this study is "informal transport", for this term best reflects the context in which the sector operates – informally and illicitly, somewhat in the background, and outside the officially sanctioned public transport sector. (Cervero 2000, p. 3)

Thus, the qualifier "informal" becomes synonymous with "illicit" or even "illegitimate". The use of this term to designate non-centralized transport only in the context of cities in the Global South is problematic, inasmuch as it carries a set of negative representations that contrast with the positive characteristics usually associated with paratransit – its technical and organizational innovation, or its flexibility. Moreover, although it rightly focuses attention on the political dimension of these transport systems, the semantic shift that the term has undergone from the economic sphere blurs its meaning with a certain amount of ambiguity. Its use has nevertheless become systematized in later works, in particular in English-language research (Cervero and Golub 2007; Evans et al. 2018).

It is precisely starting from a critique of the notion of informal transport that the French economist X. Godard forged the notion of artisanal transport which, since the late 1980s, has met with some echo in French-language research on non-centralized transport. Faced with the imprecision of a concept built largely by exclusion, he seeks a positive characterization of the transport services he observes in the cities of West and North Africa by analyzing its structures of ownership and operation of vehicles. It was in a report written for INRETS where he originally used the term "artisanal-type activity" to designate transport whose ownership is atomized between a large number of small owners (Godard 1987). In later texts, he adds a second characteristic to this fragmentation of ownership: the strong autonomy of drivers and their assistants in the field in the day-to-day operation of vehicles (Godard 2008a). The author comes to place this second characteristic at the heart of his definition, as in cases where vehicle ownership has become concentrated and where forms of collective organization of operators emerge, this is what definitively draws the line of demarcation between artisanal transport and institutional transport. The latter is based on structured and hierarchical companies, whether public or private. The precision of the concept of artisanal transport has earned it a wide dissemination in French-speaking countries, notably thanks to its adoption by organizations bringing together both researchers and transport practitioners, such as the French Development Agency (Agence française de développement – AFD), or the association Cooperation for the Development and Improvement of Urban and Suburban Transport (Coopération pour le développement et l'amélioration des transports urbains et périurbains – CODATU), which published in 2015 a synthesis report on the characteristics and development trajectories of artisanal transport systems in cities of the Global South (Ferro et al. 2015).

Other qualifiers have been developed in parallel since the 1980s, such as "unconventional", "transitional" or "intermediate" transport (Godard 2008b, pp. 11–12). This last term suggests a place for these transport services within a modal hierarchy. Special mention should also be made of the "self-produced" transport observed by Tarrius (1985) in neo-rural and immigrant communities in France, as well as the term "popular transports", used by I. Kassi in her thesis on Abidjan (2008), which has the advantage of characterizing both the socioeconomic profile of operators and that of the majority of users. This profusion of terminology testifies to the richness of the object, the difficulties encountered by researchers in describing it, but also to the diversity of approaches that can – and must – be combined to account for it.

7.2.3. *Centralization, decentralization and non-centralization*

In the remainder of this chapter, the transport referred to so far by the terms "paratransit", "informal" and "artisanal transport" will be described as "non-centralized transport". This terminological choice does not result from an intention to transcend the notions previously discussed, but rather from the search for the common factor between the functional, socioeconomic and political approaches to these transport systems. It also makes it possible to situate the latter within a broader reflection on the organization of urban services in a context of absence, insufficiency or dysfunction regarding major infrastructure networks.

The concepts of centralization and decentralization have been introduced in the context of studies analyzing modes of organization of urban services that operate outside, or at least on the margins of, these major infrastructure networks. Coutard and Rutherford (2009) use the term "centralized" to describe water distribution, energy or waste collection services, organized in a unified network and managed by public authorities – both directly and through contracting. This centralized conception of urban service management prevailed from the end of the 19th century in Europe, North America, then Japan, before spreading partially in the South, first in the big cities. In recent decades, the growing challenge to this "network ideology" (Coutard and Rutherford 2016) for mainly environmental reasons, combined with the growing fragmentation of networks under the effect of the liberalization of urban management methods (Graham and Marvin 2001), promoted the emergence of decentralized services, provided at the local level by a greater diversity of actors less directly associated with public authorities. These decentralized services are intended to be autonomous, or at least partially independent of the major technological networks.

This analytical grid of "post-network" urban planning is particularly relevant in accounting for the existence of so-called informal or artisanal forms of urban transport, insofar as these latter stand out from conventional transport precisely due to the absence of a unified network, as well as the fragmentation of the players. However, rather than decentralization, I prefer to speak here of non-centralization, taking into account the historical trajectory of these modes of transport: most of them appeared before the major infrastructure networks, a void which they filled at the level of a city or certain districts of a city. We are therefore dealing more with an "off-grid" than a "post-grid" configuration (Jaglin 2016). Non-centralized transport is therefore not an experiment in challenging or overriding pre-existing centralized infrastructure networks; it predates them and was able to substitute for them for several decades. In this way, they reveal an alternative regime of production and governance of urban spaces.

7.3. Operating and controlling non-centralized transport

The sectoral categorizations seen in the first part, whether based on functional, socioeconomic or political criteria, define non-centralized transport only by its deviation from the conventional model of transport planned, arranged and managed by public authorities. In this way, they obscure the actors, the interconnected relationships and the subtle geography of power that underlie their functioning and allow them to embed themselves in the city.

7.3.1. *Fragmented structures of operation*

One of the major characteristics of non-centralized transport, highlighted by Godard (2008a, 2008b), is the double fragmentation of the ownership of vehicles, on the one hand, and their operation, on the other hand. This fragmentation can be broken down into two operating patterns: one based solely on owners who drive their own vehicles, and another involving a working relationship between the owner and one or more drivers.

The owner-driver pattern is found in cases where the fragmentation of ownership is at its maximum, so that each owner has only one vehicle which they are then able to drive[1]. Consequently, it involves only a small number of cases. A study on large collective taxis in the Moroccan cities of Ouarzazate and Agadir reveals that the share of vehicles driven by their owners amounts to only 2% and 4%, respectively (Advanced Logistics Group 2012, quoted by Ferro et al. 2015). In the Jakarta metropolitan area, according to a survey conducted among a sample of 916 van drivers (*angkot*), only 9% also own the vehicle they drive (Darmaningtyas 2012). Motorcycle taxis do not seem to deviate from this trend, even though the small size of the vehicles and the importance of their private uses might suggest a

---

[1] Owners of a single vehicle do not necessarily choose to drive it themselves. They may still choose to delegate its operation to a driver, especially if the owner has a full-time job, or if the operating income from the vehicle is used to finance their retirement.

predominance of owner-driver figures. A study conducted in Lomé indicates, on the contrary, a strong prevalence of rental as well as leasing (*work and pay*) practices among motorcycle taxi drivers (Diaz Olvera et al. 2016).

It is therefore the owner/driver dyad that constitutes, by far, the most common operating pattern of non-centralized transport. This pattern suggests nuancing the image of a totally artisanal activity, in that it allows a certain concentration of ownership. The size of fleets remains very variable. In Jakarta alone, the average number of vans per owner is estimated at two (Darmaningtyas 2012), but some large owners have fleets that may exceed 20 vehicles. Similarly, the profiles and rationalities of owners may vary considerably, from the figure of the owner-renter operating one or two vehicles to finance their retirement or their children's higher education, to that of the entrepreneur specializing in transport activity, and heavily invested in the professional organizations of carriers. Drivers, on the other hand, are only very rarely salaried. Two main remuneration systems are used: a commission system, in which drivers receive a share of the daily operating income agreed in advance with the owner, generally around 20% (Godard 1987), and a daily rental system, where the owner transfers the operation of a vehicle to one or more drivers for a day, in exchange for a fixed rental fee. In the latter case, the driver therefore only begins to earn income for themselves once the amount of the rental cost has been covered. The two systems have the common factor that drivers are under constant pressure, in that their income depends directly on the number of passengers they carry. The strong autonomy of drivers often highlighted in studies on artisanal transport must therefore be qualified by the reality of often very unequal economic relations between owners and drivers.

This point appears decisive for understanding certain practices of drivers, frequently criticized by users and public authorities, such as engaging in speed races with their competitors, or waiting for the vehicle to be completely full before starting. Table 7.1 shows an example of a daily activity report for an intermediate bus driver in Jakarta. We may note that, in addition to the payment of daily rental costs, fuel represents an important item of expenditure that helps determine the final income.

The various vehicles of non-centralized transport, which are pivotal in the relationship between owners and drivers, reflect how transport workers appropriate the products and networks of the automotive industry. While some services, such as collective taxis or motorcycle taxis, directly use standard vehicles, minibuses of different sizes sometimes result from transformations performed by local industrial units. This is the case for vans and intermediate buses in Jakarta, made from the chassis, engines and front cabins of utility vehicles for the former or small trucks for the latter, in the assembly workshops (*karoseri*) of the Jakarta metropolitan area or other cities in Java. Some models designed for on-demand transportation have been globally diffused through the expansion of non-centralized transportation markets. One of the most iconic cases of this "bottom-up globalization" is that of the motorized three-wheeled cargo vehicles (*autorickshaw*), originally developed by the Italian manufacturer Piaggio in 1948 and then adopted in India from the end of the 1950s by the company Bajaj. Now a powerful multinational, it exports its assembled models and spare parts to a large part of Asia, as well as to several African countries such as Egypt, Mali and Ethiopia through a network of small transnational entrepreneurs (Tastevin 2012).

	Earnings (rupiahs) *Equivalent in euros*	Expenses (rupiahs) *Equivalent in euros*
Payments collected from passengers	710,000 Rp €48.78	
Rental charges		350,000 Rp €24.05
Fuel (diesel)		300,000 Rp €20.61
Daily net income (with assistant)[2]	35,000 Rp €2.40	
Daily net income (without assistant)	60,000 Rp €4.12	

Table 7.1. *Daily earnings and expenses of a Metro Mini intermediate bus driver in 2017 (driver renting a vehicle)*[3] *(source: Desmoulière 2019, p. 81)*

7.3.2. The ambivalent role of public authorities

The development of non-centralized transport is often attributed to a failure of the state and of institutional transport systems. Studies of their genesis have indeed shown that they were born of the private initiatives of city dwellers, in the blind spots or the interstices of public action. In West Africa, the rise of intermediate buses, vans and collective taxis from the 1970s and 1980s is directly linked to the crisis of public companies, or large private contracting companies operating

---

2 Until the mid-2010s, intermediate bus drivers in Jakarta systematically employed assistants (*kernet*) who helped them to collect payments from passengers or navigate the often very congested streets of the city and shared the daily operating earnings with them. The decline in the number of passengers in recent years has led most of them to abandon this practice.

3 The calculation of expenses does not include fees paid to touts or for terminal use.

institutional bus networks (Lombard 2006). South Africa has favored the development of "taxis" (which are more like vans traveling on fixed routes) due to Black people's limited access to institutional transport services, which is due to apartheid as well as a lack of smooth-running services for townships on the outskirts of big cities (Woolf and Joubert 2013). On a global scale, the neoliberal turn of the 1980s marked a major step in the disengagement of states from the transport sector and created a political and economic context that was particularly favorable to the consolidation of non-centralized transport services (Godard 1987). Structural adjustment policies led by the International Monetary Fund and the World Bank have led to the deregulation of urban transport markets which, in the 1980s and 1990s, resulted in a drastic increase in the number of small entrepreneurs, especially in African and Latin American cities (Lombard 2006; Figueroa 2013).

This observation regarding the initial development of non-centralized transport in the socioeconomic and spatial interstices of public intervention does not mean that states, at their different levels, are totally uninvolved in their dynamics. The studies cited above also show that non-centralized services have benefited from a certain tolerance on the part of the authorities, or even from official recognition associated with a process of regulation of the activity. In Jakarta, regarding the various minibus services – intermediate buses, vans, fixed-line three-wheeled vehicles – although they appeared independently of any public intervention starting from the 1930s, were subject, between the early 1960s and the late 1990s, to a policy that could be described as implicit (Desmoulière 2019). While upholding a generally hostile rhetoric toward minibuses and presenting them as short-term expedients, destined to be replaced by large mass transit networks, the local government as well as the central Indonesian state not only tolerated their development, but supported it too, all while seeking to bring it under control.

This implicit policy mobilized three complementary registers of action. First, incentives were provided to potential middle-class investors, in particular civil servants, through loans granted by public banks for the purchase of minibuses. In some cases, such as the intermediate buses which launched in the early 1960s, the state even directly supervised the import and transformation of vehicles. The second register of action consisted of the public authorities constructing a spatial frame to ensure a minimum level of control over minibuses, this frame consisting of a set of bus terminals and lines. Although the administration has never managed to control the layout of the minibus lines, which remains under the control of the entrepreneurs, it managed to gradually impose, between the middle of the 1970s and 1991, the assignment of each vehicle to a single fixed line, putting an end to the relative interchangeability of routes that previously prevailed. Regulation has been the third pillar of this implicit policy, with the imposition of a licensing system that has made it possible to subject the majority of minibuses to taxation, regulation of fares and, for owners, the obligation to join an organization of carriers – a cooperative or a company. This policy, conducted over the long term without ever being claimed as such, enabled the various levels of the state to stimulate the emergence of a dense and abundant public transport offer by limiting public investment to the strict minimum, concentrated at the time primarily on the development of road infrastructure. Most of Jakarta's public transport provision is still a direct legacy of this policy, with the development of large mass transport networks having only really started at the turn of the 2000s.

7.3.3. Intermediary organizations: popular companies or cartels?

Between the state and the fragmented sector consisting of owners and drivers, logics of collective organization appear almost systematically, originating from different types of entities: associations, economic interest groups, cooperatives, companies or even unions. The function that these entities perform in the organization and operation of non-centralized transport is sometimes difficult to determine, especially since their actual activities sometimes have no real relation to their legal form. Between the idealized image of popular entrepreneurship and the sulfurous image of the mafia, different types of organizations can be distinguished according to their degree of development and the extent of their field of activity.

Professional organizations of carriers originate from the need to curb competition by controlling operational territories. For minibuses, this means lines and, for on-demand transport, areas to compete for or wait for passengers. The most basic type of organization is therefore limited to this function, which nonetheless constitutes a major economic and political issue. In Jakarta, the first associations of van owners appeared in the 1970s when, since the previous decade, the fleet of vans in circulation experienced a sharp increase, which posed a problem when it came to regulating the number of vehicles in circulation on each line (Desmoulière 2019). These associations acquired a more official dimension during the following decade, taking two main legal forms, cooperatives and companies. Such statuses, however, were never more than purely formal, because neither the cooperatives nor even the companies own the vehicles themselves: they remain the property of each individual member. In fact, Jakarta's van organizations were formed around entrepreneurs or small groups of "founding" entrepreneurs whose social capital – both in the administration and in the neighborhoods served – was particularly strong, enabling them to open one or more lines, and obtain government approval to operate them (Panghegar 2014). The cooperative or the company thus constitutes a matrix through which this elite of entrepreneurs, on the strength of their close links with local political power, monetizes access to the lines by other owners, via the payment of contributions or membership fees. The state can help strengthen these organizations, either through regulation, by forcing individual owners to join an organization like the Jakarta provincial government did in 1991, or even by creating new organizations on its own initiative, such as the intermediate bus company Metro Mini, founded in 1976 at the initiative of Governor Ali Sadikin, whose management was entrusted to executives of the administration and the police. Organizational dynamics can therefore be supported both by owners in order to limit access to the market by territorializing it, and by the state, for whom the structuring of the sector represents a lever of control (Rimmer 1986).

In a second type of organization, this basic function of controlling services may be supplemented by more or less advanced management functions over the transport activity. This is the case for Koperasi Wahana Kalpika (KWK), the largest van cooperative in the Indonesian capital, which specializes in serving outlying neighborhoods. In addition to managing the operating licenses of its members, which reflect the grip it exerts over its 20 lines, its local branches also provide commercial intermediation functions, by buying vans just assembled in the *karoseri* to resell them to the owners, already painted in the red livery of the cooperative. Management functions also include coordination of owners and supervision of drivers in the field. As in most cooperatives, vehicle owners gather at least once a year at the general meetings of the cooperative, but different branches also organize smaller meetings, by district or even by line, dedicated to specific issues such as, for example, coordination with institutional transport on shared sections of road. Meanwhile, the work of the drivers is supervised by field coordinators (*korlap*), who monitor the smooth running of the operation of the lines and arbitrate any conflicts between competing drivers, or between drivers and residents along the routes traveled. These management functions, when properly performed by the organizations, allow them to partially compensate for the fragmentation of the non-centralized transport sector.

A third type of organization, rarer and currently absent in Jakarta, reflects a much more advanced degree of integration, particularly from an economic point of view. It corresponds to companies that have managed to concentrate the ownership of many vehicles (Godard 1987) – from about fifty to several hundred – or cooperatives in which purchase and management of the vehicle fleet are a true collective endeavor. Mention may be made in this respect of the experience of the savings and credit cooperatives (SACCO) founded by owners of minibuses (*matatu*) in Kenya from the 1990s. These co-operatives allow entrepreneurs to pool the purchase of vehicles (Orero and McCormick 2013), lowering financial barriers to entry into the business. This type of organization, with a very advanced structure, can profoundly alter the socioeconomic relations that characterize the sector, for example by establishing salaries for drivers when their resources permit, and thus gradually lead to forms of partial centralization for transport services.

7.4. What place for non-centralized transport in contemporary metropolises?

While non-centralized transport allows for the daily mobility of millions of city dwellers around the world, especially in the countries of the Global South, it also suffers from a persistent image of archaism and indiscipline. Attitudes toward them from public authorities, whose ambivalence has already been highlighted, is tending to harden today as public transport becomes a real development issue and a symbol of modernity under the influence of the sustainable city model (Reigner et al. 2013). Their sustainability therefore depends on their ability to adapt to rapid urban transformations induced by processes of metropolization, and on the possibility of integration with more centralized transport networks.

7.4.1. *"Gearboxes for metropolization?" Questions of flexibility and adaptability*

The characterization of non-centralized transport as "the gearbox of metropolization" is due to Goldblum (2001) who, based on a cross-study of different modes of paratransit in the major emerging metropolises of Southeast Asia, analyzes them as "flexible solutions" for bridging the gaps that metropolization, as a fundamentally unfinished process, produces in urban space. They provide the link between the decision-making and tertiary centers, integrated into transnational economic networks, and the peripheral areas, isolated by their distance from these centers, but especially by the weak connectivity between their cramped road network and the main roads. The mapping of minibus lines – vans and intermediate buses – in Jakarta, shown in Figure 7.4, illustrates this property of non-centralized transport. It shows that the latter offers a particularly fine coverage of popular settlements (*kampung*) and industrial areas. Institutional transport networks are present, in particular the bus rapid transit (BRT) set up from the early 2000s and the metro, whose first line was inaugurated in March 2019, but their infrastructures remain limited to the main roads. Although Jakarta minibuses have suffered the full force of competition from these new networks on the main roads, they are managing to maintain their position due to demand linked to local mobility, at the extremities of the travel chains of city dwellers.

150 Urban Mobility Systems in the World

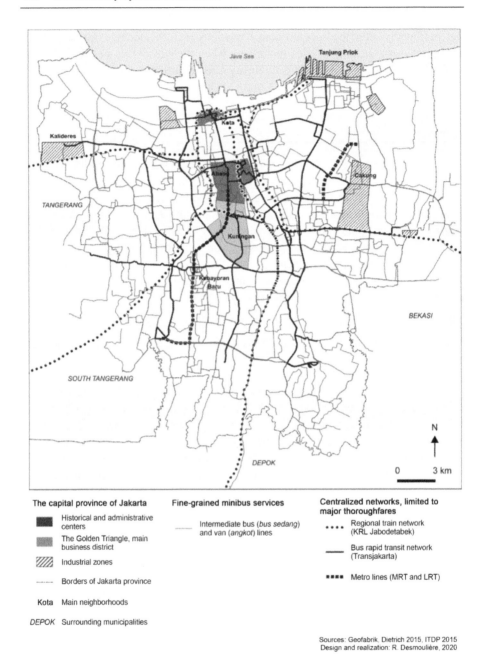

Figure 7.4. *Spatial coverage of minibus lines in Jakarta. For a color version of this figure, see www.iste.co.uk/lesteven/urban.zip*

Beyond this cartographic approach, the flexibility and adaptability of non-centralized transport can be understood by analyzing driver practices. In the absence of fixed lines, this flexibility relates to the routes themselves. Wester's (2015) study on Brazzaville, based on multi-agent modelling, shows how crews compose their itineraries on the fly, according to the destinations favored by the users found along their routes. When lines are defined in a relatively fixed way, strategies of adaptation focus more on managing travel and stop times. In Jakarta, drivers of vans and intermediate buses have little leeway to change routes, but they compensate for this by making long stops, or driving at reduced speed on sections where passengers are likely to be more numerous, or close to commercial centers or places of intermodality, such as railway stations and BRT stations. The absence of fixed stopping points also benefits these minibuses in terms of their "adhesion", that is to say by the density of contacts they allow with the spaces they cross (Amar 1993): passengers are free to hail and disembark vehicles at any point along the lines, reducing load breaks and walking distances.

However, consideration of the flexibility and adaptability of non-centralized transport must not only take into account its operational characteristics, but also the political and territorial jurisdictions in which it operates. In contexts of intense competition, it is indeed through more or less extensive and more or less exclusive territorialization of portions of urban space that carriers manage to maintain the profitability of their activity. Jakarta's minibus lines thus follow a paradoxical dynamic: initially open informal pathways that support the extension of the built-up area and functional changes in the urban space, over the long term they undergo a process of territorialization which rigidifies them, through their official registration with administration and through the control exercised by intermediary organizations over their access (Desmoulière 2019). Non-centralized transport operating on demand may also undergo processes of territorialization. Motorcycle taxi drivers, for example, collectively limit the arrival of new entrants to the "bases" (*pangkalan*) where they wait for their passengers, and, depending on the configuration of local power relations, may prohibit access by other modes of transport to the neighborhood in which they are based at certain time slots, particularly at night. These linear or areal territorialities may set limits to non-centralized transport's possibilities of adaptation. They may also function as barriers to their integration with more centralized transport networks.

7.4.2. *Integration of non-centralized transport: experiences and sticking points*

The question of integrating non-centralized transport with centralized transport networks arises mainly in the cities of the Global South, and especially in the metropolises of emerging countries. It is here, in fact, that a dualization of the provision of transport is now taking place between non-centralized transport services initially developed in the absence of any institutional provision, and centralized networks of metro, tram or bus rapid transit generally developed from the 1990s onward. Despite the initial reluctance of the public authorities to recognize the full legitimacy of services that they only partially control, reflections emerged, from the end of the 2000s, on the possibility of combining the two types of transport provision, particularly in Latin America and South Africa (Figueroa 2007; Schalekamp and Behrens 2009). The gradual application of these reflections signals the beginning of a "pragmatic turn" in urban policies (Jaglin 2016), marked by the recognition of the hybridity of transport systems.

From a functional point of view, the development of complementarity between the two types of transport provision is generally envisaged through the so-called *trunk and feeder model*, which distinguishes a set of main lines allocated primarily to centralized transport, and feeder lines allocated to non-centralized services (Ferro et al. 2012). This general principle can be broken down into several patterns: preservation, on the same axis, of the two types of service on separate tracks, especially when demand is high; sharing a reserved lane between a BRT line and non-centralized transport, either permanently (*interlining*) or only at peak times (*peak-lopping*) or the establishment of connecting points linking a BRT line to minibus lines. Several experiments of this type have been conducted in the Jakarta metropolitan area since 2015. The Kopaja intermediate bus co-operative and the BRT management company PT Transjakarta have entered into an *interlining* arrangement on four intermediate bus lines that intersect with BRT corridors. As a result, intermediate buses – with new adapted designs – are allowed to use the BRT corridors and service its stations, while continuing to use normal roads outside the overlapping sections. In 2017, PT Transjakarta also set up an integration experiment with the KWK cooperative, covering 10 van lines: with a monthly subscription, Transjakarta passengers can use vans to reach BRT terminals in the morning, or to leave in the evening. In 2015, the outlying municipality of Bogor, in the south of the metropolitan area, launched an ambitious program of total redesign of its van lines to achieve better coverage of its entire territory, and to use the vans as a feeder service for Transpakuan, the new institutional bus network which is being rolled out.

Such experiments involve sometimes difficult negotiations with non-centralized transport operators in that they challenge the systems of socioeconomic relations and the territorialities that the latter have built over the long term. This is why, 5 years after its launch, the Bogor municipality program is still a dead letter. It was confronted with the territorial inertia of lines over which the municipality has little control and which, for carriers, constitute indispensable frameworks for market sharing and management of competition. The more ad hoc experiments conducted in Jakarta worked better, in that they involved from the outset the intermediary organizations which control the lines. However, they have led to a widening of inequalities within the sector. The implementation of *interlining* for Kopaja intermediate buses has thus led to a dualization of status within the cooperative, between owners who are financially able to acquire new buses compatible with the technical standards of the BRT corridors, and others who find themselves effectively excluded from the experiment. In the experiment conducted with KWK vans, the implementation of the subscription system for passengers coming from the BRT resulted in a substantial drop in the daily income of the drivers, whose modalities of compensation had not been foreseen in negotiations with PT Transjakarta. This type of integration program, while generally beneficial to users, therefore challenges the social and territorial structures of non-centralized transport services, while producing selection and exclusion effects. Such effects contribute to increasing conflict across the whole field of public transport, and may therefore, in the long run, jeopardize the success of integration.

7.5. Conclusion

Non-centralized transport constitutes a rich and fruitful subject of study because of its diversity, the major place it occupies in urban mobility systems and the complexity of its modes of organization. This complexity is difficult to grasp in a single category of analysis, and the notion of non-centralized transport used here is no exception. The presence and pivotal role of intermediary organizations shows that the sector may experience internal dynamics of centralization around the issues of market sharing and access to lines. These internal dynamics may even serve as a crucible for more ambitious integration programs for transport services, as evidenced by the experiments conducted in Jakarta since 2015.

Beyond the problems of organization and management of transport, the case studies discussed in this chapter raise more theoretical questions for geography and urban studies. First, they make it possible to analyze atypical forms of transport organization and, more broadly, urban services. Faced with the absence or failures of public intervention and centralized networks, they represent forms of urban innovation that make it possible to mitigate the spatial fractures produced by urbanization and metropolization. As objects of social geography, they show how a world of work is rooted in urban space through the construction of territories within it that guarantee its functioning and sustainability. As objects of political geography, they question the modalities of governance of services of public interest, but developed and operated outside any state centralization. Finally, as methodological challenges, they suggest complementing quantitative approaches with qualitative approaches, such as ethnography or participatory observation, in order to account for the practices that, on a daily basis, shape the paths and places of transport.

7.6. References

Advanced Logistics Group (2012). Étude relative à l'élaboration d'une méthode pour l'évaluation des besoins en transport par taxis. Draft report, Advanced Logistics Group.

Amar, G. (1993). Pour une écologie urbaine des transports. *Annales de la recherche urbaine*, 59–60, 141–151.

Cervero, R. (1997). *Paratransit in America: Redefining Mass Transportation*. Praeger, Westport.

Cervero, R. (2000). Informal transport in the developing world. Report, UN-Habitat, Nairobi.

Cervero, R. and Golub. A. (2007). Informal transport: A global perspective. *Transport Policy*, 14(6), 445–457

Coutard, O. and Rutherford, J. (2009). Les réseaux transformés par leurs marges. Développement et ambivalence des techniques "décentralisées". *Flux*, 76–77, 6–13.

Coutard, O. and Rutherford, J. (2016). Beyond the networked city. An introduction. In *Beyond the Networked City. Infrastructure Reconfigurations and Urban Change in the North and South*, Coutard, O. and Rutherford, J. (eds). Routledge, London/New York.

Darmaningtyas (2012). Laporan Akhir – Penyusunan Strategi Penataan Angkot. Report, INSTRAN, Jakarta.

Desmoulière, R. (2019). Géographie d'un milieu : propriétaires, chauffeurs et organizations de minibus à Jakarta. PhD thesis, INALCO, Paris.

Diaz Olvera, L., Guézéré, A., Plat, D., Pochet, P. (2016). Earning a living, but at what price? Being a motorcycle taxi driver in a Sub-Saharan African city. *Journal of Transport Geography*, 55, 165–174.

Eckert, R.D. and Hilton, G.W. (1972). The Jitneys. *The Journal of Law & Economics*, 15(2), 293–325.

Evans, J., O'Brien, J., Ch Ng, B. (2018). Towards a geography of informal transport: Mobility, infrastructure and urban sustainability from the back of a motorbike. *Transactions of the Institute of British Geographers*, 43, 674–688.

Ferro, P.S., Behrens, R., Golub, A. (2012). Planned and paratransit service integration through trunk and feeder arrangements: An international review. *31st Southern Africa Transport Conference*, Pretoria.

Ferro, P.S., Breuil, L., Allaire, J. (2015). Le transport collectif artisanal : une composante essentielle dans un système dual. AFD-CODATU report, Lyon.

Figueroa, O. (2007). L'intégration des taxis à l'offre de transport collectif majeur à Santiago du Chili. *Colloque du Festival Taxi*, Institut pour la ville en mouvement, Lisbon.

Figueroa, O. (2013). Four decades of changing transport policy in Santiago, Chile. *Research in Transportation Economics*, 40, 87–95.

Godard, X. (1987). Transport privé, transport public, expériences des villes du Tiers-Monde. Report, INRETS, Bron.

Godard, X. (2008a). Transport artisanal, esquisse de bilan pour la mobilité durable. *Conférence CODATU XIII*, Ho Chi Minh City.

Godard, X. (2008b). Introduction à la question du transport artisanal en Méditerranée. In *Le transport artisanal dans les villes méditerranéennes*, Godard, X. (ed.). INRETS, Bron.

Goldblum, C. (2001). Transports "informels" et adaptations à la métropolisation en Asie du Sud-Est. *L'information géographique*, 65(1), 18–32.

Graham, S. and Marvin, S. (2001). *Splintering Urbanism: Networked Infrastructures, Technological Mobilities and the Urban Condition*. Routledge, London/New York.

Hart, K. (1973). Informal income opportunities and urban employment in Ghana. *Journal of Modern African Studies*, 11(1), 61–89.

International Labour Organization (1972). Employment, incomes and equality. A strategy for increasing productive employment in Kenya. Report, ILO, Geneva.

Jaglin, S. (2016). Is the network challenged by the pragmatic turn in African cities? Urban transition and hybrid delivery configurations. In *Beyond the Networked City. Infrastructure Reconfigurations and Urban Change in the North and South*, Coutard, O. and Rutherford, J. (eds). Routledge, London/New York.

Kassi, I. (2007). Régulations des transports populaires et recomposition du territoire urbain d'Abidjan. PhD thesis, Université Bordeaux 3, Université d'Abidjan-Cocody, Bordeaux-Abidjan.

Kirby, R.F., Bhatt, K.U., Kemp, M., McGillivray, R.G., Wohl, M. (1974). *Para-Transit: Neglected Options for Urban Mobility*. The Urban Institute, Washington.

Le Breton, E. (2001). Le transport à la demande comme innovation institutionnelle. *Flux*, 43, 58–69.

Le Breton, E., Ascher, F., Bourdin, A., Charrel, N., Ducroux, L., Prins, M., Pycha, A. (2000). Le transport à la demande, un nouveau mode de gestion des mobilités urbaines. Report, PREDIT, Paris.

Lombard, J. (2006). Enjeux privés dans le transport public d'Abidjan et de Dakar. *Géocarrefour*, 81(2), 167–174.

Mulley, C. and Nelson, J.-D. (2016). Shaping the new future of paratransit. An agenda for research and practice. *Transportation Research Record*, 2542, 17–24.

Orero, R. and McCormick, D. (2013). Cooperatives involvement in the paratransit sector: Experiences and lessons in Nairobi. *32nd Southern Africa Transport Conference*, Pretoria.

Orfeuil J.-P. (2008). *Mobilités urbaines. L'âge des possibles*. Les Carnets de l'info, Paris.

Orski C.K. (1975). Paratransit: The coming of age of a transportation concept. *Transportation*, 4, 329–334.

Panghegar, F. (2014). *Berebut ruang. Dinamika politik trayek angkot di Jakarta*. Puskapol Universitas Indonesia, Depok.

Reigner, H., Brenac, T., Hernandez, F. (2013). *Nouvelles idéologies urbaines. Dictionnaire critique de la ville mobile, verte et sûre*. PUR, Rennes.

Rimmer, P. (1980). Paratransit: A commentary. *Environment and Planning A*, 12, 937–944.

Rimmer, P. (1986). *Rikisha to Rapid Transit: Urban Public Transport Systems and Policy in Southeast Asia*. Pergamon Press, Sydney.

Schalekamp, H. and Behrens, R. (2009). An international review of paratransit regulation and integration experience: Lessons for public transport system rationalisation and improvement in South African cities. *28th Southern African Transport Conference*, Pretoria.

Tarrius, A. (1985). Transports autoproduits : production et reproduction du social. *Espaces et sociétés*, 46, 35–54.

Tastevin, Y.-P. (2012). Autorickshaw (1948-2…). A success story. *Techniques et cultures*, 58, 264–277.

Wester, L. (2015). Modélisation multi-agents de transports collectifs artisanaux : structures émergentes et stratégies individuelles. In *Proceedings of the Spatial Analysis and Geomatics Conference (SAGEO) 2015*, Hammamet.

Woolf, S.E. and Joubert, J.W. (2013). A people-centered view on paratransit in South Africa. *Cities*, 35, 284–293.

PART 3

Active Modes of Transport and Infrastructure Policies

8

The Infrastructure of Walking: The Case of Mexico City Sidewalks

Ruth PÉREZ LÓPEZ[1], Jérôme MONNET[2] and Guénola CAPRON[1]
[1] Department of Sociology, Universidad Autónoma Metropolitana-Azcapotzalco, Mexico City, Mexico
[2] Gustave Eiffel University, École des Ponts, LVMT, Marne-la-Vallée, France

8.1. Introduction: sidewalks, a special element of urban pedestrian infrastructure

In contemporary cities around the world, walking corresponds to three main functions, to which urban planning has assigned specialized and distinct spaces. During the Renaissance, there appeared the sociospatial distinction between walking-for-leisure and walking-for-travel (Monnet 2016). Walking-for-leisure has benefited from dedicated places since the 16th century, with parks and gardens created for the practice of walking: the first public park in Mexico City was created in 1592. In the second half of the 20th century, certain streets in the old heritage districts were pedestrianized. Both are comfortable and pleasant to walk in but remain limited in scope, or very small in some cities. As for walking-for-travel, this was supported by roads throughout the urban space, but in uncomfortable or even dangerous conditions, due to the coexistence of pedestrians with vehicles. This is a factor of insecurity during road crossings and inconvenience in the use of sidewalks due to pollution, noise and illegal parking (Héran 2011). At the intersection between leisure and travel, a third large group of specialized places has developed since the middle of the 19th century to provide an environment favorable to walking-for-consumption. Originally, this entailed a private setting, with shopping malls, passages and shopping centers, and even amusement parks, before expanding to pedestrian streets as part of a "revitalization" of downtown areas or neighborhoods, enacted by public authorities or as part of public–private partnerships (Capron 1998; Didier 1999; Sabatier 2006).

In this chapter, we will look at sidewalks, an important element of urban pedestrian infrastructure. This latter term refers to all the spaces of circulation that are linked to each other by users, and therefore connects sidewalks and roadway crossings with green spaces, internal circulation spaces of buildings (passages, malls and shopping centers) and isolated areas such as pathways inside large complexes (Monnet 2019, 2021). The pedestrian infrastructure is therefore not planned in a unified way by the public authorities, as each of its components is built and managed by a specific actor, without organized coordination with others. This is the case for sidewalks, which have up until today been the focus of attention paid to pedestrians by the authorities in charge of roads and transport (Blomley 2011). It is a daily space for most people who move around the city and, mainly, for those who move on foot and/or use public transport, since it allows articulation between the different modes of transport. The place of sidewalks in mobility systems varies greatly depending on local conditions. They also host a very wide variety of other uses, which often come into conflict. In the case of the United States studied by Loukaitou-Sideris and Ehrenfeucht (2009), the regulated order of pedestrian traffic seems to dominate over other uses (spending time in public spaces, commerce, vehicle parking). In contrast, in the cities of the Global South, such as Ho Chi Minh City in Vietnam (Kim 2015) or Nanjing in China (Guan 2015), where informal street selling is omnipresent in some neighborhoods, the order that seems to predominate is that of negotiation and hybridization[1]. This is also the case in Mexico City, as we will see in detail. We will begin by showing that walking-for-travel occupies a central place in this agglomeration's mobility system. However, perceived as the mode of transport of the poor, it remains marginal in urban policies, as in other countries of the Global South. Second, we will present the results of research conducted on the sidewalks of Mexico City, showing the interweaving of movement, which is a matter of traffic planning and management, with their many other uses, raising issues first of all of public order, urban atmosphere and social inclusion, among others. Finally, we will discuss the challenges of a policy for the development of walking in the city, which we believe must particularly closely combine consideration of the needs of travel with those of consumption and leisure.

---

1 Hybrid order refers to the spatial interweaving of the different regulations and social norms that govern urban order (Giglia 2016; Capron et al. 2022).

8.2. In Mexico City, the place of walking in the mobility system reflects social inequalities

In the "metropolitan area" of Mexico City, which encompasses the entire agglomeration (Figure 8.1: see central panel), 44% of travel is multimodal (INEGI 2017)[2]. Thus, while 45% of trips use public transit, these trips are combined with another mode in most cases. Journeys made by minibus (small to medium-capacity buses operated by private contractors), which provide fine-grained service and account for three quarters of journeys made by public transport, are combined in 78.3% of cases with another means of transport, motorized or otherwise. Multimodality exceeds 90% of cases for trips using high-capacity public transport (train, metro, buses, whether in dedicated lanes or not, trolleybuses). However, these high-capacity transport services cover urban areas very unevenly, and peripheral areas particularly poorly. As a result, the large disadvantaged population living in those areas can only access the main employment areas, and in particular the city center, by combining several modes of transport at the cost of long and complicated journeys. In addition, the poorest groups do not have the financial capacity to use public transport on a regular basis.

The poor service and cost thus partly explain why 32.3% of trips are made exclusively on foot, that is, just over 11 million daily trips over the whole agglomeration. If we add these city dwellers who exclusively use walking to those who use it in addition to public transport, walking is part of 77.3% of trips made each day in the agglomeration. However, we will see later that walking conditions vary greatly throughout the agglomeration depending on the presence and quality of sidewalks. This has a massive impact on people who depend in whole or in large part on walking to access the resources they need. We speak here of "walking dependency[3]", where city dwellers are too deprived to afford another mode or because the places which they need to reach are not served by any mechanized transport. These two factors often combine in the outlying neighborhoods of Mexico City, which are also those where sidewalks are the least well respected and maintained, or even discontinuous or simply absent.

---

2 For the first time, this survey includes walking, recording both journeys made entirely on foot and segments corresponding to the beginning or end of a journey using another mode. Despite this, walking as a means of access to public transport doubtless remains under-represented in the results.

3 Inspired by the expression "car dependency", proposed by specialists to show how the individual car has become necessary for many urban dwellers because of an organization of urban space and social life that disassociates residential, work and shopping areas (Newman and Kenworthy 2000; Orfeuil 2008).

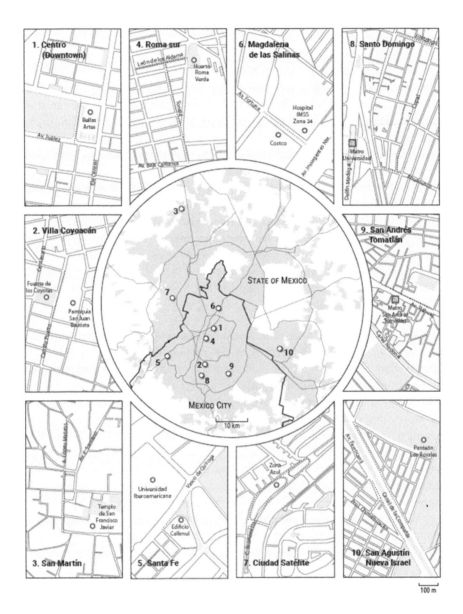

Figure 8.1. *Location of neighborhoods studied, Mexico City agglomeration. Created by: Jerónimo Diaz for the "Banquetas" project coordinated by the authors*

It has been shown elsewhere that walking reveals social inequalities. For instance, a dossier on the social and political issues of walking exposes how the City of Pamplona tried to exclude populations considered undesirable by regulating the correct way to walk in the city center; how people may feel stigma when walking through some middle- and upper-class neighborhoods in Santiago de Chile, how this stigma applies to cardboard waste pickers walking through Buenos Aires, and finally, how the practice of walking buses for children's journeys to and from school are welcomed differently according to the socioeconomic characteristics of the districts of Lausanne (Monnet et al. 2019).

In Mexico City, according to the origin-destination survey already mentioned (INEGI 2017), the people who walk the most are those who belong to the most disadvantaged socioeconomic categories of the population. Note that 45.7% and 37.3% of journeys made by the lowest socioeconomic categories (so-called "lower" and "lower-middle") are made on foot, compared to only 29.2% and 18.1% of trips in the "upper-middle" and "upper" categories. To access public transport, the more modest categories of people have to walk more and spend more time on the street.

The inequalities are even more striking when they involve gender difference: 40.3% of trips made by women during the week are made exclusively on foot, compared to only 20.3% of those made by men (Table 8.1). The intersection of inequalities weighs particularly heavily on the poorest women who make 56.7% of their journeys on foot, while 33.3% of the journeys made by men belonging to the same socio-economic category are on foot.

	On foot		By car	
	Women	Men	Women	Men
Lower	56.7	33.3	3.2	8.9
Lower-middle	46.8	26.5	7.6	15.5
Upper-middle	35.8	21.8	15.3	23.7
Upper	22.5	13.3	40.9	48.2
Total	40.3	20.3	14.4	22.4

Source of statistics: (INEGI 2017).

Table 8.1. *Percentage of trips made during the week, on foot and by car, by gender and socioeconomic category*

These differences are mainly explained by a higher proportion of men than women being identified as "economically active" because they are paid (74.2%

compared to 42.4% across the country; INEGI 2021), and by the sexual division of labor. While men's trips are mainly for commuting – 79.3% are home-work and home-study trips – the reasons for women's travel are more diversified, since accompaniment (19.3%) and shopping (17.4%) are more significant (Figure 8.2). In addition, out of every 100 trips for accompaniment and shopping, 81 and 74, respectively, are made by women.

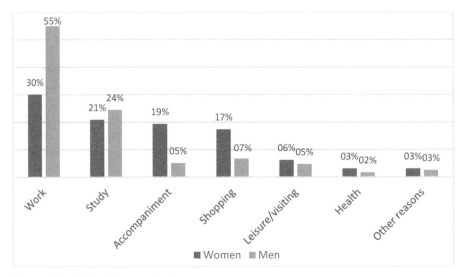

Source of statistics: (INEGI 2017).

Figure 8.2. *Reasons for travel by gender (other than "home")*

To conclude this part, it is possible to schematize the different pedestrian mobility practices of users in the Mexico City metropolitan area. Dependence on walking is highest for women in poor and under-served peripheries, while for men in the same neighborhoods, walking is combined with very long journeys by public transport to work. At the opposite end of the metropolitan area, in the central areas where jobs and services are concentrated and where all modes of transport converge, walking is a less segregative mode. Indeed, it allows all categories of the population to access everything these areas have to offer.

After having discussed walking at the scale of the metropolitan area, we will now descend to the level of the sidewalks, to see in more detail under what conditions it is possible to walk in Mexico City and its metropolitan area.

8.3. The social and material production of sidewalks: methodology

In this context, where sidewalks are designed and managed essentially as a traffic space, we have conducted research with a multidisciplinary team in social sciences[4] whose objective is to show that sidewalks cannot be understood solely as a subsystem of the transport infrastructure, but must be analyzed through the prism of a diversity of other important functions, which vary according to the urban context. For this research, we selected 10 districts within Mexico City and its metropolitan area (Figure 8.1) based on different sociospatial characteristics: central or peripheral areas, areas of activities or residence, rich or poor, old or recently urbanized, where the production and management of space are formal or informal. Apart from the ancient villages of pre-Hispanic origin where there is often no sidewalk, this feature appears in the neighborhoods studied in the form of a lateral bench (*banqueta* in Mexican Spanish), raised in relation to the central road used for vehicle traffic. In outlying neighborhoods, sidewalks are often in a deplorable and sometimes discontinuous state.

For each of the zones, a systematic program of field observations and cartographic surveys of the physical characteristics of sidewalks was carried out at all times of the week, including the weekend. Structured interviews were conducted with 18 local and municipal government officials, as well as 93 semi-structured interviews with residents, merchants and other sidewalk users. A questionnaire with open and closed questions also enabled us to collect information from 500 passers-by on the characteristics of their movements, their appreciation of various aspects of the sidewalk (maintenance, convenience, social life, surveillance, among others), feelings of security when walking in the street and the informal activities they observed in this space. These questions were selected based on ethnographic surveys prior to the project, in order to connect their results with ours. Finally, video recordings lasting 15 minutes per neighborhood were made with cameras located 6 m above ground level to automatically record the routes and speed of pedestrians.

These methods have allowed us to analyze the uses of the sidewalks that were studied, seeking to connect their physical characteristics with the behaviors of the people who use or walk upon them. A first axis of our grid of analysis combines the

---

4 Research "The social and material production of sidewalks in the metropolitan region of Mexico City" No. CB-2015-255645-S, with funding from the National Council of Science and Technology (Conacyt, Mexico), 2015-2022. Team: Guénola Capron, Jérôme Monnet, Ruth Pérez-López, Eliud Gálvez Matías, Luz Yazmín Viramontes Fabela, Perla Castañeda Archundia, Salomón González Arellano, Ángela Giglia, María Teresa Esquivel Hernández, Miguel Ángel Aguilar, Natanael Reséndiz, María Concepción Huarte Trujillo, Ana Luisa Diez García, Bismarck Ledezma Navarro.

urban landscape, the morphology and materiality of the sidewalks, the porosity of the built-up area, the fixed obstacles and the permanent occupation of land in the neighborhoods, but also phenomena that vary rapidly over time but may be recurrent, such as cleaning or mobile obstacles (parked vehicles, garbage containers, commercial stalls and so on). A second axis of analysis applies to uses and behaviors that are directly observable in situ and/or through video recordings. On the one hand, this involves characterizing the flows: circulation and coexistence of pedestrians and vehicles, density of pedestrians, pace of walking. On the other hand, it involves describing the temporalities and dynamics of activities on the sidewalks: physical and symbolic appropriation of the sidewalk, degree of legitimacy and formality of uses, power relations, conflicts, among others. We have combined these variables in order to better understand the interactions of sidewalk users with each other, with bordering actors (residents, shopkeepers or businesses), with the authorities represented by agents or by the regulatory sphere, and with the built environment.

8.4. The diversity of sidewalk functions

From the restricted point of view of transport and road policies, sidewalks are part of roading infrastructure and support the physical structures and street furniture that serve both pedestrian and vehicle traffic. In Mexico City, they are generally made of cement, an inexpensive material, but have a wide variety of surfaces (asphalt, paving, tiling), either because of specific upgrading in the central areas, or because frontage owners have modified them during work on their parcel of land, as we will see later. They are often higher than in northern countries, and in some cases it is difficult to go from the road to the sidewalk. Within them are located, in Mexico City as in the rest of the world: public lighting (not always oriented toward the sidewalks), devices for crossing the road (traffic lights, right-of-way or underground passages), street name signs, as well as advertising signage targeting the users of public space. A significant part of the street furniture installed on the sidewalk shows that it is only intended for vehicles, while another part is intended for pedestrian mobility: bus stops, benches, garbage cans, barriers channeling pedestrian flows and elements preventing vehicles from parking on the sidewalk. All these permanent installations are generally formal, that is, established by the authorities; however, there are informal installations to prevent vehicles from parking (see the next section), make the street more pleasant (Figure 8.4) or attract customers (commercial stalls).

However, the functions and uses of the sidewalk do not only relate to mobility. The sidewalk is also used to install aerial or underground technical networks (electricity, landline telephony, water supply and sanitation) and communication services (telephone booths, mailboxes). Added to this are more or less formal facilities for consumption, such as café and restaurant terraces (very common in certain neighborhoods) and a few formal kiosks (press, florists, among others). Above all, the sidewalks of Mexico City are host to many informal activities. The omnipresence of the commercial use of sidewalks is reflected in our study by the fact that 80.7% of pedestrians questioned about informal activities that they observed on sidewalks indicated "street trading".

Indeed, many formal shops informally extend their point of sale onto the sidewalk, while informal stalls selling prepared food (*tacos, tortas* and so on) are present throughout the agglomeration. Extensions of repair workshops (vehicles, furniture, household appliances, etc.) are mainly but not exclusively found in working-class neighborhoods (Figure 8.3). Often small in size, the workshops are mainly used as warehouses, while their services are provided directly on the sidewalk where the tools are installed. In a similar way, there are wooden or metal carpentry workshops operating outside, as well as artisans, sometimes itinerant, who set up on the sidewalk with their re-padding or upholstery equipment to repair or maintain customers' chairs and sofas. The sidewalk then becomes, at certain times of the day and in certain neighborhoods, a space for production as well as transactions.

Source: Photograph taken by Silvia Carbone in the Santo Domingo neighborhood for the Banquetas Project coordinated by the authors.

Figure 8.3. *Mechanic's services provided on the sidewalk. For a color version of this figure, see www.iste.co.uk/lesteven/urban.zip*

Around nodes of mobility (interchange hubs, access to hospitals or educational or administrative institutions, commercial and tourist areas, etc.) the sidewalks also welcome shoe shiners, street artists and sellers of a wide variety of goods. The intensity of pedestrian traffic and commercial density logically go hand in hand: the greater the flow, the greater the interest of merchants, both formal and informal, in setting up on the sidewalk; conversely, the more shops there are on a sidewalk, the more pedestrians it attracts (Monnet et al. 2007).

Finally, the sidewalk is one of the most important urban areas for planting vegetation, in Mexico City as elsewhere (Loukaitou-Sideris and Ehrenfeucht 2009). Since the 19th century, sidewalks have been utilized by urban policy to provide trees and plant tubs along not only the main avenues throughout the agglomeration, but also the secondary roads of the "beautiful neighborhoods" of different areas (the *colonias* of Roma or Condesa, Lomas de Chapultepec, Ciudad Satélite, Santa Fe, etc.). Added to this official greening is that carried out by locals, residents or traders, who install flower boxes, or even shrubs, in front of their buildings or around trees (Figure 8.4). To this they sometimes add seats and settle there to chat with neighbors, showing that for them the sidewalk is not simply an element of the transport system. Thanks to these amenities, the sidewalk may serve as a place of conviviality to walk, play, exercise the dog and chat. One can observe in middle and upper class neighborhoods the practice of jogging, favored in places where there exists a specific form of sidewalk, the central and tree-lined "*camellón*". In the densest of these neighborhoods, the "*eyes on the street*" (Jacobs 1961) represented by neighbors and shopkeepers offer relative autonomy for children to go to school, to see their friends or to make certain purchases.

The function of spending time is also important in poor neighborhoods where housing conditions are poor and where children sometimes play on the street, under the gaze of men who stand in groups on the sidewalk. This ability to spend time becomes vital in cases where the sidewalk serves as a refuge for the homeless and can be used to perform the activities that make it possible to survive: sleeping, consuming, socializing, begging or rendering small services to residents or traders (Pérez-López 2009).

It thus appears that the sidewalk is strongly different from the roadway within the roading network: while the roadway is a technically homogeneous space where vehicle traffic is hegemonic, the sidewalk appears as the space of a more or less conflictual cohabitation between the logics of traffic and those of spending time, working, consumption and sociability. Thus, not only can each person present in one capacity (passerby, resident, customer, stroller, worker, etc.) meet or even collide with people present in other capacities at the same time on the same sidewalk, but they can also take on a different role depending on the moment, or even by changing sidewalks.

Source: photograph taken by Guénola Capron in the Roma Sur neighborhood for the Banquetas Project coordinated by the authors

Figure 8.4. *A space of rest and freshness, created by a shopkeeper. For a color version of this figure, see www.iste.co.uk/lesteven/urban.zip*

8.5. Competition and conflict between sidewalk uses

We will now see how the accumulation of functions and the heterogeneity of uses generates competition for space and conflicts that create instability and insecurity, particularly to the detriment of certain populations, such as the poor, women, children, elderly or people with reduced mobility, who are, however, the social categories whose mobility and autonomy are the most dependent on walking.

One of the most common conflicts concerns the use of sidewalks for parking vehicles and direct and indirect obstacles to pedestrian mobility. In the affluent residential neighborhoods of central-western Mexico City, where households are equipped with private vehicles, it is common to note that the portion of the sidewalk in front of the private garage or in front of the house is considered reserved parking that avoids the need to bring the car in or out or park it elsewhere. This privatization is ensured, when the vehicle is absent, through human means (caretaker, driver) or non-human means (chains, buckets filled with cement, tires, etc.) to prevent the parking of a stranger's car, which would block access to the building or take the place of the occupant of the house.

More generally, vehicle access ramps to parking lots inside buildings represent a major obstacle for pedestrians throughout the city (Figure 8.5). Indeed, these ramps are built by local residents as often as they are by artisanal builders or large formal companies, lacking compliance with the standards in force and any effective control by the authorities. This usually results in each ramp having a specific slope between the roadway and the building, which may ascend to the raised ground floor or descend to access an underground or semi-buried parking lot. Pedestrians are then confronted with very significant differences in level and slope, as well as a great heterogeneity of materials and textures, which make walking dangerous for anyone who is not paying attention, difficult for many people carrying loads and impossible for people with reduced mobility or traveling with pushchairs, rollerblades or skateboards. Many pedestrians are then forced to descend onto the roadway.

The need to walk on the roadway also appears in the contexts already mentioned, where sidewalks are "invaded" by shops or workshops, most often informal, but also frequently by the terraces of formal restaurants. Unlike the permanent obstacles created by the heterogeneous profiles of sidewalks, commerce generally obeys temporalities which paradoxically forbid pedestrian traffic from the sidewalk when it is at its maximum during the day (Figure 8.6), while it becomes possible to walk on the sidewalk at night, when there are very few pedestrians to enjoy it.

Conflicts between different types of pedestrian use may also exist between residents concerned about tranquility and shopkeepers interested in the flow of passers-by, residents bothered by health or noise pollution from restaurants and open-air workshops, neighbors who object to cleaning or occupation of the sidewalk or who are concerned about the insecurity associated with locations of prostitution and/or drug trafficking, among others.

While these conflicts are sometimes expressed openly, there are others that are less explicit, such as that between the logic of mobility, favored by road engineers, and the logic of pausing, necessary for a variety of users such as the elderly or disabled, lovers, consumers and tourists. These do not form a coalition of actors who can ask for more benches and seats, whose absence is sorely felt in the agglomeration beyond the privileged areas of the city where a particular entity, the Public Space Agency, has intervened. This municipal agency, independent from the administration of roads and travel, was responsible between

2008 and 2018 for iconic projects for the development of public space, especially in the city center.

There are also contradictions in the formal production of sidewalks by the authorities; between the level of administration that formulates the rules and the one that gives the authorizations, between the department that designs the work and the one that performs it, between those who regulate traffic and those who manage sidewalk maintenance, etc. This vast selection of actors who are in competition, with multiple, even antagonistic interests – agents of construction of the territory who modify its morphology, residents anxious to preserve or embellish their residential space, formal and informal traders eager to attract more customers, etc. – participate in the formal and informal layout of the sidewalks, in planned or spontaneous, temporary or permanent development. The result of this is that each sidewalk is representative of a certain negotiated order subject to the different sociospatial and logical contexts of actors.

Source: Photograph taken by Jérôme Monnet in the Roma Sur neighborhood for the Banquetas Project coordinated by the authors.

Figure 8.5. *Ramp for vehicle access to a building. For a color version of this figure, see www.iste.co.uk/lesteven/urban.zip*

Source: Photograph taken by Jérôme Monnet in a street in the Historic Center of Mexico City for the Banquetas Project coordinated by the authors.

Figure 8.6. *When businesses invade the sidewalks, pedestrians invade the roadway. For a color version of this figure, see www.iste.co.uk/lesteven/urban.zip*

8.6. From uses to actors' games: the production of a negotiated order

Indeed, all these diverse and varied uses, public, private or mixed, which are observed on the sidewalks, lead to questions about how to regulate their coexistence and that of the different users, and the legitimacy of their claim to a place on the sidewalk. How does a dominant order impose itself on other orders? Under what conditions is pedestrian traffic, considered the legal norm, subject to the interests of people who make other uses of the sidewalk? Or, conversely, how are other uses dominated by the rule of mobility?

As we have seen, sidewalks are designed as a space for installing street furniture. However, in Mexico City's highway code and its "Mobility Act", sidewalks are primarily intended for "exclusive or priority circulation of pedestrians"; they must therefore be "accessible to disabled and mobility-reduced persons" (Asamblea Legislativa del Distrito Federal 2014, Art. 179, I). These standards refer explicitly to the hierarchy of types of mobility on public roads. This stipulates that people who travel on foot have priority over other modes of transport because of their vulnerability and the ecological nature of their mode of travel. In this sense, everything that is not of the order of pedestrian traffic is perceived by authorities, users and other actors, such as activists who mobilize in favor of walking in the city, as obstacles and obstructions to mobility. However, lack of respect for pedestrians by motor vehicle drivers and the weak application of this public standard do not allow this hierarchy to be respected. Thus, in practice, the local order is very rarely dominated only by pedestrian traffic.

On certain sidewalks with reduced width and a high density of pedestrians and/or commercial activities, the circulation of passers-by is subordinated to commercial activities. In the neighborhoods of Santo Domingo and San Martín, respectively, to the south and north of the city, but also in many other neighborhoods of the city, pedestrians circulate on the roadway, which does not pose any real problems when traffic is calm, but becomes a problem when it is intense. This allows them to avoid street markets and other pedestrians, perceived as obstacles by those looking to move quickly. In Figure 8.7, we see how pedestrians circulate on one side and on the other of the roadway (a), the flows of pedestrians who use the roadway as an extension of the sidewalk, modeled by red lines, and, on the right, the blue lines corresponding to vehicles (b).

In some cases, the order of car traffic dominates the sidewalks to the detriment of mobility and other pedestrian activities. Thus, we observed sidewalks where order is imposed by vehicles parked on the sidewalk or by flows of cars entering and leaving a parking lot that force pedestrians to stop, make a detour, wait or even be alert to avoid being knocked over. For example, this is the case for access to parking for a shopping mall observed in Magdalena de las Salinas, or for an office tower in Santa Fe (Figure 8.8). The low flow of pedestrians on these sidewalks (3.5 and 5.1 pedestrians per minute, respectively) thus leads to vehicle traffic taking priority over pedestrians when the two flows intersect.

Conversely, in the historic center of Mexico City, on the edge of Alameda Park, we observed that pedestrians can impose their own order and rhythm. Indeed, the high density of pedestrians on the sidewalk on a Saturday at noon (21.1 pedestrians per minute), as well as the characteristics of this space – touristic, heritage and recreational – force vehicles entering or leaving the car park to slow down and stop to give way to passers-by.

Source: Excerpts from video taken in the Santo Domingo neighborhood. 5B developed by Bismarck Ledezma Navarro for the Banquetas Project coordinated by the authors.

Figure 8.7. *Pedestrian flow on the roadway: (a) video extract; (b) pedestrian flow (in red) and vehicle flow (in blue). For a color version of this figure, see www.iste.co.uk/lesteven/urban.zip*

Source: Still from video taken in Santa Fe neighborhood for the Banquetas Project coordinated by the authors.

Figure 8.8. *Vehicle mounting a parking ramp located on the sidewalk. For a color version of this figure, see www.iste.co.uk/lesteven/urban.zip*

Thus, the social practices observed on sidewalks are far from conforming to the formal hierarchy of uses specified in the regulations. Despite its informal nature, commerce can enjoy a certain legitimacy, even domination, on the sidewalks. Indeed, it is an integral part of the urban landscape to the extent that its presence on the sidewalks is difficult to question. Successive governments that have tried to regulate or relocate it have generally failed, except in a part of the historic center from which it was "eradicated" in 2008 and where it has only stealthily become re-established. In some particularly controlled areas of the city, such as Santa Fe (Figure 8.8), the strict application of local regulations by a public–private partnership prevents any trade from setting up on the sidewalk, while some street vendors (with carriages or vans) are tolerated on the roadway.

Outside these neighborhoods, the street trade benefits from a certain flexibility in negotiating its location, its opening hours or managing the waste it produces. Despite the constraints imposed by street trading on people who move around by foot, who have to circumvent obstacles, descend onto the roadway, avoid stalls, step over an object or slow down their pace, it is fairly well accepted insofar as it provides many services to the inhabitants of the agglomeration, and particularly to those who move around (Monnet et al. 2007). As a result of the trend toward the intensification of metropolitan mobility, we may wonder whether street commerce, understood as a service offered to "ambulant" customers, will not take up even more space on the sidewalks. Nevertheless, the Covid-19 health crisis may have long-term effects, but it is too early to assess them.

8.7. Conclusion: Towards inclusive and adaptive sidewalk layouts?

While in the current regulations of Mexico City and surrounding municipalities, the sidewalk is designed and managed solely as a support space for pedestrian traffic and street furniture, the authorities in charge of planning and regulation remain blind to and therefore powerless in the face of the diversity of situations and spatial configurations of sidewalks. This situation, while particularly evident in Mexico City, is, in our view, representative of what may be observed anywhere else in the world.

This leads to wondering about arrangements that may take into account the multifunctionality of sidewalks and their heterogenous uses, but which remain to be invented. Faced with the interweaving of practices, how can we guarantee the free movement of pedestrians while making room for sociability and economic transactions? It is indeed a social inclusion issue: allowing a variety of uses on the sidewalks means making room in public space for a diversity of users, and in particular for the most vulnerable among them. The latter may be excluded by the dominant order of traffic, which marginalizes children, the elderly or those whose survival depends on the resources of the street. When the dominant order is that of commerce, this creates obstacles that do not allow certain users to pass, for example, users in a wheelchair or with a stroller, or may harm the quality of life of local residents. The challenge is therefore to counteract the domination of an order, whether formal like that of traffic or informal like that of commerce, to give more room for a greater diversity of uses and users to coexist.

There appear to be lines of thought that could be developed to design facilities differently. Should the "shared spaces" or "meeting zones" usually created in central heritage neighborhoods not be deployed first in working-class peripheral areas, where there are no sidewalks yet and where they are discontinuous? This allocation of living space for the benefit of pedestrians would have little impact on motor traffic in a context where the roads can be quite wide and where the poor population rarely owns a particular vehicle (10% of households in the lower quartile of income; Asamblea Legislativa del Distrito Federal 2017, p. 77). Should participatory approaches not include more profiles of users to be implemented in the development of sidewalks outside residential areas? There are also informal regulations that cause pedestrians to occupy the roadway during the most intense hours of commercial activity: this could perhaps be formalized by temporary traffic lane closures to temporarily "widen" the sidewalk.

These avenues of reflection involve drawing lessons from the informal production of space by users in the implementation of public policies. Conversely, the interest of pedestrians could lead to more strictly and systematically applying official regulations so that ramps for vehicle access to buildings no longer create obstacles.

The heterogeneity of practices observed on the sidewalks of Mexico City gives rise to complex configurations that are indicative of the social and political landscape of the megapolis. The different ways of confronting or avoiding conflicts, negotiating, seeking solutions and coexisting within the same space, lead to differentiated sociospatial orders in the sidewalks that we analyzed. The set of formal and informal rules that organize practices result, for each type of sidewalk, in an ad hoc order that is not fixed because it is built collectively and continuously by a great heterogeneity of actors. The multitude of these orders unsurprisingly reflects the diversity of the different cities that make up the urban patchwork of Mexico City: the villages of pre-Hispanic origin, the colonial city, the housing developments, the self-build neighborhoods, etc. (Duhau and Giglia 2008).

By building the sidewalk, as is the case in working-class neighborhoods, or by using it for various activities as may be observed in many different neighborhoods, the inhabitants appropriate it and assign it a meaning, domesticate it, modify it. Thus, sidewalks, which are far from being only an element of infrastructure for pedestrian mobility, represent an underpinning of public life and urbanity, essential for social life. This is why, with this chapter, we advocate moving from a conventional and monofunctional sidewalk design to a new approach that assumes its multifunctionality.

8.8. References

Asamblea Legislativa del Distrito Federal (2014). Ley de Movilidad del Distrito Federal. *Gaceta Oficial del Distrito Federal*, 1899, Mexico.

Asamblea Legislativa del Distrito Federal (2017). Diagnósticos de movilidad en la Ciudad de México [Online]. Available at: http://aldf.gob.mx/estudios-904-9.html.

Blomley, N. (2011). *Rights of Passage: Sidewalks and the Regulation of Public Flow*. Routledge, New York.

Capron, G. (1998). Les centres commerciaux à Buenos Aires : les nouveaux espaces publics de la ville de la fin du XXe siècle. *Les Annales de la Recherche Urbaine*, 78, 55–63.

Capron, G., Monnet, J., Pérez López, R. (2018). El papel de la banqueta (acera) en la infraestructura peatonal: el caso de la Zona Metropolitana del Valle de México. *Ciudades*, 119, 33–41.

Capron, G., Monnet, J., Pérez López, R. (2022). *Banquetas: el orden híbrido de las aceras en la Ciudad de México y su área metropolitana*. Ediciones de la UAM, Mexico.

Didier, S. (1999). Disney urbaniste : la ville de Celebration en Floride. *Cybergeo: European Journal of Geography*, 96 [Online]. Available at: http://journals.openedition.org/cybergeo/1147.

Duhau, E. and Giglia, A. (2008). *Las reglas del desorden: habitar la metrópoli*. Siglo XXI, UAM Azcapotzalco, Mexico.

Giglia, A. (2016). Reglamentos y reglas de uso de la Alameda central de la ciudad de México: un régimen hibrido. In *La ciudad y sus reglas*, Azuela, A. (ed.). UNAM-PAOT, Mexico.

Guan, L. (2015). Le commerce ambulant et son espace social à Nankin (Chine) : enjeux et perspectives urbanistiques. PhD thesis, Université Paris-Est, Marne-la-Vallée.

Héran, F. (2011). Pour une approche systémique des nuisances liées aux transports en milieu urbain. *Les Cahiers Scientifiques du Transport*, 59, 83–112.

INEGI (2017). *Encuesta de Origen y Destino*. Instituto Nacional de Estadística y Geografía, Mexico.

INEGI (2021). *Resultados de la Encuesta Nacional de Ocupación y Empleo*. Instituto Nacional de Estadística y Geografía, Mexico.

Jacobs, J. (1961). *The Death and Life of Great American Cities*. Random House, New York.

Kim, A.M. (2015). *Sidewalk City. Remapping Public Space in Ho Chi Minh City*. The University of Chicago Press.

Loukaitou-Sideris, A. and Ehrenfeucht, R. (2009). *Sidewalks: Conflict and Negotiation Over Public Space*. MIT Press, Boston.

Monnet, J. (2016). Marche-loisir et marche-déplacement : une dichotomie persistante, du romantisme au fonctionnalisme. *Sciences de la société*, 97, 75–89.

Monnet, J. (2019). Marcher en ville : technique, technologie et infrastructure (s)low tech ? *Urbanités*, #12 / La ville (s)low tech [Online]. Available at: http://www.revue-urbanites.fr/12-monnet/.

Monnet, J. (2021). Infrastructure pédestre. In *Dictionnaire pluriel de la marche en ville*, Demailly, K.E., Monnet, J., Scapino, J., Deraëve, S. (eds). L'Œil d'or, Paris.

Monnet, J., Giglia, A., Capron, G. (2007). Ambulantage et services à la mobilité : les carrefours commerciaux à Mexico. *Cybergeo: European Journal of Geography*, 371 [Online]. Available at: http://journals.openedition.org/cybergeo/5574.

Monnet, J., Pérez López, R., Hubert, J. (2019). Marche en ville : enjeux sociaux et politiques. *Espaces et sociétés*, 4(4), 7–15.

Newman, P. and Kenworth, J. (2000). The ten myths of automobile dependence. *World Transport Policy & Practice*, 6(1), 15–25.

Orfeuil, J.P. (2008). Gabriel Dupuy, *La Dépendance à l'égard de l'automobile*, 2006 – Benjamin Motte, *La Dépendance automobile pour l'accès aux services aux ménages en grande couronne francilienne*, 2006. Strates, 14, 273–275.

Pérez-López, R. (2009). *Vivre et survivre à Mexico. Enfants et jeunes de la rue*. Karthala, Paris.

Sabatier, B. (2006). La publicisation des espaces de consommation privés. Les complexes commerciaux récréatifs en France et au Mexique. PhD thesis, Université Toulouse-Le Mirail.

Secretaría de Seguridad Pública de México (2015). Reglamento de Tránsito del Distrito Federal. Report, Gaceta Oficial del Distrito Federal, Mexico.

9

Cycling Policies in Europe: The Case of Greater Lyon and Hamburg

Manon ESKENAZI[1,2]

[1] Université Paris-Est, Lab'Urba, Marne-la-Vallée, France
[2] Gustave Eiffel University, École des Ponts, LVMT, Marne-la-Vallée, France

9.1. Introduction

Long seen as a sport, a hobby, but not as a so-called "everyday" mode of travel, cycling has been increasingly prominent on the agenda of urban mobility policies for 20 years in an increasing number of European cities. The impact of the Covid-19 pandemic in 2020 and 2021 has accentuated this phenomenon: calls for physical distancing and the risks of contamination have increased this mode of travel's attractiveness to public authorities and citizens (Buehler and Pucher 2022). In France, successive re-openings after lockdowns have been accompanied by limitations on the use of public transport, and have thus led to increased use of individual modes of travel. In the wake of the crisis, many temporary or permanent cycling facilities have been set up in metropolitan areas to promote cycling in order to limit a massive return to car use and promote social distancing (Tirachini and Cats 2020; Fischer and Winters 2021).

However, cycling is not a new mode of travel. Its use was widespread in European cities in the first half of the 20th century. The rise of cycling went along with the creation of the first cycling infrastructure at the end of the 19th century.

Originally dedicated to recreational tourist use, this later became a means of separating cyclists from increasing car traffic starting in the 1920s (Briese 1993; Eskenazi 2022). However, the use of bicycles declined in all European cities after the Second World War, in parallel with the gradual establishment of the car system. Utilitarian cycling – that is, as a means of transport for daily activities – almost completely disappeared from certain cities, particularly in France and England, although its use continued in Dutch and Danish cities and in a few German cities, such as Bremen (Héran 2014). While this dynamic was common to Europe, the reactions of city and national governments, and cycling's place on the political agenda, differed greatly from place to place.

The Netherlands and Denmark, considered today to be models of good practice in terms of cycling policies and urban planning, have seen a dynamic redevelopment of cycling since the Second World War, but one based on firmly established practices and a unique context. Both countries experienced, among other things, a slower motorization of society linked to the absence of a national automobile industry (Oosterhuis 2016). Moreover, women's access to employment in the 1960s, and therefore their increased need for mobility, contributed to maintaining cycling practices (Carstensen and Ebert 2012). However, the Dutch and Danish governments did not actively implement cycling policies until the 1970s, when they were hit hard by the oil crises. Cycling then became permanently integrated into urban and territorial planning, becoming a symbol of national identity accepted and championed by political actors (Carstensen and Ebert 2012).

Outcomes for cycling in other European cities contrasted significantly. While several German cities began to develop cycling policies in the 1970s, such as Bremen and Freiburg, cycling's emergence on the political agenda generally came later in France, England, and more broadly at the European level. In this chapter, we will analyze the directions taken by cycling policies in two European metropolises since the end of the 1990s. Through the case of the metropolitan areas of Greater Lyon (France) and Hamburg (Germany), we will see that the emergence of cycling on the political agenda at the same time happened in response to similar problems of reducing car use, in cities largely organized around cars and public transport. However, this development of policies in favor of cycling took place in different contexts of mobility: while cycling in Hamburg already had a modal share of 7% in 1991 (Buehler et al. 2017), the same figure was less than 1% in Lyon in 1995 (Guidez 2007). Despite these differences in use, we will see how these policies have made cycling part of a dynamic of changing norms for mobility and road development policies.

This chapter is based on two field surveys conducted between 2017 and 2019 in Lyon and Hamburg as part of thesis work (Eskenazi 2022). Twenty interviews were conducted with local elected officials, technical actors and associations in the two metropolises. These are complemented by an analysis of the planning and communication documents of the two metropolises.

Hamburg is the third largest European port and a major German metropolis with 1.8 million inhabitants spread over 755 km^2. Composed of seven boroughs, it is a city-state (Stadtstaat) that has the powers of both a municipality and a *Land* (German federal state), like Berlin and Bremen. This particularity gives it a certain autonomy in designing and implementing public policy, particularly in territorial planning, with little involvement by the federal government. Since 1 January 2015, Greater Lyon has had the status of metropolis: it has replaced the former urban community of Lyon and has assumed the powers formerly exercised by the Rhône department over its territory. It includes 59 municipalities over a territory of 533 km^2, with a population of 1.3 million inhabitants. It has similar powers to the city-state of Hamburg in terms of spatial planning and mobility, financing and organization of urban transport networks.

9.2. Cycling infrastructure at the heart of cycling policies

Cycling policies have been the subject of a great deal of research, in parallel with the growing importance of this mode of travel for public policy (Pucher and Buehler 2008; Cupples and Ridley 2008; Aldred and Jungnickel 2014). A significant part of this work focuses on comparing so-called cycle-friendly cities with others that are less so or not at all cycle-friendly (Pucher et al. 2011; Koglin 2013), with the aim of identifying factors that explain such differences.

To implement policies aiming at increasing cycle use, local authorities may use several types of tools. Pucher et al. (2010) identify four broad categories: (i) cycling infrastructure; (ii) bicycle parking and destination services (such as showers at work, rapid repair services, etc.); (iii) coordination between cycling and public transport; and (iv) programs and legal initiatives to promote cycling. Among these tools, the most commonly featuring in cycling policies are cycling infrastructure, services and parking (Louvet and Kaufmann 2008). Local governments tend to concentrate on these tools, which show the spatial and physical results of public action.

However, there is currently no consensus on the real effect of cycling infrastructure on increasing bicycle use. In the United States, the idea that building cycling infrastructure is key for inducing new cyclists to use it is strongly rooted in the work of researchers working on cycling (Nelson and Allen 1997; Pucher and Buehler 2008; Krizek et al. 2009). Work in various contexts has sought to verify this correlation. The creation of cycle paths appears to have had little effect on the use of bicycles for commuting in Barcelona (Braun et al. 2016) but a greater impact on the use of bicycles for shopping-related travel in German municipalities (Goetzke and Rave 2011). However, improving cycling travel times by reducing stops (traffic lights, stop signs) and detours increases the competitiveness of this mode of travel compared to cars (Rietveld and Daniel 2004). While the relationship between the development of cycling infrastructure and growth in bicycle use is still debated, infrastructure policy nevertheless remains an important instrument for supporting increases in bicycle use. In the so-called model countries, such as Germany, the Netherlands or Denmark, this policy, which began in the 1970s, is said to have supported an increase in trips taken by bicycle mainly by making them more practical, safer and more comfortable (Maddox 2001; Oosterhuis 2016). Parking is also an important measure to limit the fear of theft, which is an obstacle to buying and "getting on bikes", that is, beginning to use the bicycle as a means of transport (6-t Bureau de recherche 2020). Several types of parking can be identified: home parking, work/school parking, public parking and bicycle parking near stations (the "*bike and ride*"). The ability to park a bike at home and at work increases the chances of using cycling for daily travel (Buehler 2012).

Other incentives seem necessary to support cycling awareness, notably in communication campaigns (Lanzendorf and Busch-Geertsema 2014). But some authors argue that a policy of incentives to change mobility behavior is insufficient, and to be effective must be coupled with a policy restricting the use of cars. This entails using both "*push*" tools, instruments of constraint to discourage car use (e.g. increasing parking charges or fuel taxes), and "*pull*" tools, incentives to use alternative modes (e.g. reducing public transport fares, carpool lanes, support for bicycle purchases) (Pucher et al. 2010; Wang 2018).

9.3. Hamburg: cycling planning to support the development of practices

Though Hamburg's technicians claim to have been Copenhagen's "model" of a cycling city in the first half of the 20th century (Briese 1993), today its urban government takes the Danish capital as a reference. The city of Hamburg was partly destroyed during the Second World War: the general development plan of 1950 stressed the need to see this destruction as an opportunity to significantly improve the road network and increase parking and storage spaces for motor vehicles (Bardua and Kähler 2012). In this perspective, bicycles had to be moved away from the road to make traffic flow more smoothly and cyclists were therefore restricted to the sidewalk, on narrow strips alongside pedestrians. Although cyclists became a minority in urban traffic, cycling did not disappear completely from the city. A branch of the national association for the promotion of utilitarian cycling was also founded in Hamburg in the eighties, with the primary objective of reviving city dwellers' desire to get on their bikes by organizing tours of the city. On the political side, the priority was the development of the metropolitan public transport network. It was not until the end of the 1990s that cycling found a place on the political agenda, because of the first coalition between the Social-Democratic Party (SPD) and the Greens.

9.3.1. *Integrating cycling into the urban strategy of the sustainable city: the carrot-without-the-stick approach*

In 1998, the city drew up the first plan for *Velorouten*[1], a network of structuring cycle routes designed to connect the city's residential areas, employment areas and important places. This plan called for the construction of 280 km of cycling infrastructure; although by 2016, the launch date of the Alliance for Cycling which marked a turning point in Hamburg's cycling policy, only 80 km of the network had actually been built. While the 1998 plan resulted in few concrete achievements, it outlined the cycling strategy that was implemented over the next 20 years. It particularly emphasized the political and environmental significance of this mode of travel in Hamburg, as the entry of the Green Party into urban government put cycling on the political agenda. The different strategies for cycling that followed between 2008 and 2016 also coincided with the presence of the Green Party in the city Senate, which promoted the cycling policy in the coalitions in which it participated (Figure 9.1). This initial cycle route plan emerged 4 years before the first national plan for cycling in 2002. Although the federal government does not intervene in urban planning, it provides broad guidelines and finances the construction of cycling infrastructure in cities.

From 2007, increasing bicycle use became strongly associated with strategies to combat climate change. In 2008, the Senate promulgated a cycling action plan (*Radverkehrsstrategie 2008*) in the wake of the climate action plan (*Hamburger Klimaschutzkonzept 2007–2012*) adopted the previous year. The climate action plan was renewed in 2013 and again in 2019, building on the achievements of previous plans. Developing cycling as a mode of travel is an action point for the city-state's strategy to protect the climate and reduce CO_2 emissions by half by 2030, and by 80% by 2050. A quantified CO_2 emission reduction target of 2 tons by 2020 and 9 tons by 2050 has been set to guide public action and civil society. Mobility is one of the 14 areas of action of this plan, which also covers urban development, energy, buildings and revegetation, with a view to integrating environmental issues across public policies.

---

1 The *Velorouten* imagined in the 1990s in Hamburg correspond to what are now called cycle highways in France, that is to say, routes of continuous, large-capacity and secure cycling infrastructure.

186 Urban Mobility Systems in the World

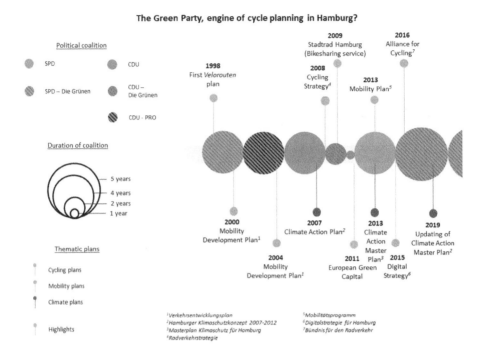

Figure 9.1. *The presence of die Grünen (the Green Party) in municipal coalitions has spurred successive strategies for the development of cycling (Eskenazi 2022). For a color version of this figure, see www.iste.co.uk/lesteven/urban.zip*

The 2007 climate action plan was the first city-state plan to really specify a strategy with quantified objectives and detailed means of action. It proposes four measures for cycling: the development of cycling infrastructure, particularly the *Velorouten*; bicycle parking; better integration of cycling into the public transport system; and improved road safety. The plan prioritizes constructing cycling infrastructure in high traffic areas, as well as in areas that attract workers and students, to support the practices of regular cyclists.

The objective of the climate plan, reaffirmed in the following year's cycling plan, is to increase the modal share of cycling from 12% in 2008 to 18% in 2015. The policy enacted by the Hamburg Senate aims to increase the supply of cycling infrastructure, without restricting facilities for cars. While measures taken to increase cycling is meant to lead to modal shift away from cars, particularly over distances of less than 5 km, they are not accompanied by measures restricting the use of cars. These plans highlight a political desire not to constrain car use, a desire that continued with the change of Senate majority in 2012. In fact, the *Climate Masterplan* of 2013 envisaged "equitable and effective parking management with priority for low-emission vehicles", but it did not provide recommendations for a reduction in the supply of parking, and above all specified that there would be no increase in pricing. Its 2019 update did not contain any restrictive measures on car use, favoring measures to encourage and optimize other modes of travel. From 1998 to 2016, the policy of increasing bicycle use in Hamburg was thus constructed as an alternative to the car, as part of an overall strategy to reduce pollutant emissions. However, the measures it contained were mainly aimed at increasing cycling infrastructure and services dedicated to cycling; few measures were introduced to constrain car use, or reduce the space dedicated to cars.

9.3.2. *Cycling infrastructure at the heart of cycling strategy*

9.3.2.1. *The Alliance for Cycling: the network of cycle routes unifying public action*

Cycling policy in Hamburg has therefore been focused since 1998 on developing cycling infrastructure, for travel and parking. The network of cycle routes was continued from the first plan of 1998 until the Alliance for Cycling (*Bundnis für Radverkehr*) launched by the Hamburg Senate in 2016. This alliance, which brings together the administrations of the city-state, its boroughs and the association Allgemeiner Deutscher Fahrrad-Club[2] (ADFC), aims to develop cycling infrastructure in order to make Hamburg a cycling city (*"Hamburg wird Fahrradstadt"*). The network of cycle routes is at the heart of the project and is the means to unify the various actors involved in implementing the cycling policy. Of the 280 km of the network initially planned in 1998, 80 km had been completed when the alliance was launched, and 50 km of new facilities were to be built each year, for the network to be complete in 2020. While this goal was ambitious, implementing it was more complex. Of the seven boroughs of the city, few already had cycling mission officers; the others had to recruit in 2016, and consequently launch studies. The construction of cycling infrastructure then confronted a lack of manpower, whether road engineers or construction companies. As part of the alliance, the city's services are supervising the implementation of the *Velorouten*

---

2 The *Allgemeiner Deutscher Fahrrad-Club* is a national association created in Bremen in 1979 to defend the interests of German cyclists. Today, it has about 400 local branches in local authorities (cities and boroughs). The ADFC-Hamburg was founded in 1981. Its activities were initially aimed at non-cyclists to encourage them to cycle in the city, through organizing bike rides in Hamburg. The association gradually turned toward lobbying and support for public policies, which are its main activities today. It has local representatives in the seven boroughs of the city-state.

plan, setting up quarterly meetings with the cycling mission officers of the boroughs, and interactive mapping to locate the works in real time in order to coordinate activity between boroughs. In fact, the simultaneous launch of several parts of the network have led to a shortage of construction companies and have delayed the construction of cycling infrastructure. In 2016, 3.3 km of facilities had been built, and 7.24 km in 2017 (Lau 2018), far from the 50 km originally planned. Priority was also given to the *Velorouten* over other cycling infrastructure for maintenance and the cleaning of the paths in autumn and winter.

9.3.2.2. *Apart from cycle routes, complex implementation of new cycling infrastructure*

While the network of cycle routes is supported by all the actors and encounters few political blocks, this is not the case for the cycling infrastructure projects supported by the boroughs. The latter have authority to plan local road developments: they manage 68% of the roads in the territory. The technical services of the boroughs can therefore set up local master plans, and propose new cycling infrastructure on off-highway routes: these are mainly cycle lanes, cycle paths, "cycle roads" or two-way cycling routes (Figure 9.2). However, implementing these secondary projects faces several obstacles, first and foremost that of funding. The city, through its Department of Economy, Transport and Innovation (*Behörde für Wirtschaft, Verkehr und Innovation* – BWVI)[3] , finances the road works. Most of the budget allocated to cycling in the Alliance for Cycling goes toward the construction of the *Velorouten*. Each year, the boroughs draw up a list of the projects they wish to implement and make a budget request to the central administration, which can then be supplemented for major projects.

Figure 9.2. *Three types of infrastructure in Hamburg: separate pedestrian and cycle paths, cycling lanes and* Velorouten *(Eskenazi 2018, 2020). For a color version of this figure, see www.iste.co.uk/lesteven/urban.zip*

---

3 After the 2020 municipal elections, the BWVI was divided into several administrations, and the *Behörde für Verkehr und Mobilität* (Department for Transport and Mobility – BVM) is in charge of transport and distribution of funding.

Local projects, excluding cycle routes, are brought to the borough councils to be approved. Each new road project goes through a complex decision-making process, and the project must be submitted for approval to all stakeholders involved in its implementation: citizens, associations, but also other departments of the boroughs and the city like the police, the units in charge of green spaces, historical monuments and so on, depending on the context in which the infrastructure is to be built. Local projects must then be approved by the borough councils. They then face local political trade-offs that are not always favorable to them. The street is a limited, bounded space, which already includes several elements: sidewalks, roadways, bus lanes, parking lots, trees, houses and so on. The creation of cycling infrastructure leads to a rebalancing of the space to the disadvantage of other elements. Any new cycle project therefore requires trade-offs that show the priorities of the actors in power. Though the cycling strategy is particularly supported by the Greens at the level of the city-state, in the boroughs, Green elected officials prefer the revegetation of public space. The issue of on-street parking is also a source of opposition for residents of neighborhoods who want to keep their parking spaces, and consequently by certain elected representatives who tend to defend positions supported by the residents and local interest groups whose support can help their reelection (Nay 2003). Public transport providers may also be a force of opposition to the creation of 30 km/h zones, complaining about decreasing the speed of their services.

The creation of new cycling infrastructure is therefore complicated and slowed down by several types of interconnected blocks: a lack of road space that leads to political trade-offs in favor of other interests (revegetation, car parking) and a lack of support from the elected officials of the boroughs for the cycling policy, apart from the *Velorouten* network. While cycling mission managers promote the borough's cycling policy through the construction of cycling infrastructure and parking, the heart of the policy is to be found at city-state level.

9.3.3. *Cycling services to build intermodality*

Although expanding the cycling network remains the priority, the 2008 and 2016 bike plans support the importance of services in the city's strategy. The launch of the Stadtrad self-service bicycle system in 2009 added a new instrument to the toolkit of incentives for public actors in the city-state and helped to raise the profile of its cycling policy. Launched with 1,000 bikes spread over 80 stations, the service was quickly adopted by Hamburg citizens and was gradually extended to cover a large part of the city. Today, the bicycle fleet has 3,100 classic bicycles, half as many as in Barcelona and 40% less than in Brussels or Lyon, which have a population of a similar size. Over the past 10 years, more and more Hamburg cyclists have started using cargo bikes to transport their children, shopping and other bulky items. The municipality and the operator of Stadtrad, Call A Bike (subsidiary of Deutsche Bahn, national rail operator), have clearly identified this change in practices and have been offering 20 self-service cargo bikes since 2019. Although the service highlights the city's action to promote cycling, the Stadtrad's share of cycling trips in Hamburg remains a minority. With a ratio of 2.7 trips per day per bike, its use remains lower than in other European cities such as Valencia (11.7 trips per day per bike), Barcelona (6.3 trips per day per bike) and especially Lyon (7.5 trips per day per bike) (Otero et al. 2018).

The second significant service offered by the city is parking. This takes several forms, operated by different actors. Residential parking is a problem mainly in the center of the agglomeration, where dwellings are mostly small. A solution was found in the 1980s with the construction of a *Fahrradhäuschen* (bicycle house) in the borough of Altona. With a capacity of 12 bicycles, this private parking space is financed by individuals, with the city-state covering one third of the cost. This type of parking is encouraged by the municipality and can be installed on private or public roads, in which case a special limited-term authorization must be issued by the borough. In order to benefit from a *Fahrradhäuschen*, applicants must prove that they have no other means of secure parking at their home. Today, there are about four hundred *Fahrradhäuschen* throughout the city.

Bicycle parking is a priority set out in the various bicycle strategies and climate plans. While improving parking needs to be taken into consideration when redesigning new cycle routes, the Alliance for Cycling focuses on parking at train stations (*bike and ride* (B+R)) and concentrates their objectives on this facility. Station parking is planned, built and managed by an operating company of the city-state that also looks after park and ride facilities. In 2015, the B+R development concept foresaw the construction of 28,000 places by 2025 to strengthen intermodality between cycling and public transport. Intermodality is a strong axis of Hamburg's cycling policy: cyclists can already carry their bicycles on the urban (U-Bahn) and suburban (S-Bahn) rail networks outside of rush hour. Fifty-two percent of Hamburg residents live within 2.5 km of a railway station (MiD 2017), a distance over which cycling is competitive with other modes (car, walking or bus) (Mathon and Palmier 2012). The progressive development of B+R facilities also aims to encourage modal shift toward rail transport on the outskirts of the urban area, in line with climate plans to reduce pollutant emissions. But if we look at the figures, the share of intermodal cycling + public transport trips remains low: it represents less than 1% of all trips, as it did in 2008 (mid 2017). However, it is not uncommon to find full bike parking near railway stations (Figure 9.3).

Figure 9.3. *On-street parking near Altona station, secure parking at the station (B+R) and Fahrradhäuschen in Hamburg (Eskenazi 2018). For a color version of this figure, see www.iste.co.uk/lesteven/urban.zip*

9.4. Greater Lyon: relaunching practice through policies, a missed bet?

In the second half of the twentieth century, cycling as a mode of travel almost disappeared from the streets of the ancient Gaulish capital. The transport system had been organized around public transport since the 1970s, in accordance with an infrastructure policy promoting the development of cars. Although the urban community of Lyon (today the metropolis of Lyon) attempted to create a cycling master plan in 1978, it resulted in only three cycle paths in peripheral municipalities (Baldasseroni 2019). Bicycle use fell in Lyon between 1975 and 1995, reaching less than 1% modal share in 1995, when it began to recover. But while in Hamburg, the policy mainly revolved around cycling infrastructure and intermodality, and it was self-service bikes that served as a showcase for Lyon's cycling policy.

9.4.1. *A cycling policy of plans*

In France, planning plays an important role in defining cycling policies, by updating political representations of cycling in the urban travel system, and introducing the tools that will define this policy at the national and local level.

9.4.1.1. *An important national regulatory framework*

Urban travel planning has been regulated since the 1982 Inland Transport Policy Act (LOTI), which established urban travel plans, which were made mandatory by the Act on Air and Rational Use of Energy (LAURE) in 1996. Through developing the various plans, the state recognized the autonomy of communities in terms of urban planning and transport, while encouraging them to be more proactive (Pinson 1998). In 2006, an inter-ministry coordinator for increasing the use of cycling was appointed, making public action on cycling an intersectoral matter. However, the development of a national cycling plan is quite recent: the first cycling plan was created in 2012. Although it has allowed cycling to become part of the state political agenda, it is simply repeating measures that had been enacted in previous years – such as the M12 sign that allows right turns at red lights, or anti-theft marking of bicycles – and does not provide dedicated funding for carrying out this plan.

In 2018, a second national cycling plan was unveiled, with 25 measures aimed at tripling the national modal share of cycling from 3% to 9%. This plan serves as a basis for coordinating action between the government and the various administrations. It is based on four axes outlining a cross-sectional view of cycling, which must be taken into consideration in several sectors of public action:

– infrastructure, by supporting communities through a call for projects for the elimination of gaps in cycling networks;

– safety, with more use of bicycle marking to combat theft;

– fiscal, through implementing several measures to finance cycling for commuting;

– integrating cycling into cross-sectoral policies: awareness-raising at school, physical activity, inclusion and return-to-work policies and so on.

State intervention into cycling policies is also present in the legislative apparatus, with communities obliged to include cycling infrastructure in any new development or road project, introduced by the LAURE law. This legislative provision is a particularly important tool for associations, which can thus rely on the law to oblige local authorities to abide by it. In 2010, the construction of bicycle parking spaces was in turn made compulsory for any new housing or office construction by the Grenelle 2 Law. First through legislation, then more recently through planning, the state therefore provides a framework of intervention for local authorities to implement cycling policies at several levels.

9.4.1.2. *Multiplication of plans at the local level*

In 2005, the launch of the Vélo'v self-service bicycle system drew attention to the cycling policy of the metropolis of Lyon and relegitimized cycling's place in the city (Guidez 2007). Though it was a sign of the importance of cycling in Greater Lyon's political agenda, it had begun in 1997 with the inclusion in the urban travel plan (PDU) of the objectives of developing the use of bicycles and cycling infrastructure. Cycling policy in Greater Lyon is a policy of plans: between 1997 and 2019, eight sectoral plans defined directions, objectives and tools for mobility (PDU), three of which focus on active mobility (Soft Mode Plans, Action Plan for

Active Mobility) with a focus on cycling (Figure 9.4). In Hamburg, cycling plans have stronger links to cross-sectoral climate action plans, or with a very infrastructure-focused approach (the Alliance for Cycling). Conversely, in Greater Lyon, planning for mobility and cycling remains a sectoral policy, although it incorporates climate objectives.

Figure 9.4. *Chronology of plans integrating cycling in Greater Lyon (Eskenazi 2022). For a color version of this figure, see www.iste.co.uk/lesteven/urban.zip*

Urban transport plans must help bring coherence to local political action and allow a more overall approach to mobility planning (Pinson 1998). Increasing cycling use is part of a vision of the "short-distance city", and a policy of modal shift from cars to active modes and public transport, which has been supported and reaffirmed by successive spatial management plans. These plans convey a vision of cycling restricted to short distances, to local areas (inter-neighborhood links and local service in the PDU of 2005), and to sharing roads. The issue of increasing bicycle use appears to be mainly linked to the supply of dedicated facilities and bicycle services, as well as to restricting the place of cars in the city through the supply of parking, aiming at changing user behavior. It therefore differs from

Hamburg's cycling policy by integrating tools to restrict car use, without however implementing any drastic policies in this regard.

9.4.2. *Infrastructure and services as the pillars of public cycling action*

Sectoral mobility plans define objectives to be achieved in terms of bicycle use and cycling infrastructure to be built over the duration of the plan. The Soft Modes Plan of 2009 provides for the construction of 200 km of additional cycling infrastructure before 2014, and 600 km before 2020, as well as a modal share target of 5% by 2014 and 7.5% by 2020. The 2015 household travel survey showed the limited impact of cycling policy on use. Although the 600 km of cycle lines have been completed – there are now more than 1000 km, regardless of the quality of the infrastructure – the modal share has stagnated at 2%, the same as in 2006.

9.4.2.1. *A development policy carried out at several levels*

The first strategic plans for cycling did not offer a coherent vision of constructing a cycling network in the territory. Structuring axes have been identified since 1996 in the city of Lyon (Baldasseroni 2019), and the Soft Modes Plan of 2009 clearly distinguishes two levels of cycle routes: a structuring network which must provide inter-municipal links, and a secondary cycle network for fine-grained service over the territory and as a feeder for public transport. The dedicated facilities are not the same for these two networks. On-road and separate facilities (cycle lanes, bus lanes and cycle lanes) are preferred for the structuring network, while mixed facilities are particularly preferred in the 30 km/h zones for the secondary network.

Figure 9.5. *Three types of cycling infrastructure in Greater Lyon: on-road strip, cycle + bus lane and two-way cycle path (Eskenazi 2019, 2020). For a color version of this figure, see www.iste.co.uk/lesteven/urban.zip*

But the realization of the network came up against the inertia of some of Greater Lyon's mayors. Although since the MAPTAM[4] law of 2014, the metropolis has jurisdiction over the entire territory, in fact the technical services do not build new cycling infrastructure without the agreement of the municipalities concerned. This includes both roading development and the creation of bicycle parking on public roads. While some municipalities and districts are driving forces in this area, others, especially those in the wider periphery, are not interested in or even resistant to the development of cycling infrastructures on their territory. This dichotomy is reflected in the cycling network, with facilities concentrated in the center and east of the metropolis, and crucially lacking in the north and west. If these areas are not seeking cycling infrastructure, it is mainly due to the lack of social demand in their territory. Here again, elected officials reflect the needs expressed by the inhabitants (Nay 2003); and when groups of cyclists come together in a municipality and express the need for infrastructure, the town halls will convey – more or less enthusiastically – this request to the metropolis. The association La Ville à Vélo, created in 1994 in Lyon, has branches in 17 communes and nine districts of Greater Lyon, which organize both local advocacy actions for cycling infrastructure, and also at metropolitan level for large-scale projects such as the redevelopment of the Part-Dieu station[5].

This "horizontality" of metropolitan public action for cycling reveals different views of cycling among local elected officials, and the metropolis' difficulties in uniting all actors around a common project. Despite an increase in the powers of the metropolis as the organizing authority for mobility, local elected representatives remain key players in cycling policy, and one of the main obstacles to its implementation. Developing the cycling network, which is the backbone of the cycling policy, therefore faces dynamics in levels of public action that do not always manage to move forward together. Because it affects roads, and therefore parking and police powers that were historically devolved to municipal level, the cycling policy has not become the subject of a metropolitan project that would rally all the actors behind it, as is the case for urban public transport. The election of the party Europe Ecology – The Greens to lead the metropolis in 2020 will potentially change this dynamic: the political project for cycling aims to build a cycling express network, similar to that of Hamburg, throughout the metropolis.

---

4 Modernization of Territorial Public Action and Affirmation of Metropolises Law of 2014.

5 During information meetings on the Part-Dieu station redevelopment project in 2017, the association La Ville à Vélo organized a welcome for political actors to remind them of the importance of giving more space to train-bicycle intermodality in the project, in particular by increasing the number of bicycle parking spaces.

9.4.2.2. Cycling and public transport: a difficult intermodality to build

While infrastructure remains the main instrument of cycling policies, the 2017 Urban Mobility Plan (UMP) signaled a new approach to public action on cycling, with a range of tools oriented toward services and knowledge of cycling practices. Previous plans already included a service dimension with the development of Vélo'v, the flagship instrument of Lyon's cycling policy, and the integration of bicycle parking into the urban transport network's park and ride facilities. But the 2017 UMP emphasizes the service dimension of the policy, aiming at shifting mobility behaviors. The Vélo'v brand remains an important instrument of Lyon's cycling policy: the service has been expanded to offer long-term rental of electrically assisted bicycles (Myvélo'v), free bicycles for low-income young people (Freevélo'v) and tricycles (Benur vélo'v).

Apart from services facilitating access to bicycles, Lyon's cycling policy includes the development of intermodality, which is mainly based on developing *"bike and rides"* with the creation of park-and-rides dedicated to cycling. Five hundred eighty-eight bicycle parking spaces are available free of charge in seven park and ride facilities located near the stations of Lyon's public transport network (TCL), while there are 21 car park and ride locations. In Greater Lyon, the Syndicat Mixte des Transports Lyonnais (SYTRAL) is the authority in charge of organizing public transport, while Greater Lyon is the authority that organizes mobility for other modes of travel.[6] Convergence between a public transport policy and a policy to encourage changes in behavior in favor of sustainable mobility seems natural in principle, but comes up against different views of the modes of transport among the actors in charge of them. Thus, while intermodality is highlighted in the plans, bicycles are still prohibited on public transport, with the exception of Line C outside rush hour. This route connects the center of Lyon to the Croix-Rousse hill, which has a steep elevation. The trains are certainly not suitable to accommodate bicycles; however, an experiment carried out since July 2020 on the Saint-Just funicular railway, which runs up the hill of Fourvières, authorizes bicycles to be carried in an adapted prototype, and signals the beginning of convergence between public transport and mobility policies.

---

6 Since 1 January 2022, SYTRAL has become the organizing authority for mobility in the territories of Lyon (AOMTL), a local public authority covering the Lyon metropolitan area, the Auvergne-Rhone-Alpes region, the Villefranche-Beaujolais-Saone and West Rhodanien communities, and all the communities of the Rhône municipalities. It retains its functions of organising regular and on-demand transport, in addition to coordination, multimodal information and overall planning of mobility in its enlarged territory.

9.4.2.3. *Understanding practices to better guide policy*

The metropolis conducts household surveys to gain knowledge of mobility practices in the territory, as well as bicycle counts (manual and automatic) on certain thoroughfares to observe changes in bicycle traffic, mobility behaviors and the usage of cycling infrastructure. These counts make it possible to guide cycling policy and the construction of infrastructure by identifying its structuring axes. They also allow technical services to justify this policy and the development of facilities, by showing evidence of increases in cycle traffic on the new routes developed (Adam 2018). They also help to emphasize the role of the Vélo'v service in cycling policy, since these counts made it possible to estimate Vélo'v's share of cycling traffic at 40% in 2017. While self-service bike systems sometimes attract criticism for their cost and levels of use, Vélo'v appears to be a success for Lyon's policy. The counts are also used by cycling associations to demand new infrastructure on routes identified as important and bring these demands before the municipalities and the metropolis.

Knowledge about practices leads to adaptation of cycling policy tools, in particular financial tools. Purchase support for electric bikes was first offered by Greater Lyon in 2012 and was extended to cargo bikes and folding bikes, which are increasingly common on the streets of the metropolis, despite their high cost. However, the metropolis offers no assistance for standard bicycles, while only 59% of Greater Lyon households owned at least one bicycle in 2015[7]. Self-service bikes can compensate for this lack but are located mainly in the center of Greater Lyon, creating spatial inequality of access to the service, especially for inhabitants of working-class neighborhoods who have little access to the second-hand market and remain very vulnerable to theft (Varin 2018). The cycling policies of Greater Lyon, whether they relate to infrastructure and services, therefore tend to impact only part of the population, those who live in the center of the agglomeration. To have lasting effects of increasing and perpetuating the practice of cycling, policies implemented to develop cycling will have to broaden their targets – geographically and socially.

9.5. Conclusion

We can see a standardization of cycling policies in the two metropolises, which mainly focus on infrastructure, parking and services. Some tools, such as self-service bicycles or express bike networks, tend to become widespread according to models of "good practice" replicated from city to city. However, the way in which these tools are used in cycling policies depends on several factors. On the one hand, the presence of more or less widespread cycling practices in the territory defines

---

7 Figures taken from our processing of the 2015 household travel survey.

objectives and therefore different ways of doing politics. In Hamburg, where the policy was launched when utilitarian cycling practices were already well established, the network of *Velorouten*, which served from the outset as a directing thread for public action, had to support and facilitate the development of practices in order to become a *"Fahrradstadt"*, a cycling city. The objective is still far from achieved: though we have observed an increase in the modal share of cycling in the latest surveys, this mode of transport is still a minority in city planning and mobility practices. In Greater Lyon, where utilitarian cycling had virtually disappeared in the 1990s, the policy relied on a combination of reference infrastructure (the quays of the Rhône, the soft modes tunnel) and the Vélo'v service to communicate a cycling "boom" linked to the policy.

On the other hand, two traditions of planning emerge. In Hamburg, the city-state has integrated bicycle planning into environmental protection but has also made it an object of targeted planning, unlike other modes of travel. Despite the Mobility Plan of 2013, it is difficult for the actors involved to have an overall vision of the city's mobility strategy (Wang 2018). Although cycle planning is built around a unifying project, it appears to be unrelated to other mobility policies, particularly those on car use. In addition, aside from the network of cycle routes that brings all the players together, the creation of cycling infrastructure faces certain local barriers, arising from residents, elected officials or other technical services in the boroughs. Conversely, the planning of cycling in Greater Lyon is broken down into a multitude of plans that respond to each other, and which gradually specify actions to be put in place to develop cycling, with a diversity of tools among the plans. However, the right of municipalities to oversee developments in their territory hampers the creation of a coherent cycling network at metropolitan scale and has resulted in a fragmented network concentrated on the center and the east.

In fact, the goals for cycling modal share set by the plans made by the two metropolises are never achieved: even if bicycle use is increasing, it remains below the expectations of public actors, even though the objectives for building cycling infrastructure seem to be reached. This paradox can be explained by a mainly technical approach to cycling policies that fails to grasp the complexity of mobility practices, and in particular their social embeddedness which goes beyond the mere materiality of the bicycle. Focusing on cycling, minimizing its non-movement aspects (repair, socializing, parking at home and at work, etc.) restricts the scope of the policies carried out. Cycling policy must therefore be carried out in a cross-sectional manner with housing, work, health and so on, to integrate this mode of travel into all policies affecting daily life and urban planning.

9.6. References

6-t Bureau de recherche (2020). Le développement du vélo et de la trottinette dans les grandes villes françaises : une tendance confrontée au stationnement dans l'espace public. Final report, 6-t Bureau de recherche.

Adam, M. (2018). Nette hausse du trafic cyclable dans la Métropole de Lyon en 2017. *CyclOPs* [Online]. Available at: https://cyclops.hypotheses.org/294 [Accessed 4 October 2020].

Baldasseroni, L. (2019). Sur la piste du vélo : des infrastructures encore marginales. *TI&M*, 514, 51–53.

Bardua, S. and Kähler, G. (2012). *Die Stadt Und Das Auto: Wie Der Verkehr Hamburg Veränderte*. Dölling und Galitz Verlag, Hamburg.

Braun, L.M., Rodriguez, D.A., Cole-Hunter, T., Ambros, A., Donaire-Gonzalez, D., Jerrett, M., Mendez, M.A., Nieuwenhuijsen, M.J., de Nazelle, A. (2016). Short-term planning and policy interventions to promote cycling in urban centers: Findings from a commute mode choice analysis in Barcelona, Spain. *Transportation Research Part A: Policy and Practice*, 89, 164–183.

Briese, V. (1993). Separating bicycle traffic. Towards a history of bikeways in Germany up through 1940. Research thesis, Kassel Gesamthochschule.

Buehler, R. and Pucher, J. (2022). Cycling through the COVID-19 pandemic to a more sustainable transport future: Evidence from case studies of 14 large bicycle-friendly cities in Europe and North America. *Sustainability*, 14(12), 7293.

Buehler, R., Pucher, J., Gerike, R., Götschi, T. (2017). Reducing car dependence in the heart of Europe: Lessons from Germany, Austria, and Switzerland. *Transport Reviews*, 37(1), 4–28.

Buehler, R. (2012). Determinants of bicycle commuting in the Washington, DC region: The role of bicycle parking, cyclist showers, and free car parking at work. *Transportation Research Part D: Transport and Environment*, 17(7), 525–531.

Carstensen, T.A. and Ebert, A.-K. (2012). Cycling cultures in Northern Europe: From golden age to renaissance. *Cycling and Sustainability*, 1, 23–58.

Eskenazi, M. (2022). Voir, faire et vivre la ville pour le vélo. Pratiques du vélo et politiques de mobilité dans deux métropoles européennes. PhD thesis, Université Paris-Est, Marne-la-Vallée.

Fischer, J. and Winters, M. (2021). COVID-19 street reallocation in mid-sized Canadian cities: Socio-spatial equity patterns. *Canadian Journal of Public Health*, 112(3), 376–390.

Goetzke, F. and Rave, T. (2011). Bicycle use in Germany: Explaining differences between municipalities with social network effects. *Urban Studies*, 48(2), 427–437.

Guidez, J.-M. (2007). Les chiffres de... 2007 : le tournant du vélo ? *Transports urbains*, 111(2), 14–15.

Héran, F. (2014). *Le retour de la bicyclette. Une histoire des déplacements urbains en Europe de 1817 à 2050*. La Découverte, Paris.

Koglin, T. (2013). Vélomobility – A critical analysis of planning and space. PhD thesis, Lund University.

Krizek, K., Forsyth, A., Baum, L. (2009). Walking and cycling literature review. Final report, Department of Transport and Planning, Victoria.

Lanzendorf, M. and Busch-Geertsema, A. (2014). The cycling boom in German cities: Empirical evidence for successful cycling campaigns. *Transport Policy*, 36, 26–33.

Lau, D. (2018). Sind wir auf einem guten weg? *RadCity*, Hamburg, 6–9.

Louvet, N. and Kaufmann, V. (2008). Le vélo en couronne dense : aspirations, usages et potentialités de développement. Final report, Club des Villes Cyclables, Paris.

Mathon, S. and Palmier, P. (2012). Vélo et politique globale de mobilité durable. Comment estimer le potentiel cyclable d'un territoire ? Une application sur l'agglomération lilloise, Research project, MEDTT/CETE Nord Picardie.

Nay, O. (2003). La politique des bons offices : l'élu, l'action publique et le territoire. In *La politisation*, Lagoroye, J. (ed.). Belin, Paris.

Nelson, A.C. and Allen, D. (1997). If you build them, commuters will use them: Association between bicycle facilities and bicycle commuting. *Transportation Research Record*, 1578(1), 79–83.

Oosterhuis, H. (2016). Cycling, modernity and national culture. *Social History*, 41(3), 233–248.

Otero, I., Nieuwenhuijsen, M.J., Rojas-Rueda, D. (2018). Health impacts of bike sharing systems in Europe. *Environment International*, 115, 387–394.

Pinson, G. (1998). Politiques de déplacements urbains : mobilisations territoriales et recherche de cohérence dans l'action publique urbaine. *Politiques et management public*, 16(4), 119–150.

Pucher, J. and Buehler, R. (2008). Making cycling irresistible: Lessons from the Netherlands, Denmark and Germany. *Transport Reviews*, 28(4), 495–528.

Pucher, J., Dill, J., Handy, S. (2010). Infrastructure, programs, and policies to increase bicycling: An international review. *Preventive Medicine*, 50, S106–S125.

Pucher, J., Garrard, J., Greaves, S. (2011). Cycling down under: A comparative analysis of bicycling trends and policies in Sydney and Melbourne. *Journal of Transport Geography*, 19(2), 332–345.

Rietveld, P. and Daniel, V. (2004). Determinants of bicycle use: Do municipal policies matter? *Transportation Research Part A: Policy and Practice*, 38(7), 531–550.

Tirachini, A. and Cats, O. (2020). COVID-19 and public transportation: Current assessment, prospects, and research needs. *Journal of Public Transportation*, 22(1), 1.

Varin, V. (2018). Le vélo dans les quartiers d'habitat social en périphérie. De nouveaux modes de gouvernance pour une mobilité inclusive. Research paper, ENPC, Paris.

Wang, L. (2018). Barriers to implementing pro-cycling policies: A case study of Hamburg. *Sustainability*, 10(11), 4196.

PART 4

Circulation of Urban Mobility Analysis Tools and Public Policy Models

10

Categorical Pitfalls for Analyzing Urban Mobility

Hadrien COMMENGES[1] and Florent LE NÉCHET[2]
[1] *UMR Géographie-cités, Université Paris 1 Panthéon-Sorbonne, Paris-Aubervilliers, France*
[2] *Gustave Eiffel University, École des Ponts, LVMT, Marne-la-Vallée, France*

10.1. Introduction

Urban mobility is linked to multiple issues, including economic, ecological and social inequalities, and the choice of methods of counting and of indicators cannot be neutral (Desrosières 2016). The formation of geographical scales of action and categories of analysis of urban mobility speaks to the issues and stakes that local actors face in regard to urban mobility (Gallez 2015). In recent decades, in the field of geography and urban planning, we can observe on the one hand a convergence toward working at the level of functional areas, that is, a delineation of cities based on commuting patterns (Bretagnolle 2015), and on the other hand, working with a tripartite modal breakdown (active modes – walking, cycling – using cars, public transport), with a wide variety of sectoral and/or single-mode monographic analyses. However, this approach has progressively become outdated, both because of the diversification of the use of modes of transport in world cities and the emergence of geographical entities that go beyond functional areas, the "polycentric mega-regions" (Hall and Pain 2006).

These reconfigurations have hindered the analysis of daily mobility, whether this means adopting a perspective of comparison between cities, or studying the local

Urban Mobility Systems in the World,
coordinated by Gaëlle LESTEVEN. © ISTE Ltd 2023.

dynamics of a given city, according to seemingly fully standardized methods. Conversely, we suggest in this chapter a number of approaches for tackling, in a localized way, urban mobility in all its diversity. Reflection on the geographical scale and on categories of mobility seems important, given the emerging desire to automate the calculation of an ever-increasing number of indicators with regard to urban mobility, in real time/with higher frequency (Miller and Goodchild 2015), at the risk of losing sight of the main orders of magnitude and metrics of urban mobility, and local issues of public action. Desrosières (2012, p. 267) introduced an important distinction between "quantifying" and "measuring". Quantifying means "expressing and bringing into existence in numerical form something which was previously expressed in words rather than numbers". On the other hand, measuring "implies that something already exists in a measurable form according to a realistic metrology, such as a physical size", which is rarely the case in social sciences. Quantification therefore entails a double task: *agreement*, that is, agreeing on the definition of conceptual objects; then *measuring* the objects thus defined, expressing them in numerical form. We will focus here on the first task, that of agreement.

The definition of objects and categories for measuring mobility practices is driven by two opposing forces: on the one hand, the creation of new categories reflecting the creation of new vehicles and services (bike and car self-service, car sharing); on the other hand, the stability of the categories, a necessary condition for studying the evolution of practices. It is necessary to define categories in order to measure and to define stable categories in order to compare measures over time. This question is particularly sensitive when the measures apply to comparison, over space or time:

– if the categories remain too stable, new practices are incorrectly attributed to residual categories;

– if the categories change too much, changes cannot be measured since the context of their measurement changes at the same time;

– if the categories are too blurred in definition, the changes observed say much more about the way categories are constructed than about the practices they encapsulate;

– if the categories are too strongly distinct, there is a great risk of missing out on changes in practices masked by abusive equivalence.

The objective of this chapter is to summarize the issues and problems in forming categories of analysis and action in the field of daily mobility. This reflection on categories is necessary in any analysis of mobility at city level and is even more necessary when comparing data between cities. In this chapter, we successively address the diversity of mobility data, the question of defining urban boundaries, the question of categories of mobility analysis and finally the connections between tools for data collection, analysis and decision-making. We detail below a few methodological pitfalls that we think are important to focus on, when beginning a monograph or an interurban comparison of mobility practices.

10.2. Which type of data for analyzing urban mobility?

A wide variety of actors produce, organize, and analyze urban mobility data for decision support, research, marketing and so on. Common factors in all of these datasets are that they cover only a portion of actual movements, their limited temporal and spatial precision, and have a finite temporal coverage. There is a very wide variety of datasets on mobility (Figure 10.1): institutional data, such as censuses and mobility surveys; disaggregated data from telecommunications or transport operators in particular; and data aggregated by institutions, private organizations and research collectives. Let us note that we are focusing on data for mobility demand and not for supply (transport infrastructure, characteristics of services, etc.).

10.2.1. *Typology of mobility data*

As it is difficult to create an exhaustive inventory of methods for quantifying daily mobility, we propose a set of criteria for definition. In this chapter, we deal with public censuses and surveys, defined by the following set of criteria:

– the survey is explicitly (but not necessarily exclusively) set up to capture daily mobility practices;

– one or more public institutions are wholly or partially responsible for its implementation;

– it is intended to be systematized, that is, reused several times, on different dates and/or in different spaces.

Criterion (1) excludes surveys which produce data that can be used for secondary purposes dealing with daily mobility, but which have nothing to do with it, such as call detail record (CDR) from mobile phones, except where such data are integrated through a dedicated mechanism. Criterion (2) excludes surveys that explicitly aim to quantify mobility practices but for purely private purposes. This is the case, for example, for surveys carried out by major advertisers and media agencies (Delage 2012). Criterion (3) excludes experimental surveys set up as part of research projects or occasional studies.

Once these criteria have been established, the next step is to establish a typology of these surveys. The typology proposed here (Figure 10.1) uses certain elements from that of the SETRA[1] manual (2010), but is more generic.

Any quantification mechanism that does not require interaction between the counter and the thing being counted is referred to as counting. Any mechanism involving verbal interaction between counter and counted is an enquiry, whether conducted face-to-face, over the telephone, or on a delayed basis via the Internet or mail.

Among quantification mechanisms, the oldest and most widespread today is a one-off: a quantification of the flow passing a given point. As soon as a mechanism identifies an individual moving past at least two time-stamped locations, it produces trajectories.

Among surveys, two types of mechanisms are distinguished: home–work commutes as measured by the population census and origin-destination surveys (also named "O-D surveys"). The census produces a pair of places which are supposed to be connected by movements, but nothing is known about the temporality of these movements (frequency, duration, time of day). The term "O-D survey" is used here in a sense that does not exactly correspond to the terms used in recent technical manuals. Indeed, in the current terminology used by SETRA and CERTU[2]/CEREMA[3], O-D surveys refer only to surveys with an interview while mobility is taking place (cordon survey, itinerary survey), thus excluding household travel surveys, where the interview takes place in retrospect. These terms used by SETRA and CERTU/CEREMA are the result of changes in vocabulary whose trace and motivations are difficult to grasp. Indeed, until the mid-1970s, the terminology designating the different types of surveys was not fixed: "origin-destination survey", "travel survey" or "traffic survey" may refer to roadside interviews as well as home surveys. In the typology proposed here, any survey that produces origin-destination pairs, or pairs of places that are located and time-stamped, is called an O-D survey.

Among O-D surveys, the main distinguishing criterion is the location of the interaction between counter and counted. When the measurement of mobility is carried out while mobility is occurring, the interaction is called "real-time": roadside surveys (cordon surveys and surveys at break points) are an example. When the measurement of mobility is held up compared to the mobility itself, the interaction is said to be "delayed": household travel surveys are an example.

---

1 SETRA: Service d'études techniques des routes et autoroutes.
2 CERTU: Centre d'études sur les réseaux, les transports, l'urbanisme et les constructions publiques.
3 CEREMA: Centre d'études et d'expertise sur les risques, l'environnement, la mobilité et l'aménagement.

Categorical Pitfalls for Analyzing Urban Mobility   209

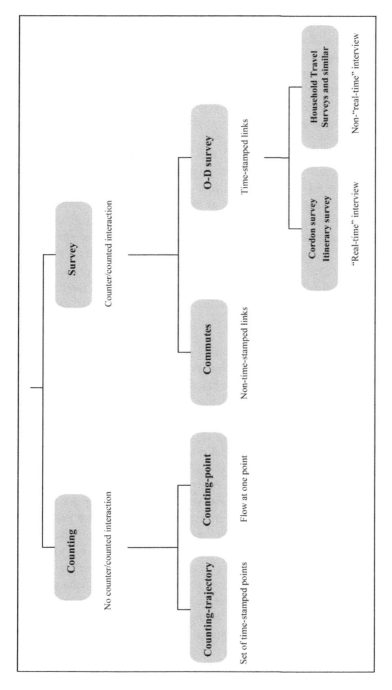

Figure 10.1. *Typology of systems for quantifying daily mobility*

Household travel surveys contain important and detailed semantic information (purpose and mode of transport), but are rarely produced (one every 10 years in large French cities, for example), have a rather small sample over a restricted perimeter (Armoogum et al. 2018) and most often – but not always – concern only residents (Belgian national survey: Cornelis et al. 2012). In addition, the sample targets adults and children over a certain age, but this threshold is variable (5 years for CERTU/CEREMA type surveys). These surveys exist in many countries and cities (Armoogum et al. 2018).

Note that while methodologies are not necessarily harmonized at the international level, or even at the national level, the two successive surveys are very similar in that they all come from the same mold: the American Household Travel Surveys were defined in the 1940s as part of the birth of American traffic engineering. The most common structure of such surveys, still used in many countries today, can be found in the American *Manual of Procedures for Home Interview Traffic Studies* of 1944. The survey is part of a larger set composed of two other elements: a model that estimates future traffic and an economic evaluation procedure that guides investment choices based on the model forecast. The three elements – survey, model and evaluation – form a *technical matrix* and are interconnected through common statistical objects (Commenges 2013).

These surveys produce cross-sectional information for an average working day, but they produce no information on intra-individual variability over the short term (routines) or the long term (changes in practice) (Hoogendoorn-Lanser et al. 2015). Some surveys, relatively rare, are created ad hoc to serve these purposes. Examples of short-term variability include an Indonesian survey (Dharmowijoyo et al. 2015), and in particular the Mobidrive survey (Schlich and Axhausen 2003). The latter, conducted in the German cities of Halle and Karlsruhe, covers each individual sampled for every day (working days and weekends) over six weeks. For long-term variation, a panel must be set up. The Puget Sound Transportation Panel Survey of the Seattle Metropolitan Area is the first American panel survey and is considered exemplary in this field. It gives an overview of the questions that household travel surveys cannot answer, in particular questions on intra-individual variations (Commenges 2015). With household travel surveys, it is possible to know if the number of trips by car has changed between two surveys; in contrast, only panel surveys allow us to understand the drivers of this evolution. For example, is there a growing number of car users or growing car use by people who already were car users? If we observe a stable number of trips by a car between two dates, we can imagine at least three scenarios: (1) the number of car users as well as their practices are stable; (2) the number of car users has increased, but they use the car less exclusively, and therefore less frequently; (3) the number of car users has decreased, but those who do use them use their car more frequently (because there is less congestion or because their lifestyles have changed). Household travel surveys are not relevant for distinguishing between these three scenarios.

10.2.2. *From local surveys to attempts at international harmonization*

While mobility surveys were first created to serve local technical engineering objectives, over the past 30 years they have been integrated into national or international comparative approaches. The work of Newman and Kenworthy (1999) certainly played a pivotal role. These authors were the first to propose a correlation, analyzed as a causal link, between urban density and energy consumption linked to mobility practices, through what is commonly called the "Newman and Kenworthy" curve. Despite numerous methodological flaws, both in the production of the curve and in its possible analysis (Raux et al. 2018), this curve became a landmark, prompting cities to question their relationship to density and compactness, at several levels, and several French-speaking authors further explored this question of the links between urban form and daily mobility (Genre-Grandpierre 2000; Pouyanne 2004; Hubert and Delisle 2010; Le Néchet 2012; Raux et al. 2018), in parallel with articles in international literature (Schwanen et al. 2003; Banister 2008; Ewing and Cervero 2010).

These studies have mostly been confined to the national level; however, over the past two decades, internationally harmonized databases have appeared. Eurostat's ex-post and even progressively ex-ante harmonization work (Urban Audit: Gourdon et al. 2019) represents the most successful attempt to compare cities at the European level. Several entities have made strong efforts – such as UITP, Eurostat, World Bank or the United Nations – to gather, organize and harmonize statistical information on urban mobility.

Apart from these institutional data, other organizations produce data through crowdsourcing platforms (the most famous example being OpenStreetMaps) or through existing private or public data aggregation initiatives such as the Geopolis database at the global level (Marius-Gnanou and Moriconi-Ebrard 2007), or the TRADEVE base at the European level (Guérois et al. 2019). Data on mobility services are available in world cities: the Shared Mobility Observatory of the École Nationale des Ponts et Chaussées (Boutueil et al. 2021).

The last two decades have seen an increase in the amount and diversity of technical data collected automatically in the transport sector (mobility operators, road managers) and elsewhere (mobile telephony, in particular). These data have the potential to reconfigure the possibilities of mobility analysis (Chrétien et al. 2018; Wang et al. 2018). However, it is important to note that automated counting data are nothing new (Baldasseroni and Charansonney 2018). Data from automated road traffic sensors (Cools et al. 2009) or ad hoc surveys carried out by transport operators or local authorities (cordon survey, origin-destination survey, etc.) date from the 1960s and 1970s, following the importation of American survey methods (Commenges 2013). This influx of technical data into the field of mobility is notable in two ways:

– because different treatments become possible with data that are more precise in time and space (Kitchin 2014) and can be used longitudinally (Järv et al. 2014), over periods of weeks or even months;

– because it produces a reconfiguration of the interaction of stakeholders concerning the production and use of urban mobility data.

The methodological challenges related to the processing of these often-called "new" data and their intersections are numerous (Armoogum et al. 2020), but these are not the focus of this chapter. Because of their non-semantic nature, that is, the absence of information about people (socio-professional category) or the trips themselves (purpose, mode), practices are gradually moving toward cross-enrichment with data from conventional surveys and from a variety of GPS or other types of data (Armoogum et al. 2020). In particular, this allows for a higher frequency of survey data, through hybridizing classic data and data from mobile sensors (Chandakas 2020). Partly and in some cases, therefore – rarely, as the operators concerned seek to maintain control of the data – second-hand data from sectors outside of transport can be integrated into an explicit chain of observation of mobility. In most cases, however, technical data are offered to local authorities for access on a fee-paying basis, such as those from Tom-Tom GPS (Nie et al. 2013) or mobile phone data from Telefonica or Orange, among others (Fen-Chong 2012; Louail et al. 2015).

It should be noted that the "Open Data" movement aims at facilitating the interoperability of data and makes it more possible to conduct rich analyses at the intersection of supply and demand data, although it mainly concerns data produced by public institutions and does not allow for the sharing of detailed data from public or private operators (Dingil et al. 2018; Kujala et al. 2018). All of these examples represent a fragmented and intentionally complex landscape (Courmont 2018) where a large amount of data are now produced on an international scale, where the data collection process is more difficult or costly and, where it is easily accessible, it can be hard to use it for comparisons because of different methods of collection, processing and aggregation between countries, regions and cities.

It is worth highlighting the variety of methodological problems that arise in processing mobility data, or even comparing them with each other. In what follows, we limit ourselves to the already vast field of so-called "classical" data, that is to say, mobility surveys, and population censuses. The questions we raise are of a more general scope, and we hope they can serve to better understand the methodological issues involved in the analysis of daily mobility.

10.3. Which objects describe mobility?

In which cities is there widespread use of cars? Which neighborhood is best for walking? It is impossible to answer such questions today due to the latent semantic complexity of this field: what is a city? What does it mean to use your car? It depends on the quantification designs and the statistical categories. If I stop during a walk to finish a phone call, my travel time inflates, when in fact I had already arrived, but early... Does it make sense to assign this time to the walking trip? If I wait for a train at a station, and I stay there for 30 minutes, modern data collection tools such as mobile phones might (but not necessarily, it depends on the algorithm used to infer movements) consider that I stopped at the station to do something. But this is not the case at all as I waited impatiently while constantly refreshing my smartphone to know when my train would arrive... All these examples show the difficulty of making events of a different nature commensurable and the difficulty of producing aggregated statistics for cities to allow for analysis and comparisons.

Here, we discuss in detail the definition of three fundamental terms in the field of urban mobility: the trip, the mode of transport and the city, the support space for urban mobility. The focus on these three terms should not cause us to lose sight of all of the issues whose definition could be debated: the purpose for travel, the household, the social group and so on.

10.3.1. *The trip*

From the 1950s to today, the main quantification designs (surveys, models, economic evaluations) have been based on the same object: the trip, defined as any movement carried out on public roads linking two places defined by the activity taking place there. The criterion for dividing the continuum of movement into a discrete series of trips is the "purpose". The latter designates much more than its name indicates: it is an *exclusive pairing between the place and the purpose* for the trip (Commenges 2013).

The instructions to investigators in the first survey conducted in the Paris region, based on American practices developed in the 1944 manual cited above, emphasize the need to combine places and purposes: "The places of origin and destination to be indicated are those where the person making the journey actually goes, such as home, office, shop, theatre, bank, school, or factory. If, because of traffic congestion, a person stops their car two or three blocks from where they want to go, the latter place should be noted and not the place where the car stopped" (Survey on the movements of people in the Paris region, Instruction to investigators, 1965). This place–purpose combination implies a strong constraint that prohibits (1) considering mobility as an activity, (2) considering multiple activities in a single place and (3) considering activity during mobility.

A new object appeared during the 1990s following work on the programs of activity issuing from *time-geography:* the loop or outing, defined as a chain of trips anchored on the home, that is, all the trips between departure from and return to the home. Indeed, it is clear that there is a problem in considering the place–purpose as an object that renders the continuum of discrete movement. Take for example the case of an individual who leaves home to go to his workplace located 10 km away, by metro, and stops at the metro exit to buy a sandwich or a newspaper before arriving at work. This would result in a 9-km metro ride for a purchase, and a 1-km walk for work. Let us take this example in the 2010 Global Transport Survey in the Paris region. We take all of the trips made in the working day (about 41 million), we choose the trips made by Parisian residents, then we select the purpose for travel as frequent purchases (daily to weekly) and finally we filter by a distance greater than 1 km. There remain 155,000 trips that, without being coding errors, are aberrations from the point of view of mobility practices. For example, there is a 20-km taxi ride from Seine-Saint-Denis to Paris for a daily purchase. In low-density areas, it is perfectly possible to travel 10 or 20 km to buy bread. On the other hand, in Paris and the inner suburbs, the massive number of bakeries accessible within a radius of 1 km makes any trip beyond this distance unlikely, a fortiori by taxi, unless this trip is part of a chain of trips that justifies it.

The division of mobility into trips based on place–purpose also poses the problem of the intrinsic incompatibility of trip and activity: in this context, a trip cannot be an activity, and an activity cannot be performed during a trip. However, it is well known that a trip, a walk for example, may constitute the activity itself

(Mokhtarian 2005; Chrétien 2019), as we know that individuals take advantage of trips to perform activities (Adoue 2015; Pajević and Shearmur 2017).

Despite the disadvantages attached to the trip as an object, this way of dividing up mobility remains predominant. There are two main reasons for this retention. First, for the transport operator, what matters is the trip. From their point of view, it is necessary to know whether a road infrastructure or a public transport service would have to support 100, 1,000, or 10,000 trips per day. Whether these trips are made by a large number of individuals who make few trips or a small number of individuals who make many trips, whether they are out-and-back trips or complex loops, these are not questions of operational importance. The second reason is linked to the first. The socio-economics of transport has built a set of mechanisms that interact with the survey, in particular a mechanism for forecasting transport demand and an economic evaluation mechanism. However, these mechanisms make up a system and also work with the trip as an object (Commenges 2013). Similarly, the place–purpose, that is to say, the exclusive pairing of place and purpose, is linked to trip modeling: it is this pairing that makes it possible to establish the link between individual mobility and the land uses that generate and attract this mobility. All of the tools involved in knowledge and public action around urban mobility are slowly changing and will probably one day be obsolete – that is to say, inoperative in their capacity to inform public action. But this is not yet the case, despite the methodological difficulties discussed in this chapter.

10.3.2. *The mode of transport*

In Europe and the United States, after several fairly quiet decades for modal diversity, the beginning of the 21st century saw an explosion in the supply of mobility, through mobility services with very dissimilar characteristics which are difficult to analyze with conventional tools. In 2000, it still seemed reasonable to consider that the field of possibilities for moving around the city included walking, bicycle, train, bus and car. Today, the situation has become more complex, with the emergence of ride-sharing, self-service electric cars, electric bicycles and free-floating fleets of bicycles or scooters. A whole section of the literature reflects these developments: shared mobility, electric mobility and so on (Frotey and Castex 2017; Huré 2019).

Before discussing these new modes, it is worth presenting two classic problems that must be faced, in particular from a perspective of comparison in time or space. The first is simply the development of modes and typologies, the implications of which have been set out above. One example, among others, is that of two wheelers. Until recently, both in the population census in France and in local or national mobility surveys, this category included all two-wheeled vehicles, whether motorized or not.

The second classic problem is that of assigning a principal mode. In the context of population censuses, individuals who are in study or employment must declare their destination municipality (for study or employment) and the mode most frequently used. This is a simple and summarized way to reduce the complexity of the modes of transport actually used.

To address the problem of changes in transport categories faced with a revolution in services (Figure 10.2), it is practical to start from common language definitions (Le Robert, French online dictionary):

– Taxi: "Motor car equipped with a meter that indicates the price of the journey".

– Bus: "Motor vehicle for public passenger transport, within cities (as opposed to a coach)".

The definition of a taxi is very partial: it refers exclusively to a certain type of vehicle, with a certain type of equipment. According to this definition, an automobile without a meter is not a taxi. The definition of a bus is both more complete and more problematic. It also refers to it as a vehicle, but with a function ("for public transport"). The addition of the notion of "city" and the relation of inclusion ("within") are of course problematic (see the next section).

Legislative and regulatory documents must include definitional elements upon which the articles of law are based. In France, this is the regulatory part of the Highway Code (Article R311-1), but similar definitions are found in other countries, resulting from the harmonization work of the UNECE World Forum for Harmonization of Vehicle Regulations (WP29). Vehicles are defined by weight, power, number of wheels, speed and so on. Thus, within the meaning of the Highway Code, a bus is a "public transport vehicle which, by its construction and layout, is assigned to the public transportation of persons and their luggage". A "public transport vehicle" is a vehicle of category M2 or M3, being a "vehicle designed and constructed for the carriage of persons, comprising, in addition to the driver's seat, more than eight seats" and a weight less than or equal to 5 tons (M2) or greater than 5 tons (M3).

These first elements highlight the limits of talking only about vehicles. How can we differentiate between a licensed taxi service and a ride-hailing service? How can we categorize the trotro (Ghana), dala dala (Tanzania), and matatu (Kenya), when all of these forms of public transport operate partly along lines, partly on demand, with vehicles of various types and sizes? These few examples clearly show the limits of considering only the nature of the vehicle. The modal categories featuring in surveys and for public action very often refer to types of vehicles and not types of use, which may hinder our understanding of mobility practices (Amar 2010).

If we are interested in the type of service rather than the type of vehicle, we have to clarify the notion of the service. The major classification used since 1945, since Colin Clark, is this three-way classification distinguishing the primary sector (direct exploitation of natural resources), the secondary sector (transformation of these resources into goods) and the tertiary sector, a residual category that encompasses everything else, that is to say, all production of services. This three-way classification is still widely used, but it has flaws, in particular the fact that it is difficult to define very clearly what a service is. Indeed, there is not a binary distinction between goods and services but rather a goods–services continuum. On the one hand, there are pure goods, for example, socks, and on the other hand pure services, for example, legal advisory services, and between the two a multitude of mixed goods or services that require the support of a good. This goods–services continuum is evolving in the direction of services: more and more goods that were pure are becoming mixed goods and then services. A car was a pure good in the 1960s, became a mixed good in the 1980s (a good whose sale is associated with after-sales services, credit sales services, etc.) and approached the nature of a service in the 2000s with the implementation of systems for monthly payments and leasing with option to purchase. This blurs the lines between the purchase of a good and payment for a rental service or car-sharing between individuals.

Over the last 10 years, mobility (urban in particular) has been affected by major changes in the context of the service economy. The movement of the functional economy into the field of urban mobility is referred to as *mobility as a service* (MaaS). This involves decoupling ownership and use, that is, replacing a vast fleet of owned vehicles with a set of mobility services. Mobile individuals cease to consume goods (vehicles), and instead consume services paid for according to use: public and/or private car-sharing systems, public and/or private bicycle-sharing systems (and other more or less heavily motorized two-wheelers) and public and/or private public transport systems. This ongoing development threatens all of the conventions established during the second half of the 20th century to describe modes of transport. Is a ride in a ride-hailing service comparable to a taxi ride? Should means of transport be aggregated according to vehicle type or by vehicle status? Indeed, there seems to be at least two ways to proceed: (1) consider that a ride on a self-service bike or scooter is comparable to a ride on a bike or scooter that is owned and (2) consider on one hand the use of both mechanized and non-motorized owned vehicles, and on the other hand these same vehicles used "as a service".

Reflecting on a typology of modes based on a series of distinguishing criteria (Figure 10.2) is a useful exercise for several reasons:

– To highlight modes that do not exist here and now but that exist elsewhere or that have existed in the past, for example, pedicabs, sedan chairs or animal-drawn buses.

– To lead to reflection on the criteria of distinction and their relative importance: for example, is positioning (sitting, standing and lying down) really important for characterizing a mode? The category "motorized two-wheelers" exists in almost all surveys at the level of the highest aggregation of modal typologies, yet it is a mechanized, motorized, individual and private mode. In the former surveys, it has been aggregated with non-motorized two-wheelers (bicycles), but we could argue it has more of an intrinsic similarity with private cars.

– To analyze cases that hide behind the aggregations and synonyms of common language. For example, it is common to talk about collective transport and public transport in an equivalent way, whereas there are four categories at the intersection of these two criteria: public and collective (metro and city bus), private and collective (company shuttle), public and individual (self-service bike) and private and individual (car and motorcycle).

It should be noted that the modal typologies derive from the work of the organizations producing the surveys and that no traces remain of the criteria and choices that led to these typologies, apart from a few memos or meeting minutes. To our knowledge, there is no research work on modal categorization.

10.3.3. *The city*

Drawing a perimeter around what we call a "city", in which mobility practices are quantified, is an operation of categorization. Traditionally, according to Guérois and Paulus (2002), there are three types of definition of cities: an administrative definition (e.g. any municipality with more than 2,000 inhabitants in France); a morphological definition (an agglomeration can be defined by grouping together places between which the built-up area is continuous); and a functional definition. A functional delimitation of a city is constructed in two stages: firstly, by distinguishing the agglomerations that house a significant number of jobs as "employment centers" or "subcenters"; and then by matching these centers with those municipalities from which a significant fraction of their residents originates. Definitions vary between countries, whether for the criterion used or the threshold chosen for a given criterion. Thus, the criterion of continuous built-up areas used to define agglomerations has been used in both Belgium and France, but were based on a different threshold, 100 m and 200 m respectively, reflecting different average building densities between the two countries and, for this chapter, leading to obvious problems of comparability.

In the context of the study of urban mobility, cities are both spaces for collecting information about travel and possible areas of action; in France, the Urban Transport perimeters, created in 1974, were effectively used as a definition of "urban" in terms of the organization of public transport. Since the NOTRe (2015) and LOM (2019) legislations, the territory has been spatially divided at several levels, with regions having the important role of organizing coordination between several local government bodies responsible for transport and mobility (AOM for Autorités Organisatrices de la Mobilité in French). Although the consequences of LOM law are still unfolding, it is interesting to note that the boundaries of the AOMs, which are used to mainly apply to urban spaces, are now at the scale of French consolidated intermunicipal areas (as of July 2022, 53% are local AOMs[4]), reflecting the wider spread of urban areas over French territory. Comparing mobility practices between cities presupposes a theoretical definition and a similar operational implementation of geographical concepts, allowing comparisons between the figures obtained. Since the 1990s, we have witnessed a movement toward standardization of production of mobility information, particularly under the influence of the American statistical institute. The Census Bureau has produced the boundaries of *Metropolitan Statistical Areas* since 1983, which have inspired statistical institutes in Europe and around the world (Bretagnolle 2015). There is no perfect match between the boundaries of functional areas as defined by INSEE on the basis of home–work commutes (Urban Areas until 2010 and from 2020 Urban Attraction Areas[5]) and the boundaries chosen for examining the mobility practices of residents (see the review of Household Travel Survey boundaries by CEREMA). Differences may arise, on the one hand, from the differences between functional spaces

---

4 Available at: https://www.francemobilites.fr/loi-mobilites/prise-competence-AOM-communautes-communes [accessed 22 November 2021].

5 Both terms refer to the concept of functional area, but there are two main methodological points of difference. For urban areas, urban poles are defined on the basis of continuity of the built-up area, whereas for urban attraction areas, urban poles are defined on the basis of the population density grid within the municipalities. On the other hand, for urban attraction areas, suburban municipalities are "directly" attached, based on a threshold of 15% of commuters working in the pole, while for urban areas, it is more complex: an iterative algorithm has made it possible to successively attach municipalities first to the urban pole, then to the entity "urban pole + municipalities already attached", etc.

related to home–work travel and functional spaces related to other trip purposes (shopping, leisure, etc.) and on the other hand, from wider (Greater Marseilles Area Travel Survey, in 2009) or smaller (Medium City of Beauvais Travel Survey, in 2010) political boundaries which were compared to the limits of functional areas. Overall, in France, and in particular since 2018 and the creation of CEREMA Certified Mobility Surveys, the geographical scope of Household Surveys has increased and is now more in line with the borders of the functional areas. However, even with this extended perimeter, a few major limitations of mobility surveys for understanding urban mobility should be underlined. On the one hand, only the residents' movements are included in the study, for obvious reasons of accessing the people concerned – the mobility of non-residents is nevertheless significant, especially in urban and/or tourist centers. On the other hand, mobility of people is not the only generator of road traffic. Freight transport in general and urban logistics, particularly in a strong growth sector and in connection with the development of e-commerce (Motte-Baumvol et al. 2017), generates many professional trips that are only partially recognized by these surveys (Toilier et al. 2018). The employee's place of residence is the factor of inclusion, which is quite inadequate for some of this mobility.

Cities are currently in the full process of transformation, with an increasingly complex spatial distribution of flows, including the most frequent ones (home–work). "The urban, metropolitan & the subnational-regional scales seem to be blending together" (Soja 2011). To quote Bretagnolle (2015):

> From this point of view, the adoption of zoning in urban areas in France, then that of Larger Urban Zones in the European Union raise many questions. In particular, it seems unreasonable to think that the European city, if such a thing exists, can be defined by the use of identical parameters in any country, given the extreme variety of urbanization processes and administrative networks (Guérois and Pumain 2008).

Figure 10.3 illustrates both the different criteria that may be used to define the city (continuity of the built-up area, commuter belts, with different possible thresholds), and the recent developments of cities, in Europe and in the United States. After a period of metropolization (from the post-war period to the 1990s), the recent period has been marked both by continuing growth of the spatial extent of cities and by the emergence of subcenters in the outskirts of most cities (Berger et al. 2014). The complexity of the functioning of cities may make it necessary to adapt the system for collecting mobility data, in particular by using data covering a period of 1–2 weeks, rather than data covering only one day, in order to account for the diversity of individual spatial anchoring within multipolar urban spaces (Cailly and Pourtau 2018).

The difficulty of separating spatial scales is increasingly evident for functional areas, with growth in medium and long-distance trips (Conti 2019). Two observations reinforce this observation: among the 548 cities with more than 1 million inhabitants in the United Nations database (2018), 160 (about a third) are located less than 100 km away at least from one other. These "spatial clusters" of cities of 1 million inhabitants are made of two, three or four cities in 30 cases, and of five or more cities in 11 cases (including a cluster made up of 27 cities around Shanghai, China!). This threshold of 100 km obviously has a very different meaning depending on the state of the underlying transport network and motorization of households, but typically entails possible frequent exchanges between cities. At the European level, in the same vein, the intertwining of identified functional areas is striking. Among the 655 Larger Urban Zones of the Urban Audit in 2020, about half (310) are isolated, that is to say, not contiguous to any other. The remaining cities (a little more than half) are contiguous to at least one other functional area, of which 148 (about a quarter of the set) form a collection of at least six cities. The largest of these, of course in the heart of Europe, represents 98 contiguous functional areas next to each other between Amsterdam and Munich: this is approximately Brunet's Blue Banana (2002). The scale at which urban mobility is measured is in no way a neutral choice in understanding urban issues. The classic example is the Randstad (between Amsterdam and Rotterdam), where each functional area taken separately is often among the most virtuous examples of urban planning leading toward sustainable mobility, but where interurban travel is largely carried out by car and contributes to significant congestion at the level of the urban system (Nello-Deakin and Brömmelstroet 2021)!

Two complementary directions of research have been the subject of numerous monographs over the last decade: the differentiation of suburban areas (Berroir et al. 2017; Pistre and Richard 2018; Raux et al. 2020) and the differentiation of polycentric mega-regions (Georg et al. 2016; Berroir et al. 2017; Pujol et al. 2017; Conti 2019), and "intermediate" territories within these mega-regions (Solís Trapero et al. 2015; Hubert et al. 2016; Berroir et al. 2017). In the current state of the literature, there is no stabilized nomenclature allowing comparison of peripheral territories with similar characteristics between cities in the world, which certainly hinders the possibility of circulating good planning practices at this level. Especially when we go beyond the national level, comparison is made difficult by the heterogeneity of data collection boundaries.

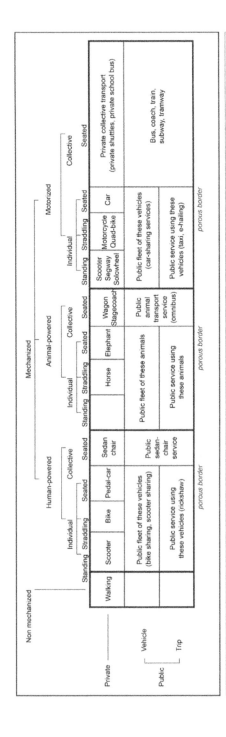

Figure 10.2. Diversity of transport modes and operations of aggregation

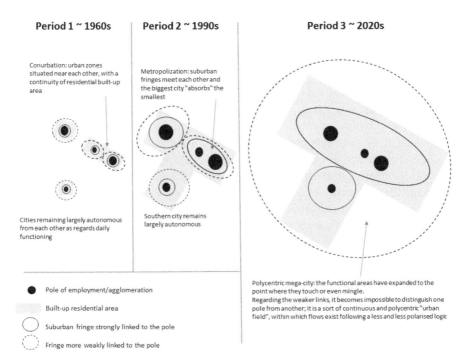

Figure 10.3. *Changes in urban polarization between the 1960s and the 2020s, in Europe or North America. While the most significant growth in built-up areas took place during the end of the 20th century, the most recent period is marked by increasing complexity of flows between centers, between residential places and centers. To illustrate this point, different geographical areas are distinguished by a method of delimiting functional areas; with different thresholds – strong links exclusively, or strong links and weak links. For a color version of this figure, see www.iste.co.uk/lesteven/urban.zip*

10.4. Categorical pitfalls: balancing diversity and comparability

Categories of analysis and public action largely determine what we know about and how we act on daily mobility. Among these categories, some are scholarly or technical categories, while others come from the shared experience of individuals. Desrosières (1992) distinguishes two types of conventions that differ based on the origins of their coding criteria. In one case, the convention already exists in the field studied before the intervention of the statistician. This is the case when counting (in 2013 in France, for example) the number of individuals who own or rent their homes, as these ownership regimes are defined by law. Alternatively, the convention is conceived by the statistician, "creating discontinuity where society sees only continuity". This is the case when counting the number of "trips" made by individuals, who do not necessarily see their mobility as divided in this way.

All of these conventions can be examined, since they have effects on analyzing the context, comparing spaces, monitoring trends or even measuring the effects of a public policy. Below, we will detail four categorical issues: the way that the determination of the main mode influences the perception of intermodal travel practices; how temporal categories influence the perception of routines of mobility; how the delimitation of the urban boundary influences the perception of the scope of travel and the importance of car use; the way in which the definition of harmonized categories is linked to objectives of inter-urban comparison defined in advance. Other categorical pitfalls are also well known and identified in the literature, such as social categorizations of residents, or the evolution of modal categorizations over time. For example: should we consider an e-bike as a classic bike or as a motorized two-wheeler? Or should we create a new category? Whichever we choose, this has consequences for which comparisons over time can be made.

10.4.1. *The category of transport: modes and purposes for travel*

In household travel surveys, the problem cannot be circumvented so easily, as these surveys are used precisely to produce detailed information on mobility. In these surveys, the convention is to divide mobility into trips, which are defined by unity of purpose (see the previous section). These trips are themselves divided into stages or journeys which are defined by the unity of mode of transport. Thus, a trip that is made entirely on foot is a unimodal trip consisting of a single journey with which a single mode of transport is associated. On the other hand, a trip made up of an approach on foot, then a bus journey, then a final journey on foot, is a multimodal trip made up of three journeys.

It is possible to work with journeys and keep all the details of the typology of modes of transport, but, as explained above, the vast majority of analyses, models and evaluations are done at the level of trips. It is therefore necessary to be able to assign only one mode to each movement, the so-called "main" mode. However, there is a very large number of possible combinations, which makes it necessary to simplify by aggregating the modes. In the 2010 Global Transport Survey (EGT), which produces information on the mobility of Île-de-France (greater Paris) residents, there are 1,931 combinations of journeys, including all uni- and multi-modal trips collected by the survey. Here are the most common combinations, given that there are 41 million daily trips on an average business day:

– walking alone: 16 million trips;

– walking–car as driver–walking: 12 million trips;

– walking–car as passenger–walking: 3.2 million trips;

– walking–metro–walking: 2.2 million trips (if we aggregate intermediate metro transfers).

These very frequent combinations represent 33 million trips, so there are approximately 8 million daily trips that may involve rarer combinations, for example, walking–bus–walking–metro–walking.

In most surveys, a hierarchy of modes of transport is used to assign a single mode, the so-called "main" mode, to multi-modal travel. In the French case, at the top of the hierarchy are heavy rail modes (train, metro), in the middle other motorized modes (car, motorcycle), and at the bottom of the hierarchy, walking. Thus, a trip that begins with an approach on foot, then a metro ride, then a final walk to the destination, will be considered a metro ride. In some surveys, the main mode is determined by the journey that is longest in either distance or time. In both cases, the first consequence of this assignment is the disappearance of journeys using "minor" modes, in particular walking. In the case of the Île-de-France EGT, the result of this assignment is to show 16 million daily trips on foot and 25 million using other modes. But if we take a closer look at these 25 million trips, 99% of them include walking. Walking is omnipresent in urban mobility, it is the glue that holds all other modes together and makes all intermodal combinations possible.

By going into more analytical detail, we can explore the effects of this assignment rule (Table 10.1) by comparing the main mode designated by the mode hierarchy and the main mode if determined by the maximum journey distance. The first conclusion is that reclassification involves relatively few trips. Out of 41 million in the survey (125,000 unweighted trips), only 500,000 are affected by the reclassification, or 1.2% of the total.

The two most affected modes are those at the two extremes of the hierarchy. In intermodal travel, walking is systematically erased while public transport is systematically made essential. For walking, 170,000 trips would be considered walking trips if the maximum distance criterion were to be used. Unsurprisingly, these are journeys of approaching public transport and, to a lesser extent, journeys to an individual motorized vehicle. As for public transport, it eliminates around 50,000 car trips, both as driver and passenger. These are mainly journeys consisting of an approach by car, parking at the station and a rail transport journey, in which the approach by car is longer than the rail transport journey.

		Distance criterion						
		Walking	Bike	Transit	Car	Car passenger	Motorbike	Total
Hierarchical criterion	Walking	0	0	0	0	0	0	0
	Bike	5 251	0	0	0	0	0	5 251
	Transit	111 250	1 459	0	21 112	28 793	498	163 111
	Car	40 566	0	222	0	8 419	1 345	50 552
	Car passenger	11 986	0	0	0	0	0	11 986
	Motorbike	603	0	0	0	42 162	0	42 764
	Total	169 656	1 459	222	21 112	79 374	1 843	273 664

Table 10.1. *Reclassification of main mode according to distance. Source: EGT 2010*

What are the operational implications of such an analysis? For producers of mobility data, this calculation must still be made to determine if the reclassification is really residual, including a finer geographical level than the entire region. It would also be wise for surveys to suggest several variables of the main mode to characterize trips: mode chosen according to the hierarchical rule, according to maximum distance, or even according to maximum travel time. From the point of view of public action, there are several elements to draw from this, starting with the relative omission of walking in the calculation of modal shares which, it should be remembered, are systematically calculated for trips and not for journeys or stages. In addition, modal shares relate to trips and not to individuals. In the 2010 EGT, the modal share of walking on an average working day is 37%. Instead of relating the number of trips on foot to the total number of trips, we can relate the number of individuals who make at least one journey on foot to the total number of individuals (Commenges 2015). Also, in the 2010 EGT, this modal split calculated at individual level is 87%: in other words, on a typical working day, 87% of Île-de-France residents are pedestrians at least once during the day. Using different conventions and measurements reveals a different reality, that of a mainly pedestrian society, and may induce a corresponding consideration of this reality (Monnet 2016).

When categories are defined in a questionnaire, it is almost certain that they will need to be aggregated in subsequent processing. Indeed, the initial categories are defined in relation to expectations or preliminary issues, but they are independent of the numbers that they will finally collect, once the questionnaires have been completed. Let us use the Île-de-France EGT once again to illustrate this. The most disaggregated variable describing the main mode of transport (after the procedure for assigning the main mode described above) contains 41 modalities. Among these modalities, some register no trips (the Orlyval airport shuttle, the Batobus river ferry), others collect a very small number of trips (the Noctilien night bus, driver of an unregistered motorized two-wheeled vehicle). These 41 methods are not used in any study report, nor will they be used in other systems such as modeling; they will be aggregated for all uses after the survey. However, to our knowledge, there is no research on aggregation criteria, the issues involved with these aggregations, or the history of these aggregation practices. Of course, there is no harmonized thesaurus of terms for these aggregations. Among the questions raised above: should taxis (private vehicles in public use) be aggregated with car travel as passenger or public transport; should a company shuttle (collective transport in private use) be aggregated with car travel as passenger or public transport?

The real contribution of mixed methods is the intersection of quantitative, qualitative and simulation methods for the study of individual trajectories. No divisions can be intrinsically relevant and unassailable. This is the real contribution of mixed methods (Berroir et al. 2018, Vincent-Geslin et al. 2019, Meissonnier and Richer 2020) to allow us to go beyond the necessarily limited descriptive results of these mobility surveys.

10.4.2. *Temporal categories: the typical working day*

The *typical working day* or *average day* is "an average day of the week [excluding] public holidays, school holidays or special days that may cause a change in behavior (severe climatic disturbances, public transport strikes)" (CERTU 1998, p. 52). The collection of data over a single day, considered to be average, predominates in systems for quantifying mobility. This mode of collection is justified by the idea that daily movements follow a fairly regular pattern and that short-term variation is residual. This assumption is however highly debatable (Huff and Hanson 1986; Commenges 2015).

As mentioned above, taking a single day into account does not make it possible to deal with the habits and routines that integrate mobility into a lifestyle. In addition, by considering a typical day, the calendar day is short-circuited, and fluctuations that take place throughout the year, and which differ from one agglomeration to another, are ignored. Other elements must be dealt with depending on the objectives pursued – for example, the fact that the typical day is defined as the 24-hour period beginning and ending at 4 am. If we are interested in populations who work shifts, in particular night workers, this definition of the time period will truncate all the working hours of the individuals concerned. Still on this finer temporal scale, analysis of urban rhythms (Lecomte et al. 2018; Munch and Royoux 2019), partly made possible by mobility surveys, often stumbles on the question of the sample; whether it is a question of studying mobility at off-peak hours in less dense zones or fine temporal synchronizations at peak hours. The size of the sample is of course connected with its primary use, as envisaged by Commenges (2013), and secondary treatments that may be imagined are not necessarily statistically possible.

In the rest of this chapter, we wish to focus on some particular aspects of these multiple methodological difficulties in comparing mobility data: the sets of scales and categories, which appear to be particularly undervalued by certain organizations which produce or provide data, although they may change the meaning of the comparative analyses produced.

10.4.3. *The spatial category: local urban systems*

In order to measure, for constant mobility categories, the effects of scale change (Figure 10.4) on the calculation of daily mobility indicators, we calculate the same set of indicators for two sets of places of residence in France, based on data from the 2015 INSEE census (for commuting only). The two scales being compared are, on the one hand, the scale of functional areas (the zoning of INSEE's Urban Areas, in 2010), and on the other hand the scale of local urban systems of Coutrot et al. (2013). Local urban systems (Berroir et al. 2017) are defined on the basis of intensity and diversity of functional relationships between functional areas: home–work links, residential migration, scientific partnerships, economic partnerships, among others. These systems typically cover 5–10 functional areas, not necessarily contiguous. Of course, these local urban systems are not primarily areas of daily mobility, and most flows between cities are infrequent and irregular. Nevertheless, the work of Conti (2016) clearly shows how interurban journeys, although a minority (about 10% of flows), account for about one third of the distances travelled for commuting, an increasing share largely not addressed by public policy. This is becoming gradually recognized by the public authorities in France, by means of the so called "mobility pools" that are being established following the LOM (2019) legislative framework. We aim to show the importance, for certain territories, of taking account of daily interurban mobility.

To do this, we calculated for the 44 French local urban systems (US) (excluding Paris, due to the particularity of that urban region), as well as for the main urban area (UA) of each US, two very classic indicators of the socio-economics of transport: the share of trips made by public transport (PT) and the average distance of home-to-work commuting. Of course, since the scale of the functional areas is more restricted and the central UA is generally the best endowed in terms of public transport, the average of the indicators between the spatial entities is 8.1% of trips using public transport (UA scale) versus 6.5% (US scale); the average range of commuting trips is thus 6.4 km (UA scale) compared to 7.4 km (US scale). But these effects of scale change are very heterogeneous between cities. In order to illustrate how such variations in scale affect the ability of local actors to comprehend local issues in their territories, we adopted a method of comparing the ranks of the two indicators used. Thus, rather than assessing the absolute variations of thresholds, we analyze relative variations in the classifications of spatial entities, with respect to each other according to these metrics. As seen in Figure 10.4, in addition to a large central bulge made up of half the cities, where the rank of indicators varies little with scale (less than 5 pts of variation on average of absolute values), there emerge two large "packages" of cities. Those located to the right of the figure (set "C" of cities) are highly polycentric urban systems where the average distance of travel and the share of travel on public transport shifts very strongly toward less relative durability, in the sense that a city that seemed energy-efficient with relatively short-range trips and moderate car use may find itself, at the level of the urban system, in the opposite situation compared to the others. One territory is symbolic of this polycentrism and the concrete problems that this poses when understanding the diversity of daily mobility issues. For Lille, the average distance of commuting is small at the level of the urban area (6 km), but this average rises to 9.4 km when calculating at the level of the urban system. These long-distance journeys are mainly made by car, and therefore on average, the modal share of public transport drops from 17.5% to 10.5% after this scale change! There follows a profound change in the "relative performance" of Lille compared to the other cities in this corpus (Lille loses six places in the ranking of the highest public transport modal shares, and 24 places – out of 44! – in the ranking of shortest average trip ranges). Conversely, to the left of Figure 10.4, for a set of territories with a more "local" polycentrism, we observe another effect of this scale change: the average range of commutes varies very little according to the scale (6.4 km for the UA versus 6.9 km for the US in Bayonne, for example), and therefore relatively, the US scale appears to underrepresent the scope of the commuting trips. For these cities, the effect on modes of transport is very variable – two sets of cities (A) and (B) in Figure 10.4, within which there are large metropolises such as Bordeaux and Toulouse whose local radial rail network is efficient, supporting some of this interurban mobility. On both sides, we can clearly see the extent to which the scale of analysis changes our perceptions of the issues of action in terms of mobility.

Is this necessarily problematic? It all depends on what you wish to do. Thus, Le Néchet (2011) shows for Paris and London that changing the scale of analysis, between hypercenter, heart of agglomeration and whole agglomeration, follows the shape of the Newman and Kenworthy curve (1999)! In other words, differences in defining cities do not necessarily impact the shape of the curve, which is an important point given the glaring lack of previous harmonization of the data of the base used, mixing different scales.

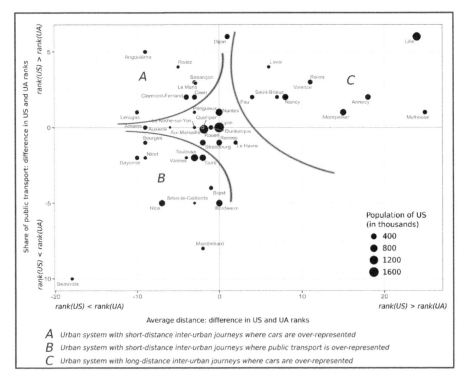

Figure 10.4. *Scale effects on calculation of modal shares and average trip distances. (The x-axis represents the difference between the classification of spatial entities when the US scale is used, and the classification of spatial entities when the UA scale is used, for the indicator "share of commuting performed on public transport". The y-axis applies the same logic, for the indicator "average distance of commute to work"). Source: MOBPRO database from 2015 and zoning in Urban Areas from 2010. For a color version of this figure, see www.iste.co.uk/lesteven/urban.zip*

This does not mean that the problem does not arise, but that it is complex to decide once and for all what is the right scale of analysis in international comparisons of mobility practices.

It is therefore advisable to be vigilant and not to take spatial nomenclatures for granted, as complex as they are, without critical hindsight or even additional work: everything is related to the context of analysis. Thus, ad hoc questionnaires could be designed at scales not specifically covered by conventional tools, such as the Habest survey, on urban, suburban and rural connections in the eastern part of France (Choplin and Delage 2014), or the Household Travel Survey specifically on large mobilities in the former Picardy region (Hasiak 2018). We end this section by emphasizing, as do Aleta et al. (2017) or Rozenblat (2020), the need for approaches combining the different spatial scales at which cities operate.

10.4.4. *Categories reconstructed for harmonization: ad hoc mechanisms*

In this section, we show, in the case of two urban regions corresponding to different functional scales (the functional area of Paris and the local urban system known as the "Rhine-Ruhr region", a polycentric system based around the cities of Cologne, Düsseldorf, Essen and Dortmund), the interest of a work of reprocessing (disaggregation and then reaggregation of statistical information) in order to harmonize the categories of mobility, and ultimately to compare certain spatial aspects of home–work mobility in these two urban regions of 12 million inhabitants and 12,000 km^2 (Le Néchet 2010). The case study areas were determined using the Knapp and Schmitt (2003) study, as well as analysis of complementary flow data. The Île-de-France region was chosen for the Paris metropolitan area, and the Rhine-Ruhr region is defined using the database from the "Larger Urban Zones" (LUZ) urban audited by Eurostat and PddV (year 2004), like the 26 *Kreis* (districts) included in these LUZ or with close commuting links to these key areas. Mobility in both regions is based on public transport networks organized at several spatial levels: there is a complex interweaving of the levels and actors that manage, plan and operate transport in both regions.

Here, we describe the harmonization of mobility datasets performed to allow comparison of the domains of relevance of motorized modes within metropolitan areas. The data used for the Paris region come from the French census of 1999 (Recensement Général de Population – RGP) and the regional transport survey 2001 (Enquête Globale de Transport – EGT), and from two databases, IGVP[6], 2000 and PddV[7], 2004 for the Rhine-Ruhr region. The harmonization procedure consists of two stages:

---

6 IGVP = Integrierte Gesamtverkehrsplanung Nord Rhein Westfalen (regional database).
7 PDDV = Prognose der deutschlandweiten Verkehrsverflechtung 2025 database (national database).

– Creating similar basic statistical areas, to avoid distorting the comparison between the two regions. The reconstructed Rhine-Ruhr areas, similar to the "municipalities" of Paris, were created according to a four-step procedure, based on 2589 North Rhine-Westphalia transport zones ("Verkehr Zones", VZ), the smallest geographical entity available in the IGVP database, and 765 "Grund" subdivisions of German municipalities.

– Creating similar mobility categories from the available databases, which requires the breakdown of modes of transport. We chose to divide the modes of transport into four categories for the two regions: car, train, other public transport and active modes, in line with the context of the research of Le Néchet (2010).

More precisely, for the Paris region, the RGP data have a specific category of "two wheelers" which has therefore been divided between car mode and active travel (cycling). To reallocate transport modes to harmonized modes, we used the EGT (2001) dataset with more detailed information on modes of transport used for commuting, but only 10,000 households were surveyed. For the Rhine-Ruhr region, the procedure was very different because the IGVP database has a very high spatial resolution but only distinguishes between individual and collective modes; whereas the PddV database is an OD matrix with six modes of transport but only available at *Kreis* level, which is spatially thin (there are 26 *Kreis* in the Rhine-Ruhr region). Additional processing was carried out to make the two datasets compatible, which involved modeling trips distinguished by their *Kreis* of origin and destination (urban/non-urban) and the distance of the trip. This method of reaggregating information has made it possible to highlight a structural difference in the areas of relevance of the different modes of transport. If, classically, public transport struggles to perform in the German region beyond 20 km, the very monocentric character of the Paris region tends to create an increasing attractiveness of public transport with distance, up to about 60 or 80 km of travel, which is unusual (Figure 10.5). This fine spatial and modal harmonization work has made it possible to produce a thematic result, but it must be specified that since the procedure is ad-hoc, a different problem would certainly have led to a different disaggregation/reaggregation procedure, making it difficult to perform systematic international comparisons for such subjects.

Beyond the methods of data production, the question therefore arises of the configuration of analysis of these data, especially when they are used for comparison purposes.

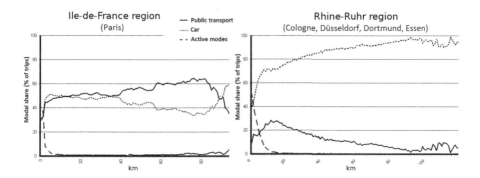

Figure 10.5. *Domains of relevance of three modes of transport reconstructed (public transport, car, active modes) by a method of disaggregation – aggregation, in two metropolises with very dissimilar spatial organizations: Paris, monocentric, and the Rhine-Ruhr region, polycentric*

10.5. Discussion

Recently, many articles have emerged in France and abroad on so-called "sustainable" mobility indicators, such as modal shares for number of trips or distance travelled, or calculations of CO_2 emissions caused by mobility (Kitchin et al. 2015, Dixon et al. 2018, Hee and Dunn 2017), and on indicators of accessibility (to jobs, services, facilities, etc.), which ignore most of the methodological issues we have raised (Zito and Salvo 2011; Gil and Read 2014; Danielis et al. 2018), which may create a wide variety of biases that are difficult to quantify. As Batty (2019) suggests, it is necessary to deal with all of the data, to put them in relation to each other and to not forget geographical and sociological theories.

The salient points that emerge from this chapter are as follows: the convergence of instrumental scale (data available at the level of the functional area) is increasingly overtaken by changes in the geography itself, which is moving toward more complex, multiscalar objects, risking the emergence of edge effects in studies carried out from the classic stance of an "isolated" city (Thomas et al. 2018). Although we have not detailed any examples, we think it is particularly important to work on the spatial and social decomposition of suburban areas (Nessi et al. 2016; Raux et al. 2020), which will certainly be an important research line in coming years. We may also mention that emerging modes, either really new ones (mobility services) or combinations of old modes, are poorly accounted for, in an unstable socio-technical context, by so-called "classical" data (household surveys), and that there is no sign that so-called "new" data (mobile phone data, etc.) solve these pitfalls. Issues of hybridization between the different existing data will necessarily involve theoretical and ontological reflections on the modalities of development and regulation of modes of transport in cities, by public actors. This is indeed the "permanent readjustment of categories of analysis" to which Barbier (2015) invites us, always keeping in mind that algorithms are not neutral (Kwan 2016): they bear the traces of a priori conceptions of mobility and its future uses, exactly like the technical matrix described by Commenges (2013) within the framework of the classic tools of the socio-economics of transport.

Immanuel Wallerstein, following others, mentions the streetlight effect: we must not, like the drunkard who looks for his lost key under the streetlight because that is where there is light, choose the problem based on the available data, but on the contrary, seek or produce the data based on the problem (Wallerstein 2009, p. 38). This injunction, which has all the appearance of common sense, in fact conveys the image of a process of data production which would perpetually start from an initial state devoid of data, devoid of questions and devoid of constraints and organizational practices: a reset with each new creation of data. However, at every moment, people and organizations seeking to produce knowledge place themselves within an area informed by existing statistical elements, by previous practices and results (Commenges and Fen-Chong 2017). As part of the analysis of urban mobility, the streetlight is increasingly determined by the needs of comparison, in time and space, by the circulation of exemplary surveys and quantification designs and by the creation of harmonized indicators. These needs for comparison are legitimate, but they should not overshadow the interest of shedding light on something else, elsewhere and in other ways, with other mechanisms.

More generally, we insist here on the need, at the level of cities or regions, for a local capacity to develop and maintain specific tools of analysis, adapted to local problems and urban trajectories. This is undoubtedly complicated for a number of cities by the context of prioritization in the system of analysis and study of mobility, due to the methods it requires. A set of tools that makes mobility into an object ultimately reveals the capacity, or otherwise, of a city to organize its way of seeing things, and therefore of acting (Gallez 2015). This is the concept of "data justice" (Sourbati and Behrendt 2020) that we believe might apply very well to the context of urban mobility.

10.6. References

Adoue, F. (2015). Information en temps réel et optimisation du déplacement. L'usage des applications pour smartphone dans et autour des transports en commun franciliens. *Netcom. Réseaux, communication et territoires*, 29(1/2), 37–54.

Aleta, A., Meloni, S., Moreno, Y. (2017). A multilayer perspective for the analysis of urban transportation systems. *Scientific Reports*, 7(1), 1–9.

Amar, G. (2010). *Homo mobilis : le nouvel âge de la mobilité*. FYP éditions, Limoges.

Armoogum, J., Tebar, M., Christian, B., Garcia, C., Nguyen, M.-H., Rendina F. (2018). Rapport de synthèse : méthodologie afin de mesurer la mobilité régionale : élaboration d'une enquête régionale. PhD Thesis, IFSTTAR-Institut Français des Sciences et Technologies des Transports.

Armoogum, J., Hasiak, F., Hivert, L., Madre, J.L., Meissonnier, J., Papon, F., Richer, C., Rizet, C., Tebar, M. (2020). Rapport de synthèse des travaux de l'ORSI observations et analyse de la mobilité (obamo) 2013–2019 [Online]. Available at: https://hal.science/hal-02938791/document.

Baldasseroni, L. and Charansonney, L. (2018). Gouverner la voirie urbaine par l'information de l'automobiliste. Une comparaison Lyon–Paris, des années 1920 à nos jours. *Flux*, 3(113), 24–40.

Banister, D. (2008). The sustainable mobility paradigm. *Transport Policy*, 15(2), 73–80.

Barbier, C. (2015). Des études urbaines comparatistes à une sociologie croisée des politiques urbaines. *Espaces et sociétés*, 4(163), 25–40.

Batty, M. (2019). Urban analytics defined. *Environment and Planning B: Urban Analytics and City Science*, 46(3), 403–405.

Berger, M., Aragau, C., Rougé, L. (2014). Vers une maturité des territoires périurbains ? Développement des mobilités de proximité et renforcement de l'ancrage dans l'ouest francilien. *EchoGéo*, 27.

Berroir, S., Cattan, N., Dobruszkes, F., Guérois, M., Paulus, F., Vacchiani-Marcuzzo, C. (2017a). Les systèmes urbains français : une approche relationnelle. *Cybergeo : European Journal of Geography*.

Berroir, S., Delage, M., Fleury, A., Fol, S., Guérois, M., Maulat, J., Raad, L., Vallée, J. (2017b). Mobilité au quotidien et ancrage local dans les espaces périurbains. *Annales de géographie*, 1, 31–55.

Berroir, S., Commenges, H., Debrie, J., Maulat, J., Bordedebat, C., Blandeau, G., Briend, E., Lanon, J. (2018). Dessine-moi une ville sans voiture : les aspirations en matière de mode de vie et de mobilité en île-de-france. *Nouvelles perspectives en sciences sociales*, 13(2), 27–73.

Boutueil, V., Nemett, L., Quillerier, T. (2021). Trends in competition among digital platforms for shared mobility: Insights from a worldwide census & prospects for research. *Transportation Research Record*, 2676(2), 69–82. doi: 10.1177/03611981211.

Bretagnolle, A. (2015). La naissance du périurbain comme catégorie statistique en France. Une perspective internationale. *L'Espace géographique*, 44(1), 18–37.

Brunet, R. (2002). Lignes de force de l'espace européen. *Mappe monde*, 66(2), 14–19.

Cailly, L. and Pourtau, B. (2018). "Faire métropole" : une analyse par les représentations et les pratiques de mobilité périurbaines des habitants de l'aire urbaine de Tours (France). *Géocarrefour*, 92(4).

CERTU (1998). L'enquête ménages déplacements méthode standard. Notes méthodologiques et annexes. Methodological guide, CERTU, Lyon.

Chandakas, E. (2020). On demand forecasting of demand-responsive paratransit services with prior reservations. *Transportation Research Part C: Emerging Technologies*, 120, 102817.

Chrétien, J. (2019). Flâner ou filer : une approche quantifiée de l'influence du contexte sur le type de pratique piétonne. *Espaces et sociétés*, 4(179), 77–91.

Chrétien, J., Le Néchet, F., Leurent, F., Yin, B. (2018). Using mobile phone data to observe & understand mobility behavior, territories, & transport usage. *Urban Mobility & the Smartphone: Transportation, Travel Behavior & Public Policy*, 79.

Commenges, H. (2013). L'invention de la mobilité quotidienne. Aspects performatifs des instruments de la socio-économie des transports. PhD Thesis, Université Paris-Diderot-Paris VII.

Commenges, H. (2015). Mesurer les pratiques modales et la dépendance automobile : à la recherche de congruence entre mesure et interprétation. *Espace populations sociétés*, 1–2, 1–15.

Commenges, H. and Fen-Chong, J. (2017). Navettes domicile-travail : naissance et développement d'un objet statistique structurant. *Annales de géographie*, 3(715), 333–355.

Conti, B. (2016). La mobilité pendulaire interurbaine en France face aux enjeux du changement climatique : caractérisation socioéconomique, analyse spatiale et potentiels de report modal. PhD Thesis, Paris Est.

Conti, B. (2019). Essai de caractérisation de la mobilité interurbaine en France : des pendulaires et pendularités hétérogènes. *Flux*, 1(115), 14–32.

Cools, M., Moons, E., Wets, G. (2009). Investigating the variability in daily traffic counts through use of ARIMAX & SARIMAX models: Assessing the effect of holidays on two site locations. *Transportation Research Record*, 2136(1), 57–66.

Cornelis, E.L., Hubert, M., Huynen, P., Lebrun, K., Patriarche G. (2012). Belgian daily mobility – BELDAM : enquête sur la mobilité quotidienne des belges. Final report, Politique Scientifique fédérale, Brussels.

Courmont, A. (2018). L'open data au Grand Lyon : l'émergence d'un gouvernement métropolitain de la mobilité. *Métropoles*, 23.

Coutrot, D., Helwig, P., Bonnet Gravois, N. (2013). Caractérisation des systèmes urbains français à partir du nouveau zonage des aires urbaines "2010". Mission d'analyse des dynamiques et des inégalités territoriales. Final report, DATAR and Groupement Systra.

Danielis, R., Rotaris, L., Monte, A. (2018). Composite indicators of sustainable urban mobility: Estimating the rankings frequency distribution combining multiple methodologies. *International Journal of Sustainable Transportation*, 12(5), 380–395.

Delage, M. (2012). Mobilités pour achats et centralités métropolitaines. Le cas de la métropole parisienne. PhD Thesis, Université Paris 1 Panthéon-Sorbonne.

Delage, M. and Choplin, A. (2014). L'est parisien, un territoire sans qualité ? *Métropolitiques* [Online]. Available at: https://metropolitiques.eu/IMG/pdf/met-choplin-delage.pdf.

Desrosières, A. (1992). Séries longues et conventions d'équivalence. *Genèses*, 9, 92–97.

Desrosières, A. (2012). Est-il bon, est-il méchant ? Le rôle du nombre dans le gouvernement de la cité néolibérale. *Nouvelles perspectives en sciences sociales*, 7(2), 261–295.

Desrosières, A. (2016). *La politique des grands nombres : histoire de la raison statistique.* La Découverte, Paris.

Dharmowijoyo, D.B., Susilo, Y.O., Karlström, A., Adiredja, L.S. (2015). Collecting a multidimensional three-weeks household time-use & activity diary in the Bandung metropolitan area, Indonesia. *Transportation Research Part A: Policy & Practice*, 80, 231–246.

Dingil, A.E., Schweizer, J., Rupi, F., Stasiskiene, Z. (2018). Transport indicator analysis & comparison of 151 urban areas, based on open source data. *European Transport Research Review*, 10(2), 1–9.

Dixon, B., Irshad, H., Pankratz, D., Bornstein, J. (2018). The Deloitte City Mobility Index gauging global readiness for the future of mobility. *Deloitte Review*, 23.

Ewing, R. and Cervero, R. (2010). Travel & the built environment: A meta-analysis. *Journal of the American Planning Association*, 76(3), 265–294.

Fen-Chong, J. (2012). Organisation spatio-temporelle des mobilités révélées par la téléphonie mobile en Ile-de-France. PhD Thesis, Université Panthéon-Sorbonne-Paris I.

Frotey, J. and Castex, E. (2017). Enjeux régionaux de la diffusion spatiale d'un équipement de mobilité : l'infrastructure de charge pour véhicules électriques. L'exemple des Hauts-de-France. *Géotransports*, 10.

Gallez, C. (2015). La mobilité quotidienne en politique. Des manières de voir et d'agir. PhD Thesis, Université Paris-Est.

Genre-Grandpierre, C. (2000). Forme et fonctionnement des réseaux de transport : approche fractale et réflexions sur l'aménagement des villes. PhD Thesis, Université de Franche-Comté.

Georg, I., Blaschke, T., Taubenböck, H. (2016). New spatial dimensions of global cityscapes: From reviewing existing concepts to a conceptual spatial approach. *Journal of Geographical Sciences*, 26(3), 355–380.

Gil, J. and Read, S. (2014). Patterns of sustainable mobility & the structure of modality in the Randstad city-region. *A|Z ITU Journal of Faculty of Architecture*, 11(2), 231–254.

Gourdon, P., Bretagnolle, A., Guérois, M., Pavard, A. (2019). Des petites villes davantage touchées par la décroissance ? Comparaison des trajectoires démographiques à l'échelle européenne (1961–2011). *Belgeo. Revue belge de géographie*, 3.

Guérois, M. and Paulus, F. (2002). Commune centre, agglomération, aire urbaine : quelle pertinence pour l'étude des villes. *Cybergeo*, 212, 15.

Guérois, M. and Pumain, D. (2008). Built-up encroachment & the urban field: A comparison of forty European cities. *Environment & Planning A*, 40(9), 2186–2203.

Guérois, M., Bretagnolle, A., Pavard, A., Gourdon, P., Zdanowska, N. (2019). Following the population of European urban areas in the last half century (1961–2011): The TRADEVE database. *Cybergeo: European Journal of Geography*.

Hall, P.G. and Pain, K. (2006). *The Polycentric Metropolis: Learning from Mega-City Regions in Europe*. Earthscan, London.

Hasiak, F. (2018). Mobilité quotidienne des grands mobiles (cas de la picardie). In *Conférence Rencontres francophones transport mobilité*, Lyon, June 2018.

Hee, L. and Dunn, S. (2017). Urban mobility: 10 cities leading the way in Asia Pacific. Report, Urban Land Institute (ULI) and Centre for Liveable Cities (CLC), 8(16).

Hoogendoorn-Lanser, S., Schaap, N.T., OldeKalter, M.-J. (2015). The Netherlands mobility panel: An innovative design approach for web-based longitudinal travel data collection. *Transportation Research Procedia*, 11, 311–329.

Hubert, J.-P. and Delisle, F. (2010). L'allongement des déplacements quotidiens contribue à l'émergence d'espaces urbains multipolaires, tandis que la mobilité baisse au centre des grandes agglomérations. *La revue du CGDD*, 3(2), 49–64.

Hubert, J.-P., Pistre, P., Madre, J.L. (2016). L'utilisation de l'automobile par les ménages dans les territoires peu denses : analyse croisée par les enquêtes sur la mobilité et le recensement de la population. *Economie et statistiques*, 483–485, 179–203.

Huff, J.O. and Hanson, S. (1986). Repetition & variability in urban travel. *Geographical Analysis*, 18(2), 97–114.

Huré, M. (2019). *Les mobilités partagées. Régulation politique et capitalisme urbain*. Éditions de la Sorbonne, Paris.

Järv, O., Ahas, R., Witlox, F. (2014). Understanding monthly variability in human activity spaces: A twelve-month study using mobile phone call detail records. *Transportation Research Part C: Emerging Technologies*, 38, 122–135.

Kitchin, R. (2014). The real-time city? Big data & smart urbanism. *GeoJournal*, 79(1), 1–14.

Kitchin, R., Lauriault, T.P., McArdle, G. (2015). Knowing & governing cities through urban indicators, city benchmarking & real-time dashboards. *Regional Studies, Regional Science*, 2(1), 6–28.

Knapp, W. and Schmitt, P. (2003). Re-structuring competitive metropolitan regions in northwest Europe: On territory & governance. *European Journal of Spatial Development*, 6(2003), 1–42.

Kujala, R., Weckström, C., Darst, R.K., Mladenović, M.N., Saramäki, J. (2018). A collection of public transport network data sets for 25 cities. *Scientific Data*, 5(1), 1–14.

Kwan, M.-P. (2016). Algorithmic geographies: Big data, algorithmic uncertainty, and the production of geographic knowledge. *Annals of the American Association of Geographers*, 106(2), 274–282.

Le Néchet, F. (2010). Approche multiscalaire des liens entre mobilité quotidienne, morphologie et soutenabilité des métropoles européennes : cas de Paris et de la région Rhin-Ruhr. PhD Thesis, Université Paris-Est.

Le Néchet, F. (2012). Urban spatial structure, daily mobility and energy consumption: A study of 34 European cities. *Cybergeo: European Journal of Geography*.

Lecomte, C., Vallée, J., Le Roux, G., Commenges, H. (2018). Le mobiliscope, un outil de géovisualisation des rythmes quotidiens des métropoles. *Mappemonde. Revue trimestrielle sur l'image géographique et les formes du territoire*, 123.

Louail, T., Lenormand, M., Picornell, M., Cantú, O.G., Herranz, R., Frias-Martinez, E., Ramasco, J.J., Barthelemy, M. (2015). Uncovering the spatial structure of mobility networks. *Nature Communications*, 6(1), 1–8.

Marius-Gnanou, K. and Moriconi-Ebrard, F. (2007). Dynamiques d'urbanisation : des megacities aux villages urbains. *Urbanisme*, 355(special edition Villes indiennes), 47–50.

Meissonnier, J. and Richer, C. (2020). Les routines automobiles à l'épreuve des perturbations. Comprendre les résistances au changement à partir de récits d'usagers dans la métropole lilloise. *Flux*, 119–120(1–2), 25–40.

Miller, H.J. and Goodchild, M.F. (2015). Data-driven geography. *GeoJournal*, 80(4), 449–461.

Mokhtarian, P.L. (2005). Travel as a desired end, not just a means. *Transportation Research Part A*, 39, 93–96.

Monnet, J. (2016). Marche-loisir et marche-déplacement : une dichotomie persistante, du romantisme au fonctionnalisme. *Sciences de la société*, 97(2016), 74–89.

Motte-Baumvol, B., Belton-Chevallier, L., Dablanc, L., Morganti, E., Belin-Munier, C. (2017). Spatial dimensions of e-shopping in France. *Asian Transport Studies*, 4(3), 585–600.

Munch, E. and Royoux, D. (2019). Synchronisations, désynchronisations : nouvelles temporalités des territoires. *Espace populations sociétés*, 2019(1).

Nello-Deakin, S. and te Brömmelstroet, M. (2021). Scaling up cycling or replacing driving? Triggers & trajectories of bike–train uptake in the Randstad area. *Transportation*, 1–29.

Nessi, H., Le Néchet, N., Terral, L. (2016). Changement de regard sur le périurbain, quelles marges de manœuvre en matière de durabilité ? *Géographie, économie, société*, 18(1), 15–33.

Newman, P. and Kenworthy, J. (1999). *Sustainability and Cities: Overcoming Automobile Dependence*. Island Press, Washington.

Nie, Y.M., Li, Q., Ghamami, M., Ma, J. (2013). Urban travel reliability analysis with consumer GPS data. Technical report, Transportation Research Board (TRB).

Pajević, F. and Shearmur, R.G. (2017). Catch me if you can: Workplace mobility & big data. *Journal of Urban Technology*, 24(3), 99–115.

Pistre, P. and Richard, F. (2018). Seulement 5 ou 15% de ruraux en France métropolitaine ? Les malentendus du zonage en aires urbaines. *Géoconfluences*.

Pouyanne, G. (2004). Forme urbaine et mobilité quotidienne. PhD Thesis, Université Montesquieu-Bordeaux IV.

Pujol, S., Arseguel, M., Alasset, S., Ance, V. (2017). Toulouse dynamise l'emploi dans son réseau de villes moyennes. Statistics report, Insee Analyses Occitanie, 47, July 2017.

Raux, C., Grassot, L., Charmes, E., Nimal, E., Sévenet, M. (2018). La mobilité quotidienne face à la contrainte carbone : quelles politiques privilégier ? *Les Cahiers scientifiques du transport*, 74, 83–116.

Raux, C., Charmes, E., Grassot, L., Sévenet, M., Maizia, M. (2020). PERITHEL. Formes (péri) urbaines, transport, habitat, énergie, environnement, localisation : un bilan prospectif. PhD Thesis, LAET, Lyon and EIFER (European Institute for Energy Research), Karlsruhe.

Rozenblat, C. (2020). Extending the concept of city for delineating large urban regions (LUR) for the cities of the world. *Cybergeo: European Journal of Geography*.

Schlich, R. and Axhausen, K.W. (2003). Habitual travel behaviour: Evidence from a six-week travel diary. *Transportation*, 30(1), 13–36.

Schwanen, T., Dieleman, F.M., Dijst, M. (2003). Car use in Netherlands daily urban systems: Does polycentrism result in lower commute times? *Urban Geography*, 24(5), 410–430.

SETRA (2010). Enquêtes de circulation. Organisation et déroulement. Guide, SETRA, Bagneux.

Soja, E.W. (2011). Beyond postmetropolis. *Urban Geography*, 32(4), 451–469.

Solís Trapero, E., Sanz, I.M., Francés, J.M.D.U. (2015). Global metropolitan-regional scale in evolution: Metropolitan intermediary cities & metropolitan cities. *European Planning Studies*, 23(3), 568–596.

Sourbati, M. and Behrendt, F. (2020). Smart mobility, age & data justice. *New Media & Society*, February 4.

Thomas, I., Jones, J., Caruso, G., Gerber, P. (2018). City delineation in European applications of LUTI models: Review & tests. *Transport Reviews*, 38(1), 6–32.

Toilier, F., Gardrat, M., Routhier, J.L., Bonnafous, A. (2018). Freight transport modelling in urban areas: The French case of the freturb model. *Case Studies on Transport Policy*, 6(4), 753–764.

United Nations (2018). The world's cities in 2018. Report, Department of Economic & Social Affairs, Population Division, World Urbanization Prospects, 1–34.

Vincent-Geslin, S., Meissonnier, J., Kaufmann, V., Rabaud, M. (2019). La mobilité en méthodes. Editorial. *Recherche transports sécurité (RTS) 2019*, 5.

Wallerstein, I.M. (2009). *Comprendre le monde. Introduction à l'analyse des systèmes-monde*. La Découverte, Paris.

Wang, Z., He, S.Y., Leung, Y. (2018). Applying mobile phone data to travel behaviour research: A literature review. *Travel Behaviour & Society*, 11, 141–155.

Zito, P. and Salvo, G. (2011). Toward an urban transport sustainability index: A European comparison. *European Transport Research Review*, 3(4), 179–195.

11

Geographical Inequalities in the Analysis of Urban Mobility

Florent LE NÉCHET
Gustave Eiffel University, École des Ponts, LVMT, Marne-la-Vallée, France

11.1. Introduction

"Tell me how you study urban mobility and I'll tell you who you are." Urban mobility is very heterogeneous around the world, and fine-grained knowledge of its fine details is local and specific. Beyond the general domination of the internal-combustion car as a means of travel, a varied range of modes of transport are available in cities, based on different modes of collective organization. At a minimum, the organization of automotive mobility requires the construction and maintenance of roadways, bridges and tunnels, and possible regulation of the types of vehicles authorized to circulate (e.g. low-emission zones in different city centers in Europe). Organization of public and private "collective" transport is more complex. In addition to ensuring the presence and quality of infrastructure, a fleet of vehicles should be purchased or rented, and fixed or modular services (bus lines, transport on demand, etc.) should be provided. For all these often-costly operations, the ability to understand the mobility of inhabitants and anticipate future needs is essential. This is the field of urban mobility analysis, which includes (i) analysis of lifestyles and how they translate into movements from point A to point B in space, in order to perform activities (mobility practices) (Massot and Orfeuil 2005; Gallez and Kaufmann 2009; Vincent-Geslin and Authier 2015; Cailly and Pourtau 2018); (ii) traffic analysis, for various modes of transport (road congestion, operational management of railway incidents, etc.) (Lesteven 2012; Leclerc et al. 2013; Commenges et Fen-Chong 2017; Alisoltani et al. 2020; Banos et al. 2021). Each of these fields explore both the question of measuring and understanding what is observable and its projection into the future, that is, the ability to imagine possible changes in lifestyles and mobility practices (choice of modes of transport, in particular), as well as anticipating the possible consequences of changes external to the mobility system, such as new infrastructures or an increase in energy costs. These fields of research and operation are more or less active depending on whether cities are experiencing significant demographic or economic dynamics, or face significant policy challenges (congestion, pollution, social inequalities and climate change) and have adequate financial resources and technical skills at their disposal.

In this context, a variety of actors are involved in the financing of mobility studies. In particular, states or public authorities, at different levels, are able to finance all or part of the investigations and technical instruments, and do so according to methodologies that are often standardized, adapted from American traffic studies from the first half of the 20th century (Commenges 2013). The most conventional components of these mechanisms are travel surveys, asking residents about trips made during a given period of time; cordon surveys, counting traffic passing through a particular place in the city; and origin-destination surveys, fixed or mobile traffic sensors (Chrétien et al. 2018).

Other actors finance the production of data and studies on urban mobility; for instance, major international donors disseminating norms (World Bank, Agence Française de Développement) (Musil 2013; Good 2020), private companies (transport operators, consulting firms), or NGOs or universities, developing ad hoc methodologies in an increasingly competitive market – for instance, location data from mobile operators or from GPS, or metadata from personal smartphone applications. Whether public or private, based on old or new technologies, these survey mechanisms have a cost of production, unevenly distributed between different territories. Accessing existing datasets is not always possible, even for local stakeholders (Baldasseroni and Charansonney 2018), and technical capacities for using the data are unequally distributed, often requiring the use of specialized private consultancies. Among stakeholders involved in the production, dissemination and use of data, interactions vary between territories, and not necessarily to the advantage of public authorities (Courmont 2018). At the global level, the capacity of public actors to organize the production, dissemination and use of local mobility data is uneven.

From this fragmentation of the modalities and instruments of knowledge derives a fragmentation of knowledge on urban mobility, which we seek to demonstrate through two empirical quantitative analyses at French and global levels. The exploratory inductive approach we have adopted is as follows. Which actors build, disseminate and use urban mobility databases, and for what purpose? In which cities may the study of urban mobility be considered particularly significant? What do these observations say about the interplay between actors associated with the production of urban mobility?

Because of the multiplicity of elements of local context that must be taken into account to understand mobility practices in a city, it is understandable that mobility studies are mainly local and specific. In fact, relatively few efforts have been made to share data and procedures openly and globally to help public decision-making around urban mobility (Haghshenas and Vazari 2012). Among the international literature on mobility data (McIntosh et al. 2014; Rode et al. 2017; Danielis et al. 2018; Braga et al. 2019), there is little international comparative work on the methods and instruments of knowledge of mobility of goods and people (Commenges 2013). According to Guilloux et al. (2015), "surveys themselves remain little studied as an instrument of 'representing' territorial reality in the service of public policy". This remark applies to both the use of traditional tools such as "household travel surveys", or innovative data such as mobile telephone data (Tempelmeier et al. 2019).

It is not easy to grasp the geographical inequalities of analysis of daily mobility, as this field is at the same time a research and an operational field. It appears to be segmented both geographically and by mode of transport. Rail and road modes in particular may appear as two different worlds between which exchanges are surprisingly weak. In this context, we seek to shed light on the unequal investment in the study of mobility at the urban scale using two different methods, each allowing only a partial look at such a complex and multifactorial issue. For the French case, we will analyze the spatial distribution of a particular tool, the CEREMA mobility survey, for French cities of 50,000 inhabitants or more. At a global level, we propose an exploratory bibliometric analysis of English-language publications on urban mobility in global cities with more than 1 million inhabitants (data source: *lens.org*). These two approaches aim to collect observations, or even certain factors explaining inter-urban inequalities in the analysis of urban mobility: inequalities in terms of measuring instruments on the one hand, differences in terms of issues and possible actions on the other hand.

11.2. Analysis of the implementation of CEREMA-type surveys in France

In this first exploration, we discuss the presence or absence of a CEREMA-type travel mobility survey to support mobility studies in major French cities. CEREMA

(Centre for Studies and Expertise on Risks, Environment, Mobility and Development) is a French public institution created in 2014 through the merger of several pre-existing entities. This includes CERTU (Centre for Studies on Networks, Transport, Urban Planning and Public Buildings), which published the protocols for mobility surveys, involving three tools: the Household Travel Survey (HTS), the Medium City Travel Survey and the Large Territory Travel Survey, which are substantially similar variations of HTS (the protocol for data collection varies, but not the general philosophy of the survey). These three surveys all aim to collect information on the mobility practices of residents of a territory. A total of 190 such surveys have been conducted in France since 1976 (source: CEREMA, 2021[1]).

Producing such a survey is often a prerequisite for local planning or actions targeting mobility. However, producing such a survey is expensive (around 1 million euros for Bordeaux Métropole (2019), for instance). These data may be used by the various urban planning agencies or private consultancies that specialize in transport and mobility. Conversely, not being covered by a CEREMA-type survey does not prevent a municipality or group of municipalities from performing actions around mobility, especially since the organization of French public stakeholders is complex: the state, regions, departments, urban-rural regions and municipalities may all intervene, at different levels, around urban mobility. It is an "essential tool for the development of PDUs[2]" according to Guilloux et al. (2015), authors who note the "rise in importance of the planning dimension of surveys […] perceptible in the coincidence of the outlines of surveys with those of large-scale territorial planning documents" (SCOT[3] in particular).

In this chapter, we propose to interpret the realization of a CEREMA-type survey in a given city as a proxy for proactive local public activity concerning urban mobility. In particular, we will investigate whether cities with a larger population are more likely to have been subject to a mobility survey than less populated cities, or whether other geographical and sociodemographic factors play a role in explaining variations in this indicator.

The following database was compiled manually from information available on the CEREMA website[4] and data on functional areas from INSEE (2020). Functional

---

1 Available at: https://www.cerema.fr/fr/activites/mobilites/connaissance-modelisation-evaluation-mobilite/enquetes-mobilite-emc2 [Accessed 26 October 2021].
2 Urban Travel Plans.
3 "Schéma de Cohérence Territoriale" (Territorial Consistency Plan).
4 Available at: https://www.cerema.fr/fr/activites/mobilites/connaissance-modelisation-evaluation-mobilite/enquetes-mobilite-emc2 [Accessed 26 October 2021].

urban areas (FUAs) are defined according to criteria of regular home-work travel[5]. Among the 699 FUAs defined by INSEE, we examine those located in metropolitan France, excluding cross-border areas (whose configuration is more complex to study). In addition, only FUAs with more than 50,000 inhabitants are included in the database, smaller cities being a priori less likely to finance such costly studies about the mobility of their residents. In fact, in the CEREMA database, only one survey involves a territory of less than 50,000 inhabitants. In the end, 170 FUAs remain. Next, by cross-referencing the files extracted from the CEREMA website and the FUA location map, each FUA is assigned the following two indicators: (i) presence of at least one HTS (since 1976) and (ii) is the city under examination the main city within the HTS boundaries?

For the first variable, it should be noted that there is generally no match between the FUA and the area covered by an HTS. We have chosen to consider an FUA to be covered when the central city "commune" was covered (even if in most cases, especially in the most recent surveys, in particular the so-called "large territory" surveys, the boundary of the HTS is wider than that of the FUA).

For this second variable, we made interpretations based on the name and boundaries of the survey. Take the example of the CEREMA-type mobility survey for Bas Rhin (2009): as FUAs with more than 50,000 inhabitants, Strasbourg and Sélestat are included in the database we compiled. The "main city" indicator is entered with value 1 for Strasbourg and value 0 for Sélestat because Strasbourg is, by far, the most important city in this department (a quarter of the inhabitants of the department, nearly 10 times the population of the second most populous municipality, Haguenau). Conversely, the survey carried out in Corsica in 2017 led us to set the indicator "main city" at 1 for both Ajaccio and Bastia because the population gap between the two is relatively small, and together, these two cities contribute two-thirds of the population of the department. These choices, made manually, are of course debatable, but are only relevant for a limited number of territories.

Finally, we have added to this table an indication of the population growth of the FUA between 1982 and 2018. This information aims to differentiate cities according to their demographic dynamism. Two contrary hypotheses can be made: either for

---

5 "A functional urban area defines the extent of its influence on the surrounding municipalities. This zoning replaces the 2010 zoning in urban areas. An area is composed of a pole, defined on the basis of population and employment criteria, and a fringe, made up of municipalities in which at least 15% of the active workers work in the pole." Definition available on the INSEE website: https://www.insee.fr/fr/information/4808607 [Accessed 30 November 2021, then translated into English].

the same size of city, the most demographically dynamic would also be those cities featuring more proactive local public policies relating to urban mobility, leading to these cities having a greater propensity to produce HTSs; or on the contrary, the state and/or regional stakeholders would seek to compensate for inequalities in local public finance through investments such as the production of mobility surveys.

11.3. Size effects and context effects explaining why an HTS is carried out

Figure 11.1 shows the gradual growth in CEREMA-type surveys, driven by the "progressive decoupling between the production of data and the construction of a travel model" (Guilloux et al. 2015). This growth is accompanied by a spatial spread of the tool from the largest cities to smaller cities. Thus, four of the six cities that completed an HTS in 1976 (first year) are the four main French metropolises: Paris, Lyon, Marseille and Lille (the other two are Nancy and Orléans). The eight surveys carried out in 2018 involved smaller cities (Rennes, Le Havre, Alençon, Brest, Poitiers, Besançon, Evreux and Gap).

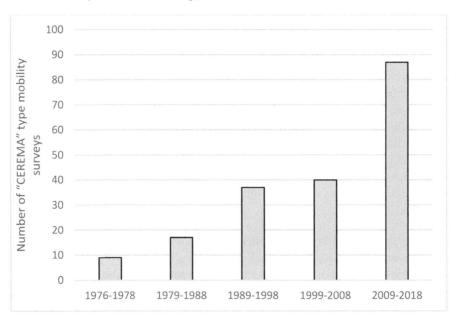

Figure 11.1. *Changes in the production of CEREMA-type mobility surveys, in France, 1976–2018. Source: CEREMA, the division into 10-year segments is intended to correspond to the latest year for which data is available*

Table 11.1 first confirms, as expected, the importance of city size effects in explaining the presence of an HTS. Overall, two thirds of cities were covered by an HTS (119 out of 170). All cities with more than 200,000 inhabitants have been covered, at one time or another, by an HTS. Note that we do not analyze the frequency of coverage here. On the other hand, for smaller cities, coverage is heterogeneous: 65% of cities with between 100,000 and 200,000 inhabitants and 52% of cities with between 50,000 and 100,000 inhabitants were covered, at least partially. Coverage by region is also heterogeneous, with the following five regions having the smallest share of FUAs covered by a CEREMA-type HTS: Centre Val-de-Loire, Occitanie, Grand Est, Bourgogne Franche-Comté and Nouvelle Aquitaine[6], corresponding to the location of less well-served cities in the geographical center of the country.

The geographical spread of this tool is accompanied by changes in the spatial structure of the survey boundaries. As Guilloux et al. (2015) say: "it is the evolution of the urban territorial structure, through suburbanization and metropolization, but also the rise of new issues, such as sustainable development, which seem to contribute to the upturn in terms of mobility surveys". Thus, in the corpus studied, half (52%) of the cities with between 100,000 and 200,000 inhabitants were primarily covered by an HTS, compared to only 14% of the cities with between 50,000 and 100,000 inhabitants. Above all, and perhaps most importantly, cities that were not covered have different socio-demographic characteristics to covered cities. Indeed, for the smallest cities (50,000–100,000 inhabitants), being covered by a survey is associated with an average population growth between 22 and 24%, while cities not covered have very low population growth, 4% on average.

Half of the FUAs with declining populations during this period were not covered by an HTS (13 out of 26 cities). For cities with between 100,000 and 200,000 inhabitants, the effect is different, with the lowest population growth for cities still not covered (12% growth), but this figure is very similar to the growth of cities primarily covered (16% growth). In this category of cities, metropolization seems to play a role, since it is the cities covered by the HTS of another city (often a larger city) that have the strongest population growth (31%). They undoubtedly benefit from the effects of residential migrations of inhabitants of the largest city towards this networked "periphery", which is subject to ad hoc public policies, including in particular the production of "larger territories"-type surveys. "Out of 32 territories which carried out at least two surveys, 28 took the opportunity to widen their survey boundaries" (Guilloux et al. 2015).

---

6 Whether the counting involves all FUAs or only those between 50,000 and 200,000 inhabitants.

Size of urban attraction area	Main city of an HTS		City is included but is not the main city of an HTS		City is not included in any HTS	
	Number of cities (% of category)	Cumulative population (2018)/growth 1982–2018	Number of cities (% of category)	Cumulative population (2018)/growth 1982–2018	Number of cities (% of category)	Cumulative population (2018)/growth 1982–2018
Between 50,000 and 100,000 inhabitants	10 (14%)	0.7 M (+24%)	27 (38%)	1.7 M (+22%)	34 (48%)	2.3 M (+4%)
Between 100,000 and 200,000 inhabitants	28 (57%)	4.3 M (+16%)	4 (8%)	0.5 M (+26%)	17 (35%)	2.2 M (+12%)
Between 200,000 and 400,000 inhabitants	24 (92%)	7.1 M (+18%)	2 (8%)	0.6 M (+31%)	–	–
More than 400,000 inhabitants	24 (100%)	32.0 M (+27%)	–	–	–	–

Table 11.1. *Descriptive statistics of the demographic growth of cities according to their size and the presence or absence of a CEREMA-type HTS*

What can we learn from an analysis of such a specific corpus? Care should be taken against any causal and simplistic interpretation of these figures. Of course, coverage of a city by an HTS cannot have a direct and unequivocal impact on its demographic dynamism. Mobility analysis is a marker among others of inequalities between cities and of one level in the urban hierarchy. In fact, despite the presence of national entities like CEREMA that can provide all local authorities with skills and technical guides, and despite specific funding, mobility seems to be more studied in the most populated cities on the one hand, and in the most demographically dynamic on the other. This is not necessarily a problem: it may even be logical, in that it is probably where congestion problems are most prominent that it may be important to plan heavy transport infrastructure. Faced with the challenges of global warming, and the social problems resulting from it (fuel poverty of travel), this argument is, however, questionable. The medium-term planning measures recommended by Raux et al. (2018), aimed at offering less carbon-intensive mobility solutions to areas outside major urban centers, typically require the local knowledge of mobility resulting from this type of survey.

11.4. Bibliometric analysis of research on urban mobility

Spatial unevenness of urban mobility analysis is even greater at a global level. In order to better grasp the diversity of local studies of urban mobility, we carried out a bibliometric analysis, focusing both on the presence or absence of academic work on urban mobility, city by city, for the main cities of the world (Eckert et al. 2018).

This approach also aims to qualify, beyond "raw" bibliometric counts, the main mobility challenges that a given city may face. We manually performed systematic queries on all 548 cities with more than 1 million inhabitants according to the UN database (United Nations 2018). For this exploratory work, two categories of queries were made on the *lens.org* platform:

– a query of the number of publications, with the keyword of each city (in the title or abstract), and also containing the keyword *urban mobility*, *urban transportation*, *daily mobility* or *commuting* (in the title or in the summary);

– a query of the number of publications, by city, containing one of the previous keywords, and one of the additional keywords in the list below, to reflect the modes of transport being searched (title or abstract):

- in the field of automotive mobility: *car* or *automobile*,

- in the field of public transport: *bus*, *train*, *transit*, or *public transport*,

- in the field of soft mobilities: *walking*, *cycling*, *bicycle*, *pedestrian* or *active modes*.

We chose to work only with references in English because it is the main language of publication of scientific articles at a global level. This does introduce a bias; therefore, let us reformulate our research question as follows: "How significant is scientific publication activity in English, city by city, on this theme?" This has at least two consequences: it leads, of course, to an over-representation of cities in English-speaking or partially English-speaking countries (several dozen countries including South Africa, Australia, the United States, India, and the United Kingdom); this leads to an over-representation of cities in which public or private groups from English-speaking countries or globalized groups are present.

The choice to restrict the analysis to cities with more than 1 million inhabitants, of course a debatable one, is linked to the desire to work on cities that a priori have the financial or political capacity to organize transport infrastructure or mobility services within their own boundaries. This may involve total or partial financing of transport infrastructure, for example. Finally, it should be noted that the methodology used is based solely on the occurrence of a word in a textual database and that consequently, nothing can be said about the actual geographical area to which each publication refers. It is not even certain that the article actually deals with urban mobility in this city: however, by restricting the search for occurrences to the title and the abstract, we believe that this bias is rather limited.

In total, 59,000 scientific publications were identified by the site *lens.org* as having one of the key words referring to issues of urban mobility, 14,500 of which are attached to one of the 548 cities in the corpus. We have decided to retain all types of publications, including gray literature and reports appearing in this corpus. A majority of the publications (57%) are scientific articles, but 30% of the publications cannot be categorized by *lens.org*. This site, which was chosen because of its large collection of articles (more than 200 million references since 1950) and the technical ease of working with queries, is certainly not exhaustive or unbiased: some of these publications may be articles in unreferenced journals, press articles and working papers whose scientific value has not been assessed and so on. Despite this possible bias, we continue in our exploratory work.

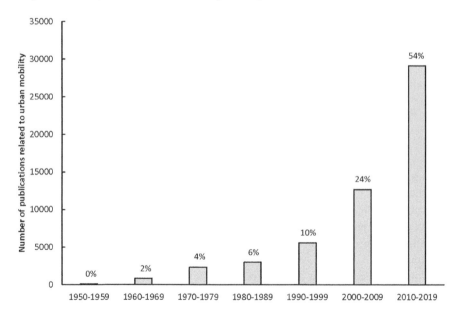

Figure 11.2. *Distribution of articles in the corpus, by year of publication*

The fact that 54% of publications are from the most recent period (2010–2019) tells us two things: (i) the pace of research activity on urban mobility is quite similar to that of research activity in general (among the 217 million publications identified by *lens.org* over all areas of knowledge, 48% come from the period 2010–2020) and (ii) the interpretation we can make of the values obtained must take into account the fact that nearly three-fourths of the corpus dates from the 21st century, at a time when the challenges of climate change related to transport and mobility have already been very well identified (Banister 2008). We will therefore, except in special cases, subsequently interpret the values obtained as corresponding to a recent period, around 2010, the median date of the corpus of bibliographical references.

11.5. Global heterogeneity of urban mobility analysis

The observed average of 30 publications per city related to urban mobility conceals a very large geographical disparity (Table 11.2). Of the 548 cities with more than one million inhabitants in the corpus, 34 cities are the subject of half of the publications related to urban mobility, and 157 cities (less than one third) are the subject of 90% of the publications. This organization of research and reporting on the issue of urban mobility therefore leaves out a large number of cities, for which methods of data collection and processing have probably been of secondary importance, either duplicating existing methods that are not adapted to the local context, or even making no study of them at all. Thus, 117 cities, or about a quarter of the cities of more than one million inhabitants in the world, have no specific scientific publications in English about the territory of their city and about urban mobility. Let us recall that these cities may appear in comparative studies at a global level or in technical publications, as well as in publications written in a language other than English.

This concentration is more related to geographical context than to size effects. Using UN nomenclatures (United Nations 2018), the sub-continents "North America", "Western Europe", "Northern Europe" and "Southern Europe" were the subject of 48% of publications for 14% of the urban population in 2018; conversely, the sub-continent "Asia" (containing China, Japan and South Korea) accounts for 29% of the urban population and only 19% of publications.

We observe that the proportion of cities with no publications is highest in East and Central Africa, echoing what Jerven and Johnston (2014) call Africa's "statistical tragedy". Overall, the distribution of the number of publications per city follows a hierarchical law of the "rank-size" type (Figure 11.3), that is to say, a distribution in which the cities most covered are more covered than those following according to a power law (cf. formula (1), where q_n is the number of publications associated with the city of rank n in the distribution). The exponent parameter of the power law is greater than 1. Conversely, the parameter of the rank-size law linking the population of cities p_n to their rank is slightly lower than 1 (cf. formula (2), for the same corpus of cities with at least one publication). In other words, the largest cities are very clearly favored as subjects for scientific publications about their territory, even more than in proportion to their population.

Rank-size law for number of publications related to urban mobility:

$$q_n \propto n^{-1.52}.$$ [11.1]

Rank-size law for population of cities

$$p_n \propto n^{-0.77}.$$ [11.2]

Continent	Countries according to the UN database, with at least one publication in the corpus studied	Number of cities	Number of publications	Ratio of publications to city (*)	Proportion of cities with no publications (%)
Asia	China, North Korea, South Korea, Hong Kong, Japan, Mongolia and Taiwan	150	2,758	18.4	34
South Asia	Afghanistan, Bangladesh, India, Nepal and Pakistan	83	769	9.3	31
East Asia	Saudi Arabia, Armenia, Azerbaijan, United Arab Emirates, Georgia, Iraq, Israel, Jordan, Kuwait, Lebanon, Oman, Syria, Turkey and Yemen	32	258	8.1	16
South-East Asia	**Burma, Cambodia, Indonesia, Malaysia, Philippines, Singapore, Thailand** and **Vietnam**	30	831	27.7*	13
Oceania	**Australia** and **New Zealand**	6	522	87.0*	0
Central Asia	Kazakhstan and Uzbekistan	3	2	0.7	33
Eastern Europe	Belarus, Bulgaria, Hungary, Poland, Romania, Russia, Czech Republic and Ukraine	24	224	9.3	13
Western Europe	Germany, Austria, **Belgium, France, Netherlands** and **Switzerland**	14	1,006	71.9*	0

Southern Europe	Spain, Greece, Italy, Portugal and Serbia	10	800	80*	0
Northern Europe	Denmark, Finland, Ireland, Norway, United Kingdom and Sweden	10	1,127	112.7*	0
North America	Canada and United States	51	4,065	79.7*	2
South America	Argentina, Bolivia, Brazil, Chile, Colombia, Ecuador, Paraguay, Peru, Uruguay and Venezuela	46	1,278	27.8*	11
Central America	Costa Rica, Guatemala, Honduras, Mexico, Nicaragua, Panama and El Salvador	22	225	10.2	23
Caribbean	Cuba, Haiti, Puerto Rico and Dominican Republic	4	19	4.8	0
West Africa	Burkina Faso, Ivory Coast, Ghana, Guinea, Liberia, Mali, Mauritania, Niger, Nigeria, Senegal, Sierra Leone and Togo	22	178	8.1	18
East Africa	Ethiopia, Kenya, Madagascar, Malawi, Mozambique, Uganda, Rwanda, Somalia, Tanzania, Zambia and Zimbabwe	14	112	8.0	50
Central Africa	Angola, Cameroon, Congo, DR Congo and Chad	11	16	1.5	45
North Africa	Algeria, Egypt, Libya, Morocco, Sudan and Tunisia	10	150	15.0	0
South Africa	South Africa	6	115	19.2	0
World		548	14,455	26.4	21

Table 11.2. *Number of publications associated with cities in the countries mentioned, on the topic of urban mobility. (*: sub-continents for which the ratio of number of publications per city is higher than the world average are shown in bold)*

256 Urban Mobility Systems in the World

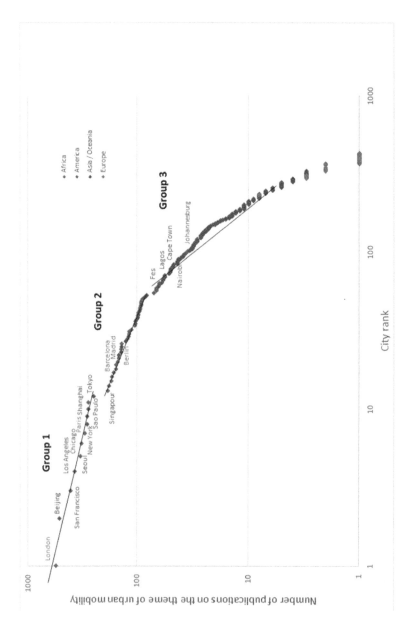

Figure 11.3. *Hierarchy of the number of local publications on urban mobility. The five cities with the most publications per continent are represented. For a color version of this figure, see www.iste.co.uk/lesteven/urban.zip*

By analyzing the breaks in slope in Figure 11.3 more finely, using a method similar to that of Guérois and Pumain (2008), the distribution of the number of articles by city can be broken down into three groups. Group 1 consists of 12 cities with, by far, the most publications, which we call "star cities". These cities are quite close to each other (in the sense that the slope of the curve connecting these cities is close to horizontal). Our interpretation is that these cities are a sort of scientific playground and sites of methodological innovation for researchers and operational actors, as cities for which academic publications are linked to effective activity around urban mobility, requiring an analysis of local mobility issues. These cities are of course more or less the same as in most international rankings of "world cities"[7] (Sassen 2009), and are mainly in the United States and Europe, representing 29% of publications for 10% of the urban population of the corpus. Group 3 corresponds to a higher slope, characteristic of a process of selection within a hierarchical network of cities. Group 2 is intermediate and may correspond to a mixture of the two situations.

11.6. Thematic specializations revealing issues for local action on mobility

The study of keywords relating to modes of transport reveals forms of specialization within the cities of the corpus studied. This latter semantic analysis aims to give elements of answers to the question: what are the challenges facing cities in terms of mobility planning (reducing congestion, modal shift to public transport, pedestrian safety, reducing car dependency in suburban areas, for example), and how can publications on these topics reflect this? To do this, we simplified our corpus of bibliographic references by indicating, for each publication, whether the article mentions a particular mode of transport (note that the answer may be "yes" several times). We then proceeded to a hierarchical bottom-up classification based on three variables: "share of articles mentioning cars"; "share of articles mentioning public transport"; "share of articles mentioning walking or cycling", for the 152 cities, with at least 20 publications associated with the field of urban mobility. This threshold was chosen so that the calculated ratios may reveal something other than statistical fluctuations (Figure 11.2). This classification is distinguished between six classes (Figure 11.4).

– Class C2, "Average Profile", includes cities that have been the subject of the majority of publications, and with a diversity of themes covered. The so-called "playground" cities of mobility research are two-thirds of those in this class.

---

7 See the entry "Global Cities, World Cities" on the Geoconfluences site: http://geoconfluences.ens-lyon.fr/glossaire/globales-mondiales-villes [Accessed 14 November 2021].

– Classes C3, "Public Transport", and C5, "Mechanized Transport", include cities with significant population growth, and which have featured recent public transport projects or activities, notably BRT (bus rapid transit), as in Cape Town (2010), Chengdu (2013), Dar es Salaam (2016) or Lagos (2008). Several of these have been financed by international donors such as the World Bank, actively participating in the organization of urban mobilities at city level.

– Classes C4, "Active Modes" (overrepresentation of active modes), and C6 "Individual Modes" (overrepresentation of active modes and the car), include cities with a particular interest in the issue of individual mobility and its regulation (in particular Helsinki or Amsterdam, cities advanced in the regulation of service mobility).

– C1, "Other Themes", a final class of cities, in blue in Figure 11.4, includes a number of cities where innovation in electric vehicles appears to be significant (Seoul, Shenzhen and Nagoya).

This suggests a heterogeneous landscape, where challenges vary according to cities and countries, which should ideally benefit from ad hoc methodologies of counting and analysis adapted to local specificities, which is far from being the case as we have explained.

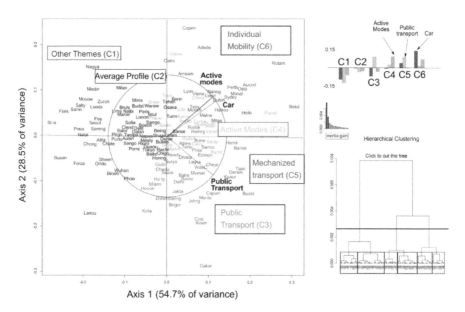

Figure 11.4. *Thematic specializations of articles on urban mobility. For a color version of this figure, see www.iste.co.uk/lesteven/urban.zip*

These observations are of course only valid in the exploratory framework of this chapter, and many methodological problems would need to be solved in order to draw thematic conclusions from this work. We use this corpus for framing purposes, to illustrate both the very great inequality of treatment of urban mobility in the international literature, and the diversity of the challenges facing cities and continents around the world. It should be noted that the classes obtained are relatively unrelated to geographical variables, the continent with the highest concentration of cities being America with 35% of cities in the "average profile" class (C2). In our opinion, the results obtained suggest a form of specialization of research themes on urban mobility that may involve cross-overs between approaches. The issues concern both unequal access to mobility data, and unequal capacity for processing the available data, due to the technicalities of mobility data processing procedures. This observation is important in a context where, whether it is mobility survey data derived from a relatively standardized protocol, or data from mobile telephony, GPS and so on, the local and specific issues of each city are difficult to fully address using the complex and rigid existing methods.

11.7. Discussion

The approaches we have taken aimed to answer the following questions: what is the level of heterogeneity in the analysis of urban mobility? What does this heterogeneity reveal about mobility issues in these cities? Which factors seem likely to explain the importance of investigating urban mobility in one city compared to another? In light of the two exploratory surveys carried out, we can outline some elements of response to the problem which we had formulated.

The first observation is as follows: levels of analysis of mobility are very uneven and do not depend only on the effects of population size. At the outcome of this exploratory work, while the answers we propose are not definitive, we observe forms of specialization among cities, for cities of similar size. Thus, small French cities that are well covered by the "HTS" tool are mainly cities with strong functional links with a larger city, a form of residential specialization requiring specific treatments in terms of mobility policy. Some global cities are emerging as playgrounds for global research on urban mobility, while others are in a "data desert." In terms of mobility policies, some cities are subject to operational implementations of urban planning, sometimes financed by international organizations (such as the case of bus rapid transit in a number of cities with strong population and infrastructure growth, which emerged in our corpus). To some extent, they can be seen as a playground for financing by major international donors such as the World Bank (Baffi 2017).

The second observation is as follows: the study of daily mobility can be seen as revealing a diversity of models of public action, sets of public and private actors, at different scales. They may be top-down national visions, as in France, supported by public bodies such as CEREMA, or top-down international visions, such as development aid. It may also relate to the logic of financial investments in emerging technologies, such as the case of electric and connected cars in Seoul or Nagoya, suggested by our corpus. This therefore raises the question of the degree of control by the public authorities of data concerning urban mobility (Commenges 2013). At the level of inter-territorial cooperation, the changes in HTS boundaries illustrate new forms of cooperation between local authorities, as mentioned by Guilloux et al. (2015).

Of course, we should not expect too much from these systematic quantitative studies, given the many possible biases and methodological pitfalls (Raimbault 2021). Among these, the questions of delimitation of cities, segmentation of modes of transport and corpus construction are debatable in both exploratory approaches, even if this is sometimes implicit. Thus, for example, by focusing on HTSs at the urban level, we largely leave aside the specific challenges of "pedestrian urban mobility" (Monnet et al. 2019), which are poorly collected by HTSs. Nevertheless, it seems to us that the points that emerge are not too sensitive to these methodological pitfalls, so evident is the heterogeneity of the means invested in understanding and acting around urban mobility, at all levels of the world cities system (Sassen 2009). Specific observatories such as that dedicated to mobility platforms (Boutueil et al. 2021) may help to better identify and understand these inequalities, at a time when all cities will have to adapt, in particular through policies related to mobility, to the challenges of climate change. Beyond these initiatives, a more effective sharing of data would without doubt help reconcile the necessary adaptation of mobility surveys to the local context. Their intersections and comparisons, at a regional, continental or global level, would enable us to better understand the complexity of the local formation of daily mobilities.

11.8. References

Alisoltani, N., Zargayouna, M., Leclercq, L. (2020). Real-time autonomous taxi service: An agent-based simulation. In *Agents and Multi-Agent Systems: Technologies and Applications*, Jezic, G., Chen-Burger, Y.-H.J., Kusek, M., Šperka, R., Howlett, R.J., Jain, L.C. (eds). Springer, Singapore.

Baffi, S. (2017). La mise en place d'un bus à Haut Niveau de Service au Cap, un outil de normalisation de la ville sud-africaine ? *EchoGéo*, 40 [Online]. Available at: http://journals.openedition.org/echogeo/14945 [Accessed 12 June 2023].

Baldasseroni, L. and Charansonney, L. (2018). Gouverner la voirie urbaine par l'information de l'automobiliste. Une comparaison Lyon–Paris, des années 1920 à nos jours. *Flux*, 113, 24–40. doi: 10.3917/flux1.113.0024.

Banister, D. (2008). The sustainable mobility paradigm. *Transport Policy*, 15(2), 73–80.

Banos, A., Commenges, H., Debrie, J. (2021). Modelling and gaming urban mobility: Île-de-France's Post-Car Project. In *Complex Systems, Smart Territories and Mobility*, Sajous, P. and Bertelle, C. (eds). Springer, Cham.

Bertolini, L. and le Clercq, F. (2003). Urban development without more mobility by car? Lessons from Amsterdam, a multimodal urban region. *Environment and Planning A: Economy and Space*, 35(4), 575–589.

Bon, B. (2020). Aide internationale et grands projets urbains en Afrique sub-saharienne. Le cas de la Ville du rail à Nairobi. *Cybergeo: European Journal of Geography*, Regional and Urban Planning, 951 [Online]. Available at: http://journals.openedition.org/cybergeo/35186 [Accessed 12 June 2023].

Bordeaux Métropole (2019). Demande de subvention. Réalisation d'une Enquête Ménages Déplacements à l'échelle du département de la Gironde 2020–2021. Report, Bordeaux Métropole.

Boutueil, V., Nemett, L., Quillerier, T. (2021). Trends in competition among digital platforms for shared mobility: Insights from a worldwide census and prospects for research. *Transportation Research Record*, 2676(2), 69–82.

Braga, I.P.C., Dantas, H.F.B., Leal, M.R.D., de Almeida, M.R., dos Santos, E.M. (2019). Urban mobility performance indicators: A bibliometric analysis. *Gestão & Produção*, 26(3), e3828.

Cailly, L. and Pourtau, B. (2018). "Faire métropole" : une analyse par les représentations et les pratiques de mobilité périurbaines des habitants de l'aire urbaine de Tours (France). *Géocarrefour*, 92(4) [Online]. Available at: http://journals.openedition.org/geocarrefour/10394 [Accessed on 12 June 2023].

Chrétien, J., Le Néchet, F., Leurent, F., Yin, B. (2018). Using mobile phone data to observe and understand mobility behavior, territories, and transport usage. *Urban Mobility and the Smartphone: Transportation, Travel Behavior and Public Policy*, 79, 79–141.

Commenges, H. (2013). Socio-économie des transports : une lecture conjointe des instruments et des concepts. *Cybergeo: European Journal of Geography*, Regional and Urban Planning, 633 [Online]. Available at: http://journals.openedition.org/cybergeo/25750 [Accessed 12 June 2023].

Commenges, H. and Fen-Chong, J. (2017). Navettes domicile-travail : naissance et développement d'un objet statistique structurant. In *Annales de géographie*. Armand Colin, Paris.

Courmont, A. (2018). L'open data au Grand Lyon : l'émergence d'un gouvernement métropolitain de la mobilité. *Métropoles*, 23 [Online]. Available at: http://journals.openedition.org/metropoles/6501 [Accessed on 12 June 2023].

Danielis, R., Rotaris, L., Monte, A. (2018). Composite indicators of sustainable urban mobility: Estimating the rankings frequency distribution combining multiple methodologies. *International Journal of Sustainable Transportation*, 12(5), 380–395.

Eckert, D., Grossetti, M., Jégou, L., Maisonobe, M. (2018). Les villes de la science contemporaine, entre logiques locales, nationales et globales. Une approche bibliométrique. *Les ancrages nationaux de la science mondiale XVIIIe–XXIe siècles*, 37–64.

Gallez, C. and Kaufmann, V. (2009). Aux racines de la mobilité en sciences sociales : contribution au cadre d'analyse socio-historique de la mobilité urbaine. In *De l'histoire des transports à l'histoire de la mobilité*, Flonneau, M. and Guigueno, V. (eds). Presses Universitaires de Rennes.

Guérois, M. and Pumain, D. (2008). Built-up encroachment and the urban field: A comparison of forty European cities. *Environment and Planning A*, 40(9), 2186–2203.

Guilloux, T., Rabaud, M., Richer, C. (2015). De l'enquête-ménage aux enquêtes-déplacements : comment l'action publique a fait évoluer ses instruments d'évaluation. CEREMA – IFSTTAR. Mobilité en transitions. Connaître, comprendre et représenter. Study and research report, halshs-01386610f.

Haghshenas, H. and Vaziri, M. (2012). Urban sustainable transportation indicators for global comparison. *Ecological Indicators*, 15(1), 115–121.

Jerven, M. and Johnston, D. (2014). Statistical tragedy in Africa? Evaluating the database for African economic development. *The Journal of Development Studies*, 51(2), 111–115.

Leclerc, B., Trépanier, M., Morency, C. (2013). Unraveling the travel behavior of carsharing members from global positioning system traces. *Transportation Research Record*, 2359(1), 59–67.

Lesteven, G. (2012). Les stratégies d'adaptation à la congestion automobile dans les grandes métropoles : analyse à partir des cas de Paris, São Paulo et Mumbai. *Confins. Revue franco-brésilienne de géographie/Revista franco-brasilera de geografia*, 15.

Massot, M. and Orfeuil, J. (2005). La mobilité au quotidien, entre choix individuel et production sociale. *Cahiers internationaux de sociologie*, 118, 81–100. doi: 10.3917/cis.118.0081.

McIntosh, J., Trubka, R., Kenworthy, J., Newman, P. (2014). The role of urban form and transit in city car dependence: Analysis of 26 global cities from 1960 to 2000. *Transportation Research Part D: Transport and Environment*, 33, 95–110.

Monnet, J., Pérez-López, R., Hubert, J.P. (2019). Éditorial. Enjeux sociaux et politiques de la marche en ville. *Espaces et sociétés*, 4(179), 7–15.

Musil, C. (2013). La coopération urbaine et l'aide publique au développement à Hanoi : un appui à la fabrication de la ville par la structuration du réseau de transport métropolitain. PhD Thesis, Université Paris-Est.

Rabaud, M. (2018). EMC² : vers une nouvelle génération d'EMD en France. *MSFS 2018*, Tours.

Raimbault, J. (2021). An interdisciplinary bibliometric analysis of models for land-use and transport interactions. arXiv preprint, arXiv:2102.13501.

Raux, C., Grassot, L., Charmes, E., Nimal, E., Sévenet, M. (2018). La mobilité quotidienne face à la contrainte carbone : quelles politiques privilégier ? *Les Cahiers scientifiques du transport*, 74, 83–116.

Rode, P., Floater, G., Thomopoulos, N., Docherty, J., Schwinger, P., Mahendra, A., Fang, W. (2017). Accessibility in cities: Transport and urban form. In *Disrupting Mobility*, Meyer, G. and Shaheen, S. (eds). Springer International Publishing, Cham.

Sassen, S. (2009). Cities in today's global age. *The SAIS Review of International Affairs*, 29(1), 3–34.

Tempelmeier, N., Rietz, Y., Lishchuk, I., Kruegel, T., Mumm, O., Carlow, V.M., Dietze, S., Demidova, E. (2019). Data4UrbanMobility: Towards holistic data analytics for mobility applications in urban regions. *Companion Proceedings of the 2019 World Wide Web Conference*, New York.

United Nations (2018). The world's cities in 2018. Report, Department of Economic and Social Affairs, Population Division, World Urbanization Prospects.

Vincent-Geslin, S. and Authier, J.Y. (2015). Les mobilités quotidiennes comme objet sociologique. *Cahiers de recherche sociologique*, 59–60, 79–97 [Online]. Available at: https://id.erudit.org/iderudit/1036787ar.

World Bank (2013). Annual report 2013. Report.

12

Circulation of Models in Africa: The Example of Bus Rapid Transit in Cape Town

Solène BAFFI[1,2]

[1] UMR Géographie-cités, Université Paris 1 Panthéon-Sorbonne, Paris-Aubervilliers, France
[2] Stellenbosch University, South Africa

12.1. Introduction

The transformation of Africa into a predominantly urban continent is already one of the major societal changes of the 21st century, with the UN projecting nearly 1.5 billion urban residents in 2050, or 62% of the continent's total population. This process, of intense magnitude and speed, often occurs without a real planning framework and notably results in pronounced urban sprawl and unequal access to urban services, including public transport. In addition, another trend has been emerging for several years: motorization rates are rising across the continent. Although these remain low compared to cities in Asia and Latin America, the rapid rise in these rates in relation to household incomes suggests strong growth over the coming decades (Stucki 2017). In addition, after decades of investment almost exclusively dedicated to road construction (Porter 2007), public transport is becoming a priority on the political agenda in order to promote sustainability and inclusion. Since the 2000s, public transport projects have been spreading over the African continent in various forms. Moroccan cities have adopted the tramway (Rabat-Salé, Casablanca), a regional express train was inaugurated in Dakar and a metro is under construction in Abidjan, while a high speed train has run between Johannesburg and Pretoria since 2012. However, it is the bus rapid transit (BRT)

Urban Mobility Systems in the World,
coordinated by Gaële LESTEVEN. © ISTE Ltd 2023.

projects, high-capacity buses on dedicated lanes, that are spreading quickly: from Dakar to Nairobi, from Lagos to Johannesburg, many African cities are adopting or considering to adopt this mode of transport. This phenomenon is not new: model transfer is common in the urban transport sector and is based on dissemination of urban planning standards and technologies (the proliferation of local digital platforms similar to Uber is an example). Among all these models, BRT stands out due to its capacity to jointly address issues common to all cities in the world (congestion, pollution and road safety) as well as specific characteristics of African cities (connections between planning and mobility, opportunity to initiate reforms and reduced costs).

The high adaptability of the BRT model is one of the key factors explaining its increased diffusion over recent decades. However, its spread is not linear – after a strong diffusion throughout Latin America and Asia from the 1970s, it was not until 2007 that BRT appeared in Africa (Poku-Boansi and Marsden 2018). This time lag then brings into question the ways in which the BRT model is diffused – how it was constituted, who the stakeholders involved in its circulation are, and what their interests and objectives are. Additionally, examining the circulation of a model also leads us to consider the local adaptations of the model. This eventually enables us to question whether the "BRT wave" that has been observed for more than a decade on the continent has resulted in the emergence of an African BRT model, driving its own circulation. These different questions are examined here in a South African context, and the city of Cape Town is examined in particular. For several reasons, South African metropolises are indeed exemplary in taking an interest in the circulation of an urban transport model. First of all, mobility is a central issue in cities still marked by the legacy of apartheid urban planning and the separation of part of the population. In addition, these metropolises now have considerable human, financial and technical resources to implement policies of social and spatial rebalancing. Thus, ambitious urban policies, particularly in the area of urban transport, have emerged since the 2000s (Musil et al. 2014). It is in this context that two South African metropolises, Cape Town and Johannesburg, decided to adopt the BRT model in 2007 by offering original versions of this model developed in Latin America.

12.2. The diffusion of BRT in Africa

12.2.1. *Diffusion of an efficient transport model as a planning and urban planning tool*

After the inauguration of the first African BRT project in Lagos in 2008, other networks were then created: in Cape Town (2011), Johannesburg (2013) and Pretoria (2014), then in Dar Es Salaam (2016). As of the start of 2021, other networks are being built in Dakar, Abidjan, Accra, Nairobi and Kigali. In all of these cities, the choice of this mode of transport is part of the projects in place to modernize existing public transport, or even real urban transport reforms. Among the arguments suggested to explain the choice of BRT, the relationship between passenger capacity, commercial speed and investment costs makes this mode a very competitive choice. In particular, the cost of BRT is much lower compared to other modes of public transport on dedicated routes, such as trams or the metro[1]. In addition, the BRT model comes in several categories of varying cost: namely the BRT Classic model and the BRT Lite. The latter is less expensive and simpler to build because it requires less infrastructure, since the isolation of the dedicated route is not continuous and therefore costs less to build (Venter et al. 2020). Indeed, it is the possibility of using a dedicated route that differentiates BRT from conventional bus networks and allows satisfactory commercial speeds by avoiding congestion, which is frequent in cities of the Global South[2]. The capacity performance of BRT, superior to that of tramways, makes it a more suitable mode of transport for metropolises with still high urban growth rates. Finally, rapid construction is another advantage of the BRT: in Lagos, it took 15 months from design to operation of the network (Kaenzig et al. 2010).

Apart from the intrinsic performance of this mode, BRT is also valued for its ability to facilitate intermodality and improve travel conditions for city dwellers. Indeed, in many cities of the Global South, modal integration is weak or even non-existent, which results in long and costly travel for urban dwellers (Stucki 2017). Transport costs are also often proportionally higher for the poorest. Very often, public transport is supplied by informal transport, and in some cases, there are also private bus companies whose quality of service is mediocre due notably to low fare revenues that do not allow reinvestment. The paratransit sector brings together many private operators, federated under the aegis of professional organizations with various statuses (unions, associations and cooperatives). These operators have a complex relationship with local authorities, who do not always recognize their legal existence, and struggle to regulate it and impose quality standards. However, as has occurred in several Latin American cities, BRT offers opportunities for the integration and reform of the paratransit sector. In Bogota, for example, the implementation of the BRT was accompanied by a process of professionalization to help owners form legal entities, with the objective of operating the new BRT service. Over the long term, intermodality takes the form of integrated fares

---

1 For example, while BRT construction costs range from $1.7 million/km in Lagos, $8–10 million/km in Johannesburg, and $12.5 million in Bogota, costs of construction for rail systems are 3 to 10 times higher (Kaenzig et al. 2010).
2 For example, the BRT service deployed in Istanbul reaches a maximum operating speed of 42 km/h (Hidalgo and Gutierrez 2013).

facilitated by the introduction of new technologies. Improving traffic and intermodality conditions results in time and budget savings for users, and the imposition of BRT standards introduces a higher quality of service than that of the existing supply.

Very often, the introduction of BRT is part of a planning process: it involves first identifying the main trunk corridors along which densification and diversification of urban functions are to occur. BRT fits more generally into the perspective of *transit-oriented development*, which tends to prioritize urban development around mass transport networks, to improve accessibility for urban activities and amenities. In return, the use of this mode of transport over short distances optimizes usage rates and guarantees the economic profitability of the service. BRT is therefore a tool for considering both mobility planning and urban planning, while these two types of planning often remain disconnected in many African cities (Helluin et al. 2018). This results from the existence of siloed professional environments, isolating engineers on the one hand and urban planners on the other, due to the absence of urban planning agencies, and of the absence of planning documents articulating master plans for urban development and travel plans. Finally, shortcomings in terms of planning lead to the wider question of urban governance and transport governance. Institutional fragmentation in the urban transport sector, regulatory difficulties and dispersion of funding are common features of many African cities. The implementation of BRT networks is also an opportunity to instigate governance reform. It is in the context of these projects and financing granted by international donors that several local authorities have emerged over the last few years. In Lagos in particular, the BRT project was led by LAMATA – Lagos Metropolitan Area Transport Authority – which has become the organizing authority for transport at the metropolitan level. A similar process has been followed in Nairobi, with the establishment of NaMATA – Nairobi Metropolitan Area Transport Authority. Parallel to the creation of these structures, regulatory and legislative frameworks are created or updated to regulate the entire sector. Although the success of BRT on the continent seems to be explained by the multiple objectives associated with it, this plural tool is also supported by diversified interests and an ideological underpinning which in turn gives it direction.

12.2.2. *Stakeholders supporting this model*

Although the term BRT was coined already in the first half of the 20th century (Hidalgo and Gutierrez 2013), the urban model refers more directly to the service as first deployed in cities of the Global South; in Curitiba, from 1982, then in Bogota in 2000. These cities have gradually established themselves as showcases for this mode of transport, and the starting point for the export of the BRT model (Wood 2015a).

Indeed, Peyroux and Sanjuan (2016) argue that the notion of an "urban model" refers to a material but also the ideal production of the city. However, in the case of BRT, by the use of its model, cities of the Global South seek to demonstrate their ability to implement an integrated planning and mobility policy, as well as the possibility of sharing global issues, as demonstrated by the desire to include these developing cities in the rhetoric of sustainability. Like any model, the image of the originating space is promoted first to create a record of norms and values that will then be transferred to other spaces.

The circulation of the BRT model then leads us to examine how an established system functions, organized around several key actors and institutions. At the origin of the model is the former mayor of Bogota, Enrique Penalosa, leader of the Transmilenio BRT project. Bogota's "success story" is widely attributed by international decision-makers to this actor, who has become for several decades a true champion of the BRT model (Wood 2014, 2015b). This individual's activity fits more broadly into a system of actors that Rizzo (2014) does not hesitate to call "*the BRT evangelical society*". At the heart of this "society", two actors play a major role: the World Bank, which provides loans to developing countries for BRT projects, and the NGO Institute for Transportation and Development Policy (ITDP). Initially, the ITDP specialized in lobbying decision-makers to promote the merits of BRT. Nowadays, the ITDP produces guides to assist the implementation of BRT, conducts pre-feasibility studies, produces significant research on BRT and its impacts and identifies funding opportunities for these projects (Rizzo 2014). The interests of these institutions are also largely intertwined: as Rizzo (2014) illustrates, in 2011 among the members of the ITDP board of directors were representatives of both Goldman Sachs and the World Bank. The geopolitical scope of these networks of actors is therefore coupled with economic interests, since BRT projects very often open up new markets for manufacturers and international transport operators. Among these manufacturers, Volvo, a supplier for several BRT networks, also funds BRT research, in particular through the Embarq Centre of Excellence, backed by the World Resource Institute. This intersection of funding and interests results in a significant promotion of BRT through an extensive bibliography, and a portal giving access to precise data on BRT worldwide, "Global BRT Data". While the system of actors exposed by Matteo Rizzo is not specific to BRT, it is notable that it is a closed circuit of actors in which former "receivers" (like Enrique Penalosa) then become "producers" of the model (Allal 2010).

The model then circulates because of the use of specific tools. Study tours to these Latin American cities enable executives and decision-makers to travel from cities that might potentially establish BRT; or, conversely, BRT actors from promoting cities are sent to potentially receiving cities, to praise the merits of the model and evaluate its implementation in the local context. These trips are promoted in the framework of technical cooperation, or financed by institutions such as the ITDP or Embarq, and contribute greatly to transforming iconic projects into "best practice". This term, "best practice", refers directly to political science and the notion of "policy transfer" (Allal 2010), as well as to the work of Eugene McCann and Colin McFarlane. If these promotion activities and the dissemination of public policies aim to capitalize on the experiences of certain cities, they often lead to the omission of the negative impacts, which reinforces the "ideal" dimension of urban models. Best practice ultimately refers to the adaptable dimension of urban models. Through the circulation of these models, only their assets are exposed and appropriated by local decision-makers. Regarding BRT, its adaptability is at the heart of the spread of the model, in particular as advocated by the ITDP. The distinction between BRT Classic and BRT Lite (see section 12.2.1) reflects this desire to propose adequate infrastructures according to political, economic and social contexts, as well as the Guide published by the ITDP for decision-makers and technicians who would like to build a model appropriate for their city.

12.2.3. *Limits of the circulation of the model in Africa*

Despite the construction of a solid mechanism to disseminate the BRT model in Africa, after more than a decade, observers and researchers have identified the limitations of this model and proposed a critique of the methods of implementation for these projects. First, the works of Rizzo (2014), Wood (2015a) and Klopp, Harber and Quarshie (2019) converge to show that the export of the BRT model is based on supposed advantages that very often are not demonstrated, making the *success story* of BRT (Rizzo 2014) more of a fable rather than an evidence-based narrative. Here again, this observation is not specific to the BRT model and is part of a broader area: many development models are based on the trickle-down theory strongly promoted by the World Bank, whose effects in terms of growth remain largely to be demonstrated (Giraut 2009; Didier et al. 2012). Variations in this discourse may be observed in particular around the question of the costs of BRT. Due to the effectiveness of the arguments produced by the ITDP and the World Bank, the profitability of this transport service is not questioned, and even explains why in some cases, such as in Cape Town (Schalekamp 2015) or Johannesburg (Klopp et al. 2019), no pre-feasibility study was carried out[3]. However, in most

---

3 Indeed, discussions between local decision-makers and model promoters quite often concern the performance of existing BRTs, rather than their economic viability. In accordance with the vision of donors – including the World Bank – BRT's economic viability is mainly due to the establishment of public–private partnerships to operate the service. This relieves

African cities, profitability of the service is not guaranteed in practice, with ridership often overestimated in preliminary studies, requiring the subsequent intervention of the public authorities to compensate for operator losses. Paget-Seekins (2015) underlines the contradictions underlying the model: it creates an international market for bus manufacturers and operators at the cost of strong state involvement, both for investment in infrastructure building and support in the formalization of informal and artisanal actors. Finally, despite the stated objective of adapting to local contexts, the standards promoted by the ITDP and the World Bank almost systematically involve the use of international companies and consultants to design and implement BRT infrastructures (Klopp et al. 2019).

Another identified limitation of the model involves its orientation toward the poorest urban dwellers. Among the elements traditionally used to justify the need for a BRT service, the poorest households' possibility of access to good quality transport at a low cost is identified as a priority. However, several studies show that BRT services instead benefit the middle classes, and the upper fringe of households are considered to be poor (Ferbrache 2018; Venter et al. 2018). Several elements of analysis are suggested: first, the lack of subsidization of BRTs by the public authorities translates into high prices for the poorest households (Vermeiren et al. 2015). Second, the layout of the BRT networks tends to exclude the poorest households because of poor intermodality and the need for spatially relegated households to use feeder services outside of fare integration (Vermeiren 2015; Venter et al. 2018).

Finally, from the point of view of governance, the effects expected from BRT projects must again be qualified. The establishment of governance structures in the context of BRT projects must be assessed in hindsight: in several cases, the imposition of a structure at the metropolitan level has been superimposed on pre-existing levels of regulation, without replacing them, thus reinforcing the fragmentation and tensions that already exist between levels of power and regulation. This is notably the case in Nairobi, where Nairobi's transport authority, NaMATA, is struggling to assert its role and its competency at the local level (Klopp et al. 2019). Other configurations exist, such as in Lagos where the affirmation of LAMATA's role is based more on the flexibility of its legislative framework. Klopp et al. (2019) also illustrate the case of Johannesburg, where the BRT project was financed by the National Treasury and implemented without the existence of any transport authority for the Pretoria–Johannesburg conurbation. Poku-Boansi and Marsden (2018) offer a similar analysis by highlighting the path dependencies that exist in the organization of governance and sets of actors, and which very often result in institutional inertia. In this context, the imposition of

---

the local authorities of the need to grant public subsidies, since the services' high frequency of use guarantees sufficient fare revenue for the operators.

structures developed within the framework of exogenous models then leads to the establishment of "empty shells", which may result in discrediting both the project and public action.

12.3. South Africa, laboratory for urban mobility projects

12.3.1. *A long-awaited reform*

At the level of the African continent, taking an interest in urban transport projects in South Africa may, at first glance, seems inadequate. South Africa completed its urban transition several years ago, and South African metropolises have a relatively extensive supply of urban transport compared to other cities on the continent; in large cities, this will consist of regular buses, trains and paratransit services. However, these cities remain marked by the legacy of apartheid urban planning, which is still evident today and has resulted in a persistent dual mobility system (Wilkinson 2008): households with access to private vehicles are contrasted to those who cannot afford it, the latter being dependent on public transport. This duality explains the high rate of motorization in the country, while using public transport involves long, costly and painful travel and remains a marker of socio-economic disadvantage inherited from apartheid. Indeed, one of the main consequences of apartheid urban planning was the distancing of formerly segregated populations in the townships, which have poor access to urban opportunities concentrated in the city center. Since 1994, this inherited structure has been reinforced by a rural exodus, immigration and natural growth, which have led to an increase in the population of these neighborhoods and the development of new informal settlements on the periphery (Turok 2001). This disjunction between residential areas and areas of economic activity justifies talking about a *spatial mismatch* to discuss the structure and functioning of South African cities (Naudé 2008; Sinclair-Smith and Turok 2012; Budlender and Royston 2016). In Cape Town, Khayelitsha – the main African township – and Mitchell's Plain – the main township[4] of the so-called "Colored" population – have the highest densities and the highest number of households without access to motor vehicles (Figure 12.1). For these households, the travel budget is proportionally larger than for middle- and upper-class households (Venter 2012).

---

4 Townships are neighbourhoods planned during apartheid under the Group Areas Act, which established strictly-defined residence areas in the city for each of the different population groups (White, Black, "*Colored*" – or mixed-race – and Asian) in the racial classification established by the regime, the "Colored" and African townships being the furthest away from the city centre. This law was abolished in 1991 but persists in practice.

Circulation of Models in Africa 273

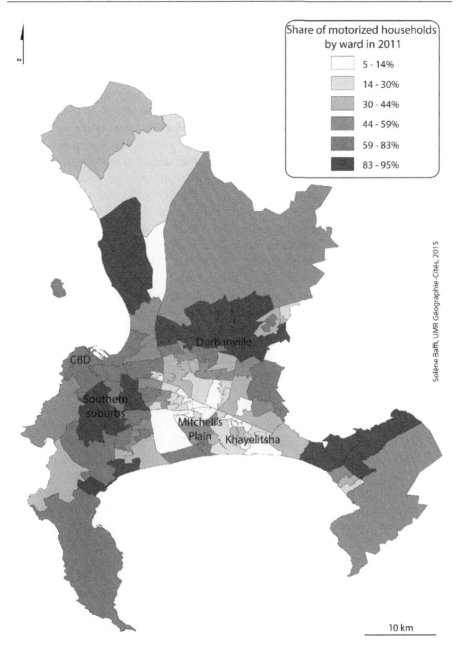

Figure 12.1. *Share of motorized households in 2011 in Cape Town (according to municipal subdivisions of wards). Source: Baffi (2016). For a color version of this figure, see www.iste.co.uk/lesteven/urban.zip*

These urban and mobility characteristics made reform of the transport system part of the agenda of the post-apartheid government as early as 1996 and made reform a component of the newly elected democratic government's redistribution program. In that period, the National Transport White Paper formulated the objective "to provide safe, reliable, effective, efficient and fully-integrated transport operations and infrastructure which will best meet the needs of freights and passenger customers". However, despite the investments made, at the turn of the 2000s, the situation had not changed. The quality of public transport services remains mediocre, as reflected in an increase in the number of individual motorized vehicles on the one hand, and a modal shift toward minibus taxis (paratransit services) on the other. In parallel, at the end of the 1990s, the national government set up a major program to modernize and professionalize the paratransit industry, which first consisted of creating a dialogue with operators via the National Taxi Task Team. In addition, another program was introduced, the Taxi Recapitalization Program, whose objective is twofold: to regulate operating conditions and to encourage owners to renew their fleet. Despite the mixed record of this program, initiated in 2006 – the renewal of the fleet not having reached the expected number of vehicles (Schalekamp 2015) – this measure represents a step in the opening of a dialog between public authorities and operators from the paratransit industry.

In addition to sectoral reforms, the country is also undertaking a profound process of decentralization. From 2000, the country's largest metropolises saw their boundaries change to become "Unicities", that is, metropolitan governments (Jaglin and Dubresson 2008). These new administrative units were born from the merger of old municipalities to promote fiscal equalization at the level of urban territories, and thus facilitate redistributive measures. In Cape Town, the metropolitan territory therefore extends over nearly 2,500 km² as of 2,000 and, like the other Unicity in the country, the metropolitan government has significant technical, fiscal and legislative means to construct a vision and a planning framework for the city. However, although decentralization of responsibility for urban transport regulation is foreseen in the Unicity framework, this has not been immediately implemented. In addition, transport regulation remains fragmented between the different levels of government: trains are regulated at the national government level, the bus network is under the authority of the provincial government and the municipality is responsible for issuing licenses for minibus operators. Moreover, from a political perspective, the transfer of powers to the metropolises enables the national government, whose activity is strongly pro-rural because of its electoral base, to relinquish responsibility for intervening in the largest metropolises (Turok 2014).

12.3.2. *BRT: symbol of post-apartheid South Africa*

It was with South Africa's selection as host country of the World Cup in 2010 that urban transport reform gained new momentum. The prospect of welcoming hundreds of thousands of tourists from all over the world and bringing them from airports and hotels to stadiums prompted the national government to develop reliable and efficient urban transport services. The challenges associated with this need were multiple. First, it involved demonstrating the country's hosting capacity, as the first country in Africa to organize such an event according to the principle of continental rotation that had just come into force, and the first country in the South in general (Brazil organized the 2014 World Cup). In addition, South Africa is also the country displaying the greatest inequalities with the highest Gini coefficient in the world according to World Bank data (63.4 in 2010). Thus, part of the scientific literature produced around this event concerned the use and appropriation by the local population of the infrastructures built for this "mega-event" (Pillay and Bass 2008; Haferburg 2011). One of the objectives associated with the World Cup was therefore building urban services that could benefit the local population beyond the event, to justify massive investments made by the government and to avoid scandals related to constructing "white elephants" (Cubizolles 2011). Indeed, infrastructures built as part of major events equally offer an opportunity for elected officials to leave a legacy, and the risk of becoming a real burden if the economic, social and cultural benefits are not acknowledged.

In the transport sector, 10 years after the White Paper setting out the objectives of urban transport reform, a new impetus was given with the publication of the National Land Transport Strategic Framework (NLTSF). This document identified the World Cup as a catalyst for urban transport reform. At this stage, several cities, including Cape Town and Johannesburg, were planning to improve their mobility system by promoting better connections between high-capacity modes (rail) and paratransit services (Venter et al. 2020). Shortly after, the 2010 Transport Action Agenda published in 2006 specified the projects and methods of implementation linked to the investments. For the first time, public money was allocated by the government to South African municipalities to finance urban transport (Van Ryneveld 2018). Among the conditions to obtain the Public Transport and Infrastructure Systems Grant (later the Public Transport Network Grant), municipalities were required to incur expenses related to the construction of a BRT system. Thus, it appears that the priority was not to reform existing systems, but rather to promote BRT as a solution to transport problems. Moreover, the deadlines set by the World Cup also made this mode of transport an appropriate response. According to Wood (2014, 2015b), the importance given to BRT in public policy as early as 2006 was not unrelated to the presence in South Africa at this time of Lloyd

Wright, international expert, consultant for the ITDP and a fervent advocate and promoter of the BRT.

Beyond the deployment of a new bus service, one of the corollaries of the BRT is to support the densification of metropolises around structuring corridors. This is not a recent idea in South Africa: in the 1970s, municipal planners identified the corridors along which development of the Cape Town metropolis should focus on in order to allow spatial rebalancing (Watson 1990, 2002; Vanderschuren and Galaria 2003). BRT is also a tool for implementing the urban planning principles of *transit-oriented development*. Although this term only appeared from the 2010s in planning documents for the Cape Town metropolitan area, coordination between urban planning and transport planning is one of the levers identified to promote the development of economic activities and of mixed areas close to transport networks, and by doing so, to fight against urban fragmentation and the distancing of the poorest. The objectives allocated to BRTs are therefore multiple, and the BRT has quickly asserted itself as the appropriate mode of transport for addressing the challenges of post-apartheid South Africa, for the use of all urban dwellers. Paget-Seekins (2015) notes that BRT services are invoked to create a sense of belonging among city dwellers, as shown for example by the name of the transport network deployed in Ahmedabad, "Janmarg, The People's Way". In Cape Town, the name chosen for the BRT network, "MyCiti", plays on a double meaning: belonging to a common territory, and the reference to the English initials of the city (C.T.).

12.3.3. *The Capetonian version of the BRT project: MyCiti*

By virtue of its adaptability, the BRT model adopted in South Africa presents specific characteristics. When choosing to install BRT in South Africa, South African decision-makers decided to opt for the BRT Classic model rather than the less expensive Lite version. The Classic model variation implies construction of stations isolated from the road in the middle of the dedicated sections, the purchase of buses with doors on each side to allow the loading and unloading of passengers, and high platforms (Figure 12.2). This model, favored by the ITDP by virtue of its qualification as a "Gold Medal", is supposed to present greater advantages over the long term. However, Venter et al. (2020) recall the criticisms made by many observers at the time that this standard seemed less appropriate to the characteristics of South African cities[5]. One of the arguments advanced by Wood (2015a) to justify this choice would be the desire of South African decision-makers to reproduce as

---

5 Since then, new phases of network deployment have been enacted according to the principles of the Lite model.

faithfully as possible the Transmilenio model, the standard for obtaining the ITDP "Gold Medal". Despite efforts to develop sophisticated networks, Cape Town was awarded a Silver Medal and Johannesburg the Bronze Medal .

Figure 12.2. On the left, MyCiti buses at the Table View stop on the dedicated corridors; on the right, older generation buses in traffic. Source: Baffi (2014). For a color version of this figure, see www.iste.co.uk/lesteven/urban.zip

In addition to the model chosen, concerning the operation of vehicles, the cities of Cape Town and Johannesburg considered BRT a lever to promote reform of the paratransit industry. In both cities, the principle adopted was identical: minibuses must not travel on the sections where the BRT operates. Minibus operators were encouraged to form Vehicle Operating Companies to respond to calls for tenders from the municipality and operate BRT services, or apply for buy-back of their license, in exchange for the obligation to leave the sector. For several months, tough negotiations were held in Cape Town and Johannesburg between the public authorities, representatives of minibus associations and negotiators chosen by the minibus associations (Schalekamp 2015; Witting and Wegener 2016). Eventually, several vehicle operating companies emerged and obtained the right to operate the BRT network for 12 years. This process of consultation and negotiations – notably to set the amount of the license buyback – was perceived very differently among observers. In Cape Town, a professionalization program was established in partnership with several minibus associations, the Cape Town Municipality and the University of Cape Town, giving operators the opportunity to obtain certification (Schalekamp 2017). Several researchers (Venter 2013; Woolf and Joubert 2013) nevertheless suggest that the process of professionalization implemented was largely based on a top-down approach by the local authorities.

In terms of regulation, Cape Town is notable for the creation of a Board in charge of the regulation of urban transport, Transport for Cape Town. Although establishment of this local authority had been foreseen in legislation for several years under the decentralization movement, until then a lack of funding meant that these structures had not yet emerged – except in Durban, where it remained an empty shell as it lacked the means necessary to implement its activity (Bellangère et al. 2004). With the provision of financing for the investment and operation of BRT networks, it became possible for the Cape Town municipality to create an authority in charge of the regulation of BRT, and eventually urban transport. Transport for Cape Town (TCT) was set up at the beginning of 2012, with the provision of the Public Transport Operating Grant for a 5-year period by the national government, with the aim of facilitating the commissioning of BRT before it became fully profitable. With TCT, the municipality also sought to develop the planning framework and create an authority with broad and cross-functional competences, to facilitate integration with the planning and development department and to go beyond a "silo" concept of urban development (Baffi 2016).

Finally, the choice of orientation for the BRT network differs between the two South African metropolises. In Cape Town, the priority given to the network was initially, as in Johannesburg, to serve the most disadvantaged neighborhoods and/or the most distant from existing public transport services (rail in particular). This orientation justified the choice to deploy the network in a first phase toward the northern districts of the city, which are not connected to the intra-urban rail network (Baffi 2016). However, this objective was rapidly doubled by a second objective, to encourage the modal shift of motorized populations. Indeed, Cape Town contrasts with the model implemented in Johannesburg due to its emphasis on urban development, particularly in the framework of the Energy and Climate Action Plan published in 2010. From then on, the choice of route for the first corridor of the network – also due to other considerations – evolved from the Klipfontein corridor, identified for several decades in the planning documents, toward the West Coast corridor, where rush hour congestion is a recurrent phenomenon. In Johannesburg, the social objective of the project remained central: the first BRT corridor connects the city center to the stadium, and beyond the township of Soweto, where a significant part of the city's public transport-dependent population resides.

12.4. Between strong appropriation and poor adaptation, MyCiti's mixed record

12.4.1. *An international model reappropriated to assert local power*

The choice to make BRT a central element of urban transport reform in South Africa reflects the rapid appropriation of this model by local experts and politicians. This choice may be read, on several levels, as an affirmation of the power and ambition of South African cities. Internationally, Wood (2015) highlights the deliberate choice of South African decision-makers to draw inspiration from the BRT model developed in South America rather than the pragmatic and less costly model developed in Lagos (BRT Lite), which would have enabled the promotion of an African identity in the wake of the African Renaissance advocated by Nelson Mandela. This desire to be part of international best practices and to claim assimilation to the Transmilenio model, consecrated by a "Gold Medal", denotes the position of South African cities in the hierarchy of global metropolises. This status of a "world class African city", claimed by Johannesburg but also applicable to the city of Cape Town, is indeed based on bringing post-apartheid cities up to international standard and could be understood as a desire to "normalize" and abandon the stigmatizing legacy of apartheid (Guinard 2013). In this perspective, the adoption of international norms, standards and models changes the analytical framework historically attached to South African cities and demonstrates the ability of these metropolises to integrate into a globalized economy and the international geopolitical scene.

For several decades, the affirmation of the role of metropolises at the international level has also been reflected by the deployment of high-capacity urban transport projects, whose objective seems equally to respond to a rapid increase in demand and to underline the capacity of local authorities to deploy substantial human and financial resources. This international trend has been notably analyzed in Delhi by Siemiatycki (2006). In Cape Town, the MyCiti network also appears as a demonstration of power by the local government, which is also projected onto the national level. Indeed, this new mode of transport contrasts with the train, bus and minibus networks, all three inherited from the apartheid period. As a symbol of renewal, MyCiti is deployed throughout the vast territory of the Unicity, whose strong heterogeneity fades under the unifying action of the municipality. In addition, it is important to remember that the Cape Town mayoralty has been the main bastion of political opposition at the national level (at least throughout the implementation of the first phase of MyCiti), this metropolis having been the first to come under the control of the Democratic Alliance (DA) party since its constitution in 2000. The possibility of setting up an urban service for all city dwellers therefore represents an opportunity for the DA's bastion to demonstrate its ability to provide urban services, one of the central arguments of the post-apartheid political debate. Although not the main reason for this choice, the location of the MyCiti network hub being directly outside the municipal buildings is a strong symbol (Baffi 2017).

Local appropriation of the BRT model must also be considered in the light of local transport governance in Cape Town. In particular, a major change occurred at the end of 2017, when Transport for Cape Town (TCT) evolved into the Transport and Urban Development Authority (TDA). With this change, a new upheaval took place within the municipality: the urban planning department and the transport authority merged into this new local authority, whose creation enshrines the orientation of the urban development of the city around transport projects and infrastructure. While the objective allocated to the emergence of the TDA aligns with the operational principles dictated by transit-oriented development, in practice the urban planning department comes under the control of the transport department. This process, although it was implemented to undo the spatial and functional structure of apartheid, was also denounced in 2018 by several observers who considered the preponderant weight given to transport policy at the metropolitan level to be unbalanced. Beyond the goal of promoting the principles of transit-oriented development, the central place given to the BRT in metropolitan planning in 2018 was certainly due to the large deficits caused by the operation of MyCiti, as subsidies from the national government came to an end. Focusing urban development actions around the BRT then appears to be a desperate attempt to preserve the metropolitan flagship.

12.4.2. *A project ill-suited to South African specificities*

While the BRT model in Cape Town was rapidly adopted by local policy makers, the local adaptation of the BRT appears to be inadequate in several respects. Indeed, several strategic choices made during the design phase do not seem appropriate to the constraints and functioning of the South African metropolis. For the most part, these choices result from the desire to deliver the project within the timetable set by the FIFA World Cup for phase 1 (2010), or within the schedule imposed by the municipal elections for phase 2 (2016). A first question, mentioned by one of the former executives of the municipality interviewed in 2017, concerns the choice of location for the main hub of the network in the city center. Beyond the hub function, the site also houses the main bus depot of the network, which is where all buses are brought back every evening. However, in a city marked by very unbalanced flows between the center and the periphery, the location of the bus depot in the city center rather than at the end of the line implies that they travel empty at least twice a day, while the operator subsidy is based on mileage. The argument put forward by the local authorities relates to the possibility of using publicly owned land to reduce costs for the project. This argument is, however, debatable; the increase in property values in the city center would have been greater than the acquisition of land in the outskirts connected to the BRT service, but the ability to use this land certainly contributed to delivering the project on time.

A second criticism relates to the layout of the lines and the choice of corridors identified in phases 1 and 2 for running the buses on dedicated routes. In phase 1, the choice of route (the R27 road) proved counterproductive, according to the words of a former Transport for Cape Town executive (interview, June 2017). Indeed, the chosen route runs for several kilometers along a marsh and an undeveloped coastal zone, so the possibility of creating densification seems limited. According to him, this choice is explained by arguments put forward by the municipal engineers, namely the possibility of optimizing traffic and top speed due to the distances between traffic lights. In addition to this priority given to performance, the northern districts of the city also benefit from having fewer minibus associations in the paratransit industry. Due to this lower number, negotiations carried out before the World Cup were completed in time. A similar approach was adopted as early as 2014 to prepare the deployment of phase 2 to the southeastern suburbs of the city where the main townships are located, and thus the populations most dependent on public transport. To ensure services for these districts were running before the municipal elections of 2016, the mayor of Cape Town decided to integrate a provisional variation of phase 2, called "N2 Express", before the implementation of phase 2 itself, which was complex to implement. As part of this interim phase, a BRT service was set up to Mitchell's Plain and Khayelistha townships. Because of the speed with which this phase – which was not initially planned – had to be implemented, it was not possible to establish the required consultation and negotiation process with the paratransit industry (interview with a TDA executive, March 2018), especially since there are many minibus associations in these neighborhoods. Consequently, the "N2 Express" only offers a partial connection to the inner neighborhoods of the large townships,

A third criticism concerns the speed with which the transport network was integrated, under a "big bang" approach, in contrast to the "incremental" approach that was initially preferred (interview with a former TCT executive, June 2017). This speed had the main disadvantage of not learning from design errors at the beginning of the project and did not facilitate the acculturation of South African city dwellers, unaccustomed to using public transport in the case of motorized households, and unfamiliar with new modes of transport. A first obstacle identified concerns the possibility for users to obtain and reload transport tickets. Indeed, as a TDA executive explains, the decision to use a specific type of chip in transport cards dates back to 2007, when the national government did not have a complete vision of what the system could become and therefore opted for a technology that facilitates interoperability between BRT services in different cities across the country. Since then, this use has no longer been a priority, while the technology used places a strong constraint on the municipality, which depends on a national banking institution to offer points of sale. However, several studies and surveys show that the difficulty of obtaining a ticket is a major obstacle when it comes to city dwellers (Ugo 2014) and tourists (Baffi et al. 2019) wanting to use the BRT. In addition, the "big bang" approach led to the implementation of many feeder lines, especially in the northern suburbs of the city, which have very low densities. In these neighborhoods, as transport demand is mainly concentrated during peak hours, the feeder services run almost empty for several hours each day. This weak demand justifies a rapid decrease in supply during off-peak hours, accelerating the modal shift of users to minibus services, which are better suited to serving this type of suburban area.

12.4.3. *Feedback effects at different levels*

Among the criticisms leveled at the ways the MyCiti service was deployed, the lack of profitability of the model is ultimately what shines through. In 2017, the number of passengers per day stood at 66,115 (Van Ryneveld 2018) and according to a former Transport for Cape Town executive, operating costs amounted to 4% of the revenue of the metropolis, while the deployment of the network has not yet reached 10% of the total project (interview, June 2017). In 2018, when the fund granted by the National Government came to an end, the operation of the BRT was therefore far from sustainable, fare revenues covering only a small part of the operating costs. The financial gap created by the operation of the BRT, combined with strong political tensions within the municipality (partly due to the preponderant role granted to the TDA) led to the dissolution of the TDA a few years later, and fed into the various scandals that compelled mayor Patricia De Lille to resign in 2018. Beyond these local political consequences, the mixed record of the BRT service can be seen in the northern suburbs of the city, served since phase 1, and where the network is most developed. While the implementation of the system was conditioned by the withdrawal of minibus operators from the sections served by the BRT, in 2018, many minibuses are back on the roads served by the BRT. This is due in particular to the fact that BRT pricing fluctuates during the day to encourage use of the service during off-peak hours. However, for many households, rush hour fares are too high, recreating unmet demand. As explained by a TDA executive in charge of the regulation of minibuses (interview, March 2018), a survey conducted in the Du Noon neighborhood in 2010, before the implementation of the BRT, counted 3,800 regular users at the minibus loading point. In 2018, the same survey identified 7,108 minibus users. In addition, the legal framework having changed, it is no longer possible to grant a license to these operators, which obliges the municipality to tacitly recognize the functioning of these essential services for a segment of urban dwellers.

Among the consequences of the introduction of the BRT service, the massive use of the service on the trunk corridor linking Table View to the city center reflects, at peak times, the popularity of this transportation mode. While a significant portion of South Africa's population has never used public transport (Baffi 2016), the introduction of the BRT is one of the elements introducing a change in urban practices among city dwellers. Several surveys conducted in Cape Town in 2017 and 2018 testify, on the one hand, to the sense of pride expressed by some residents, felt due to the fact that before there was "no public transport in Cape Town", and now the MyCiti service is comparable to European city standards (Baffi et al. 2019). The use of MyCiti by categories of users who did not previously use public transport, although still limited, is visible in the vicinity of BRT stations and stops for observers accustomed to South African transport spaces: the white population mixing in with regular passengers. This field observation, as well as comments reported from the municipal executive in charge of the regulation of minibuses, corroborates analyses showing that BRT, although identified as a "pro-poor" service, is generally used by the upper fringe of disadvantaged populations (Paget-Seekins 2015; Venter 2018). Questioning the social dimension and the impacts of the project on the poorest populations of the city, we can also take into account the mechanisms of land speculation in the neighborhoods served by the BRT. Although there are no studies yet, the reference to the BRT as an amenity in most offers of housing downtown and in the northern suburbs suggests that such a mechanism may be at work (Figure 12.3). The existence of a similar process in the townships served by BRT could also be an area for future research work.

Beyond changes in urban practices, one of the consequences of the introduction of the BRT – and its partial failure – concerns changes in the standards and norms of South African decision-makers. Indeed, several executives and former executives of the Cape Town municipality recalled that at the time of the implementation of the BRT, the underlying objective of the project was to eradicate the paratransit industry, considered inadequate in the context of an international metropolis. Due to the large deficits generated by the operation of MyCiti – in particular the feeder services – the municipality has been considering for several years the possibility of setting up a feeder service provided by minibus operators (interview, March 2018). According to this "hybrid" concept (Boutueil and Lesteven 2018), it is indeed a connection between existing services that is envisaged for future phases, in order to offer an on-demand, lower capacity transport service on certain sections. This concept marks an important turning point. The integration of the minibus sector is not seen as its disappearance, but as a service able to complement a regular service adapted to the standards and needs of the metropolis. Schalekamp and Klopp (2018) identify this paradigm shift as moving from a "displace and replace" strategy to one of "embrace, engage, improve and integrate". Though this orientation followed by the municipality since 2018 is based on pragmatic considerations, the fact remains that this approach seems innovative on the scale of the African continent and could, in the long term, constitute an appropriate urban model based on the characteristics of African metropolises.

Figure 12.3. *In a MyCiti bus shelter in downtown Cape Town (the City Bowl), an advertisement from a South African real estate agency: "How has your City Bowl property performed?". Source: Baffi (2017). For a color version of this figure, see www.iste.co.uk/lesteven/urban.zip*

12.5. Conclusion

In 2019, Harvey Scorcia and Ramon Munoz-Raskin, researchers affiliated with the World Bank, published an article comparing the implementation of BRT in Johannesburg with the earlier experience of Latin America. They emphasize the extent to which the model developed in Latin America is not suitable for the context of South African cities, due in particular to low densities, and to functional and morphological specificities inherited from apartheid. Throughout this chapter, the problem associated with the transfer of urban models stands out: how to replicate a project that has proven to be a success in a different context? How long does it take for a model to "take root" and to adapt to a new context? Beyond these pragmatic questions, this chapter also recalls the role played by institutions – the World Bank in particular – as well as consultants and experts who contribute not only to producing knowledge but also a discourse, even in some cases a "fable".

The mixed experience of the transfer of the BRT model to South Africa, too quickly appropriated by decision-making elites and experts, and poorly adapted to the local context, does not reflect the inadequacy of the BRT model or an intrinsic failure of this mode of transport. On the contrary, by analyzing the stumbling blocks, reorientations and errors of the project, it is mostly path dependencies that are revealed above all, which remind us of the diversity of trajectories of the metropolises of the Global South (Shatkin 2007). In addition, the instabilities of local urban governance in Cape Town, as well as the influence of motorized populations in guiding the orientation of the BRT network, cannot be decoupled from public policies and the dynamics of South African society in recent decades. The introduction of the BRT thus marks a crucial step in post-apartheid urban transport reform and indicates a fundamental social transformation.

Finally, putting the South African case into perspective with the spread of BRTs at the continental level finally raises the possibility of seeing the emergence of an African variation of this model. As Christo Venter et al. (2020) point out, some feedback from the experience of projects in Lagos, Cape Town and Johannesburg is already guiding the design of future services in Abidjan and Dakar. Although here again these good practices are based on closed-circuit processes promoted by a small circle of actors, forms of cross-capitalization emerge, in particular concerning the financial models of these services, the deployment of feeder services and the integration of the paratransit industry. On this last point, the limitations observed in the implementation of the BRT projects in South Africa mark the end of a conception of mobility systems "cleansed" of paratransit operators. On the contrary, faced with the limits of the model, new innovations are appearing in terms of regulation and planning of paratransit services, demonstrating, once again, that South African cities are laboratories for urban transformations and that new models are emerging across the continent.

12.6. References

Allal, A. (2010). Les configurations développementistes internationales au Maroc et en Tunisie : des policy transfers à portée limitée. *Critique internationale*, 3(48), 97–116.

Baffi, S. (2016). Le chemin de fer et la ville dans les processus de territorialisation en Afrique du Sud : de la séparation à l'intégration territoriale ? Geography PhD Thesis, Université Paris 1 Panthéon-Sorbonne.

Baffi, S. (2017). La mise en place d'un bus à Haut Niveau de Service au Cap, un outil de normalisation de la ville sud-africaine ? *EchoGéo*, 40 [Online]. Available at: http://echogeo.revues.org/14945.

Baffi, S., Donaldson, R., Spocter, M. (2019). Tourist mobilities in Cape Town: Unveiling practices in the post-apartheid city. *Tourism Planning & Development*, October 17, 2019.

Bellengère, A., Khan, S., Lootvoet, B., Vermeulin, S. (2004). Privatiser pour mieux réguler ? Le pari de Durban en matière de transport public. *Autrepart*, 32(4), 75–93.

Bertrand, M. (2010). Introduction. *Revue Tiers-Monde*, 201(1), 7–23.

Budlender, J. and Royston, L. (2016). Edged out. Spatial mismatch and spatial justice in South Africa's main urban areas. Report, SERI.

Cubizolles, S. (2011). Marketing identity and place: The case of the Stellenbosch Kayamandi economic corridor before the 2010 World Cup in South Africa. *Journal of Sport Tourism*, 16(1), 33–53.

Diaz-Olvera, L., Plat, D., Pochet, P. (2010). Pauvreté, mobilité quotidienne et accès aux ressources dans les villes subsahariennes. In *Dynamiques de pauvreté et vulnérabilités en démographie et en sciences sociales : Actes de la Chaire Quételet 2007*, Masquelier, B. and Eggericks, T. (eds). Presses Universitaires de Louvain, Louvain-la-Neuve.

Dubresson, A. and Jaglin, S. (2008). *Le Cap après l'apartheid : gouvernance métropolitaine et changement urbain*. Karthala, Paris.

Ferbrache, F. (2018). Developing bus rapid transit. *Journal of Transport Geography*, 70, 203–205.

Giraut, F. (2009). Les ambiguïtés de la nouvelle doctrine spatiale de la Banque mondiale. *Cybergeo: European Journal of Geography* [Online]. Available at: https://journals.openedition.org/cybergeo/22695, October 2, 2009.

Guinard, P. (2013). L'art, un outil de normalisation de la ville ? Le cas de Johannesburg. *Urbanités* [Online]. Available at: https://www.revue-urbanites.fr/chroniques-lart-un-outil-de-normalisation-de-la-ville-le-cas-de-johannesburg/.

Haferburg, C. (2011). South Africa under FIFA's reign: The World Cup's contribution to urban development. *Development Southern Africa*, 28(3), 333–348.

Helluin, J-J., Berger, P., Descroux, T., Dols, M. (2018). La planification de la mobilité urbaine dans les pays en développement pour des villes plus économes en énergie : la nécessaire alliance entre objectifs globaux et besoins locaux [Online]. Available at: http://www.codatu.org/wp-content/uploads/final_fr.pdf.

Hidalgo, D. and Gutierrez, L. (2013). BRT and BHLS around the world: Explosive growth, large positive impacts and many issues outstanding. *Research in Transportation Economics*, 39, 8–12.

Kaenzig, R., Mobereola, D., Brader, C. (2010). Africa's first bus rapid transit system. *Transportation Research Record*, 2193(1), 1–8.

Kassens-Noor, E. (2012). Transport legacy of the Olympic games, 1992–2012. *Journal of Urban Affairs*, 35(4), 393–416.

Klopp, J., Harber, J., Quarshie, M. (2019). A review of BRT as public transport reform in African cities. Paper, VREF Research Synthesis Project, Governance of Metropolitan Transport.

Lesteven, G. and Boutueil, V. (2018). Is paratransit a key asset for a sustainable urban mobility system? Insights from three African cities. *97th Annual Meeting of the Transportation and Research Board*, Washington.

Musil, C., Ninot, O., Baffi, S., Drevelle, M. (2014). Évolutions des systèmes de transport urbain en périphérie du Cap et de Hanoï – Entre pragmatisme et ambitions métropolitaines. In *Métropoles aux Suds. Le défi des périphéries ?*, Chaléard J.-L. (ed.). Karthala, Paris.

Naudé, W. (2008). Is there a spatial mismatch in South Africa's metropolitan labour market? *Cities*, 25, 268–276.

Paget-Seekins, L. (2015). Bus Rapid Transit as a neoliberal contradiction. *Journal of Transport Geography*, 48, 115–120.

Peyroux, E. and Sanjuan, T. (2016). Stratégies de villes et "modèles" urbains : approche économique et géopolitique des relations entre villes. *EchoGéo*, 36 [Online]. Available at: http://echogeo.revues.org/14642.

Pillay, U. and Bass, O. (2008). Mega-events as a response to poverty reduction: The 2010 FIFA World Cup and its urban development implications. *Urban Forum*, 19, 329–346.

Poku-Boansi, M. and Marsden, G. (2018). Bus rapid transit systems as a governance reform project. *Journal of Transport Geography*, 70, 193–202.

Porter, G. (2007). Transport planning in Sub-Saharan Africa. *Progress in Development Studies*, 7(3), 251–257.

Rizzo, M. (2014). The political economy of an urban megaproject: The Bus Rapid Transit project in Tanzania. *African Affairs*, 114/455, 249–270.

Schalekamp, H. (2015). Paratransit operators' participation in public transport reform in Cape Town: A qualitative investigation of their business aspiration and attitudes to reform. PhD Thesis, Department of Civil Engineering, University of Cape Town.

Schalekamp, H. (2017). Lessons from building paratransit operators' capacity to be partners in Cape Town's public transport reform process. *Transportation Research Part A: Policy and Practice*, 104, 58–66.

Schalekamp, H. and Klopp, J. (2018). Beyond BRT: Innovation in minibus-taxi reform in South African cities. *37th South African Transport Conference Proceedings*, July 9–12, 2018, Pretoria.

Scorcia, H. and Munoz-Raskin, R. (2019). Why South African cities are different? Comparing Johannesburg's Rea Vaya bus rapid transit system with its Latin American siblings. *Case Studies on Transport Policy*, 7(2), 395–403.

Shatkin, G. (2007). Global cities of the South: Emerging perspectives on growth and inequalities. *Cities*, 24(1), 1–15.

Siemiatycki, M. (2006). Message in a metro: Building urban rail infrastructure and image in Delhi, India. *International Journal of Urban and Regional Research*, 30(2), 277–292.

Sinclair-Smith, K. and Turok, I. (2012). The changing spatial economy of cities: An exploratory analysis of Cape Town. *Development Southern Africa*, 29(3), 391–417.

Stucki, M. (2017). Politiques de mobilité et d'accessibilité durables dans les villes africaines. Report, SSATP.

Turok, I. (2001). Persistant polarization post-apartheid? Progress towards urban integration in Cape Town. *Urban Studies*, 38(13), 2349–2377.

Turok, I. (2014). *The Evolution of National Urban Policies – A Global Overview*. UN Habitat, Nairobi.

Ugo, P.D. (2014). The bus rapid transit system: A service quality dimension of commuter uptake in Cape Town, South Africa. *Journal of Transport and Supply Chain Management*, 8, 1–10.

Van Ryneveld, P. (2018). Urban transport analysis for urbanisation review. *South African Urbanisation Review*, Paper no. 9.

Vanderschuren, M.J.W. and Galaria, S. (2003). La ville sud-africaine après l'apartheid : vers l'accessibilité, l'équité et la durabilité ? *Revue internationale des sciences sociales*, 176(2), 297–310.

Venter, C. (2013). The lurch towards formalization: Lessons from the implementation of BRT in Johannesburg, South Africa. *Research in Transportation Economics*, 39, 114–120.

Venter, C., Jennings, G., Hidalgo, D., Valderrama Pineda, A.F. (2018). The equity impacts of bus rapid transit: A review of the evidence and implications for sustainable transport. *International Journal of Sustainable Transportation*, 12(2), 140–152.

Venter, C., Barrett, I., Zuidgeest, M., Cheure, N. (2020). Public transport system design and modal integration in Sub-Saharan Africa cities. The state of knowledge and research. Paper, Volvo Research and Educational Foundations, Gothenburg.

Vermeiren, K., Verachtert, E., Kasaija, P., Loopmans, M., Poesen, J., Van Rompaey, A. (2015). Who could benefit from a bus rapid transit system in cities from developing countries? A case study from Kampala, Uganda. *Journal of Transport Geography*, 47, 13–22.

Watson, V. (2002). *Change and Continuity in Spatial Planning. Metropolitan Planning in Cape Town under Political Transition*. Routledge, London.

Wilkinson, P. (2008). "Moving ahead ?" : la difficile transition des systèmes de transport urbains au Cap. In *Le Cap après l'apartheid*, Dubresson, A. and Jaglin, S. (eds). Karthala, Paris.

Witting, A. and Wegener, D. (2016). Looking beyond the plan and understanding the process: Lessons from Rea Vaya. *African Politics & Policy*, 2(1), 1–16.

Wood, A. (2014). Moving policy: Global and local characters circulating bus rapid transit through South African cities. *Urban Geography*, 35(8), 1238–1254.

Wood, A. (2015a). The politics of policy circulation: Unpacking the relationship between South African and South American cities in the adoption of bus rapid transit. *Antipode*, 47(4), 1062–1079.

Wood, A. (2015b). Multiple temporalities of policy circulation: Gradual, repetitive and delayed processes of BRT adoption in South African cities. *International Journal of Urban and Regional Research*, 39(3), 568–580.

Woolf, S.E. and Joubert, J.W. (2013). A people-centred view on paratransit in South Africa. *Cities*, 35, 284–293.

List of Authors

Solène BAFFI
UMR Géographie-cités
Université Paris 1 Panthéon-Sorbonne
Paris-Aubervilliers
France
and
Stellenbosch University
South Africa

Bérénice BON
IRD-Cessma (French National Research Institute for Sustainable Development)
Paris
France

Sophie BUHNIK
Graduate School of Environmental and Information Studies
Faculty of Urban Life Studies
Tokyo City University
Japan

Guénola CAPRON
Department of Sociology
Universidad Autónoma Metropolitana-Azcapotzalco
Mexico City
Mexico

Hadrien COMMENGES
UMR Géographie-cités
Université Paris 1 Panthéon-Sorbonne
Paris-Aubervilliers
France

Rémi DESMOULIÈRE
ACP (Comparative Analysis of Powers)
Gustave Eiffel University
Marne-la-Vallée
France

Lourdes DIAZ OLVERA
Laboratoire Aménagement Économie, Transports (LAET)
Université de Lyon
ENTPE
France

Manon ESKENAZI
Université Paris-Est
Lab'Urba
Marne-la-Vallée
and
Gustave Eiffel University
École des Ponts
LVMT
Marne-la-Vallée
France

Sylvanie GODILLON
UMR Géographie-cités
Université Paris 1 Panthéon-Sorbonne
Paris-Aubervilliers
France
and
INRS
Montreal
Canada

Florent LE NÉCHET
Gustave Eiffel University
École des Ponts
LVMT
Marne-la-Vallée
France

Gaële LESTEVEN
Laboratoire Aménagement Économie,
Transports (LAET)
Université de Lyon
ENTPE
France

Jérôme MONNET
Gustave Eiffel University
École des Ponts
LVMT
Marne-la-Vallée
France

Benjamin MOTTE-BAUMVOL
ThéMA
CNRS
Université de Bourgogne
Dijon
France

Ruth PÉREZ LÓPEZ
Department of Sociology
Universidad Autónoma
Metropolitana-Azcapotzalco
Mexico City
Mexico

Didier PLAT
Laboratoire Aménagement Économie,
Transports (LAET)
Université de Lyon
ENTPE
France

Pascal POCHET
Laboratoire Aménagement Économie,
Transports (LAET)
Université de Lyon
ENTPE
France

Index

A, B, C

accessibility, 88, 103
accompaniment, 68, 73–75
active mobility/transportation, 70–73, 77, 78
Africa, 265, 266, 270, 272, 275, 276, 279, 283, 285
aging, 85–93, 96–100, 102–105, 108, 109
artisanal transport, 137, 140–142, 144
automobile dependency, 26, 28
autonomy, 73, 77, 78
bibliometric analysis, 245, 251
bike, 184, 185, 187, 189–191, 196, 197
Brazil, 23, 24, 32–34, 37
Bus Rapid Transit (BRT), 265–271, 275–285
Cape Town, 265, 266, 270, 272–285
category, 212, 216–218, 224, 228, 232
child, 67–75, 77, 78
comparability, 219, 223

D, E, F

Dakar, 45–49, 52, 55, 59, 60, 62–64
depopulation, 85, 88, 90, 93, 96
diversity, 206, 207, 212, 215, 220, 223, 228, 229
exclusion, 23, 24, 26, 27, 29
France, 67–78

G, H, I

good practices, 285
governance, 113, 114, 116, 118, 119, 122, 125–129, 131, 132
Hamburg, 181–191, 193–195, 198
health, 67, 68, 71, 72, 74, 76–78
India, 114–116, 118–120, 122–125, 127–129, 131, 132
informal transport, 136, 137, 140, 141
instruments, 184, 189, 196
  of knowledge, 244, 245

J, L, M

Jakarta, 135, 136, 138, 143–153
Japan, 85, 87, 88, 90, 91, 93, 94, 96, 98, 101, 103–108
Lyon, 181–183, 189–198
metropolization, 136, 139, 149, 154
metros, 113–132
Mexico, 159–169, 172, 173, 176, 177
minibus, 135, 136, 139, 144, 146–152
mobility
    analysis, 243, 250, 251, 253
    data, 207, 212, 213, 220, 226, 228, 231, 244, 245, 259
modal share, 4, 9–13, 17

N, P, Q

non-centralized transport, 136, 137, 139–147, 149, 151–153
pedestrians, 159, 160, 164–170, 172–174, 176, 177
pitfall, 205, 207, 223, 224, 233
planning, 182–185, 191–193, 196, 198
policy, 183–187, 189–198
poverty, 45, 46, 48–55, 57–63
public
    space, 160, 166, 170, 171, 176
    transport, 46–48, 52, 53, 56–59, 61, 62, 64
Quebec, 67–78

R, S, T

railway(s), 113–120, 122–126, 131
    networks, 93, 104
severance effects, 35, 36
sidewalk, 159–161, 164–173, 175–177
Sub-Saharan African, 46, 63
technical engineering, 117, 132
trade, 168, 171, 175
transport,
    expenditure, 52, 53, 63, 64
    mode of, 3, 4, 8, 10, 11, 13, 17, 18
    planning, 276
travel, 4–7, 9–14, 16–18

U, W

urban
    boundary, 207, 224
    decline, 87, 97, 105
    density, 7, 10, 15, 17
    form, 6, 8, 10, 18
    model, 268–270, 284, 285
    users, 160, 164–166, 170, 172, 173, 176, 177
walking, 46, 51, 52, 56–58, 60, 63, 64

Printed and bound by CPI Group (UK) Ltd, Croydon, CR0 4YY
19/12/2023

08211689-0002